Music in the
Hispanic Caribbean

Music in the Hispanic Caribbean

∞

EXPERIENCING MUSIC, EXPRESSING CULTURE

∞

ROBIN MOORE

New York   Oxford
OXFORD UNIVERSITY PRESS
2010

Oxford University Press, Inc., publishes works that further Oxford University's
objective of excellence in research, scholarship, and education.

Oxford   New York
Auckland   Cape Town   Dar es Salaam   Hong Kong   Karachi
Kuala Lumpur   Madrid   Melbourne   Mexico City   Nairobi
New Delhi   Shanghai   Taipei   Toronto

With offices in
Argentina   Austria   Brazil   Chile   Czech Republic   France   Greece
Guatemala   Hungary   Italy   Japan   Poland   Portugal   Singapore
South Korea   Switzerland   Thailand   Turkey   Ukraine   Vietnam

Published by Oxford University Press, Inc.
198 Madison Avenue, New York, New York 10016
http://www.oup.com

Library of Congress Cataloging-in-Publication Data

Moore, Robin, 1964–
Music in the Hispanic Caribbean : experiencing music, expressing culture / Robin
Moore.
    p. cm. — (Global music series)
Includes bibliographical references and index.
ISBN 978-0-19-537505-3 (pbk. (main)) — ISBN 978-0-19-537506-0 (hardback)
1. Music—Caribbean Area—History and criticism.   2. Music—Social
aspects—Caribbean Area.   I. Title.
ML3565.M66   2010
780.9729—dc22   2009018152

Printing number: 9 8

GLOBAL MUSIC SERIES

General Editors: Bonnie C. Wade and Patricia Shehan Campbell

Other titles in this series:

Music in East Africa, Gregory Barz
Music in Turkey, Eliot Bates
Music in Central Java, Benjamin Brinner
Teaching Music Globally, Patricia Shehan Campbell
Native American Music in Eastern North America, Beverley Diamond
Music in Pacific Islands Cultures, Brian Diettrich, Jane Freeman Moulin, and Michael Webb
Music in Mainland Southeast Asia, Gavin Douglas
Carnival Music in Trinidad, Shannon Dudley
Music in Bali, Lisa Gold
Music in Ireland, Dorothea E. Hast and Stanley Scott
Music in Korea, Donna Lee Kwon
Music in China, Frederick Lau
Music in Egypt, Scott L. Marcus
Music in the Hispanic Caribbean, Robin Moore
Music in Brazil, John Patrick Murphy
Music in America, Adelaida Reyes
Music in Bulgaria, Timothy Rice
Music in North India, George E. Ruckert
Mariachi Music in America, Daniel Sheehy
Music in West Africa, Ruth M. Stone
Music in the Andes, Thomas Turino
Music in South India, T. Viswanathan and Matthew Harp Allen
Music in Japan, Bonnie C. Wade
Thinking Musically, Bonnie C. Wade

Contents

Foreword

∞

In the past three decades interest in music around the world has surged, as evidenced in the proliferation of courses at the college level, the burgeoning "world music" market in the recording business, and the extent to which musical performance is evoked as a lure in the international tourist industry. This has encouraged an explosion in ethnomusicological research and publication including production of reference works and textbooks. The original model for the "world music" course—if this is Tuesday, this must be Japan—has grown old, as has the format of textbooks for it, either a series of articles in multiauthored volumes that subscribe to the idea of "a survey" and have created a canon of cultures for study or single-authored studies purporting to cover world musics or ethnomusicology. The time has come for a change.

This Global Music Series offers a new paradigm. Instructors can now design their own courses; choosing from a set of case study volumes, they can decide which and how much music they will teach. The series also does something else: Rather than uniformly taking a large region and giving superficial examples from several different countries within it, case studies offer two formats—some focused on a specific culture, some on a discrete geographical area. In either case, each volume offers greater depth than the usual survey. Themes significant in each instance guide the choice of music that is discussed. The contemporary musical situation is the point of departure in all the volumes, with historical information and traditions covered as they elucidate the present. In addition, a set of unifying topics, such as gender, globalization, and authenticity, occur throughout the series. These are addressed in the framing volume, *Thinking Musically* (Wade), which sets the stage for the case studies by introducing those topics and other ways to think about how people make music meaningful and useful in their lives. *Thinking Musically* also presents the basic elements of music as they are practiced in musical systems around the world so that authors of each case study do not have to spend time explaining them and can delve immediately into the particular music. A second framing volume, *Teaching Music Globally* (Campbell), guides teachers in the use of *Thinking Musically* and the case studies.

The series subtitle—Experiencing Music, Expressing Culture—also puts in the forefront the people who make music or in some other way experience it and through it express shared culture. This resonance with global studies in such disciplines as history and anthropology, with their focus on processes and themes that permit cross-study, occasions the title of the Global Music Series.

BONNIE C. WADE
PATRICIA SHEHAN CAMPBELL
GENERAL EDITORS

Preface

∞

This brief volume provides the reader with an introduction to the music of Cuba, Puerto Rico, and the Dominican Republic, as well as to various common themes and tendencies that have informed music making in those countries. Immigrant communities from all three islands have expanded greatly within the United States in recent decades, and for that reason, among others, music from the Hispanic Caribbean deserves our attention as never before. Of course, each island boasts a variety of unique musical forms and certainly merits an independent volume of its own. The traditions cannot be treated comprehensively here, and additional reading is strongly recommended for those who desire greater familiarity with the specific heritage of particular groups and/ or regions. Yet writing about the three countries together has certain advantages. A comparative approach helps us to think of the Hispanic Caribbean as an interconnected whole. The interrelated yet distinct histories of these countries point to the commonalities and disjunctures that are both so characteristic of the region. And the fact that a comprehensive overview of musical forms is not possible forces us to think more about issues, themes, and relationships.

It may not be obvious why the editors of the series and I made the decision to group these particular countries together. The reasons go beyond the fact that each shares a language and common ties to Spain and that Catholicism represents a significant influence on all three. In fact, the countries share political and intellectual histories that date back to at least the mid-nineteenth century. Cuba and Puerto Rico have been described famously as "wings of the same bird"; they remained Spanish colonies long after most others gained their independence, eventually plotting together to fight against Spain in the 1860s. Dominicans, though they attained independence (from Haiti) in the 1840s, took up arms at roughly the same time in order to maintain their independence in the face of Spanish interest in assuming control of their country once again. One of the most famous generals of the Cuban struggle for independence, Máximo Gómez, was himself Dominican, having been radicalized against the Spanish as the result of their aggressive tactics on his home soil in the 1860s. In the late nineteenth century, intellectuals in Cuba and Puerto Rico expressed interest in forming an "Antilles confederation" whereby Cuba, Puerto Rico, and the Dominican Republic would unify and contribute jointly to a national project for the Hispanic Caribbean (Rivero 2005, 29).

In the realm of music as well, exchanges between all three islands have been significant. Nineteenth-century *contradanza* and *danza* repertoire, derived from Spain and France, influenced all three. Popular artists of the early and mid-twentieth century, including Sindo Garay, Rafael Hernández, and the Trío Matamoros, toured all three locations and attracted loyal audiences in each. The Dominican *merengue* has become popular in Cuba and in Puerto Rico as well as at home; Cuban traditions such as *son* have proven to be similarly influential on neighboring Spanish-speaking islands, as have Puerto Rican *salseros*. In the mid-twentieth century, performers from Puerto Rico (Daniel Santos, Bobby Capó, Ruth Fernández, etc.) worked frequently in Cuban nightclubs; Cubans Dámaso Pérez Prado, Guillermo Portabales, Xiomara Alfaro, and others likewise visited Puerto Rico on a regular basis. Puerto Rican Mirta Silva actually sang lead in the famous Cuban Sonora Matancera dance band for years in the 1940s before being replaced by Celia Cruz. More recently, *reggaeton* artists from Puerto Rico have inspired an entire generation of young performers in Cuba and the Dominican Republic as well as in other Spanish-speaking areas, including the United States.

The reader should note that my own expertise relates primarily to Cuban popular music from the 1920s to the present in Havana and the cultural initiatives of revolutionary Cuba; while I have spent time in Puerto Rico and the Dominican Republic, my firsthand exposure to traditions there is much less substantial. As a result, discussions of Dominican and Puerto Rican music in this volume draw more heavily from the work of others. In the case of Dominican repertoire, I rely on writings by Paul Austerlitz, Martha Ellen Davis, Deborah Pacini Hernández, Daniel Piper, and others. In the case of Puerto Rico, I likewise owe a debt to research by Frances Aparicio, Marisol Berríos-Miranda, Rafael Figueroa Hernández, Emanuel Dufrasne González, Peter Manuel, Angel "Chuco" Quintero, and César Rondón, to mention only a few.

My research on Cuban music began in earnest with a two-month summer trip to Havana in 1992, followed by nine months of dissertation research from the fall of 1993 through the spring of 1994, and has continued in summer trips every two years or so since that time. Investigations in Cuba have been divided between archival and ethnographic work and have familiarized me with major musical forms and artists. Even in the case of Cuban traditions, however, the complexity of many styles of music and the constant emergence of new ones are too much for any single researcher to study. I continue to learn substantially from others about African-derived religious traditions (e.g., Katherine Hagedorn, Elizabeth Sayre, María Teresa Vélez), Cuban rap (Geoff Baker, Sujatha Fernandes, Alan West-Durán), and traditions from eastern Cuba (Olavo Alén, Judith Bettelheim, Ben Lapidus, José Millet).

Three overarching themes have been selected for this study as a means of relating the topics of various chapters and of underscoring the relationships between musical forms on the islands considered here. The first is the legacy of colonization and slavery. This broad theme encompasses a number of related issues including the many cultural contributions of West Africans and of Europeans to the Caribbean, the context of plantation labor in which many musical forms first developed, the often oppressive conditions under which people of African descent have maintained their heritage, and the many negative or ambivalent attitudes associated with African heritage that continue to manifest themselves in the Caribbean today. The second theme is that of hybridity or creolization. While it is generally accepted now that "pure" cultures do not exist and that all have been influenced by external elements, the Caribbean nevertheless represents an especially creolized area. Countless West African, European, and other traditions have fused together in endlessly complex ways over the centuries, resulting in unique musical forms that transcend their individual components. The third theme is that of diaspora, movement, and musical exchange. In part because the Caribbean lies along intercontinental trade routes, because it stands at the geographic center of the Western Hemisphere, and because it is so fragmented and diverse, musical forms from the region constantly dialogue with others. There could be no New York salsa, for instance, without North American jazz or Spanish-language *reggaeton* without the influence of Jamaica or Dominican *bachata* without the bolero. Caribbean music exists because of a dynamic, ongoing process of borrowing and assimilation. These borrowings may result from a perception of commonly shared aesthetics, may support an ideology of pan-Africanism, or may simply represent an imposition of the mass media. But the music of the region cannot be understood without an appreciation for processes of cultural exchange.

Music in the Hispanic Caribbean is divided into seven chapters. Chapter 1 notes the rich heritage of the Caribbean in terms of music and other cultural fields, then proceeds to explore various key terms (race, ethnicity, creolization, diaspora, the notion of the Caribbean itself) that serve as a basis for discussion in later sections. Chapter 2 provides a brief historical overview of the Caribbean, considering the sorts of music brought to the islands by immigrant groups from Spain, both elite colonizers and the laboring poor. Chapter 3 includes background on the trans-Atlantic slave trade and the sorts of music associated with African heritage. Chapter 4 compares various forms of creolized dance music including Dominican *merengue*, Cuban *son*, and Puerto Rican *plena*, with additional discussion of Rafael Cortijo and Ismael Rivera and of New York salsa. Chapter 5 shifts focus from music on individual islands to consider the history of genres strongly influenced from abroad, including the *contradanza*, bolero, *bachata*, and *reggaeton*. Chapter 6 examines the ways in which the Caribbean's turbulent political history has inspired music making of various kinds. It focuses on song associated with the Puerto Rican independence movement, with the Dominican Republic in the aftermath of Rafael Trujillo's assassination, and of Cuban *nueva trova* and rap. Chapter 7, a concluding section, explores various ways that notions of race and national character have been represented musically through the years. It analyzes music of the Cuban blackface theater of the early twentieth century, classical compositions in a nationalist vein, and Latin jazz. A glossary and a list of additional sources for further study appear at the end.

The manuscript ended up being longer than expected, and in order to reduce its overall size the editors and I decided to print only partial listening guides (approximately the first minute of each) in the book itself, moving the full listening guides to a special page of the Oxford University Press website (www.oup.com/us.moore). The full listening guides represent an important resource in analyzing the recordings on the CD that accompany this book; readers are strongly encouraged to access the site and to download pdf files of the full listening guides from the outset so they will be on hand as necessary.

Sincere thanks are due to the many individuals who have guided me in my investigations of these subjects, especially in terms of music making in the Dominican Republic and Puerto Rico and the history of the Atlantic slave trade. Specifically, I have been helped immensely by conversations and communications with, and publications by, Paul Austerlitz, Martha Ellen Davis, Robin Derby, Cristóbal Díaz Ayala, Héctor Fernández L'Hoeste, Carlos Flores, Juan Flores, Liliana González, Kim Kattari, Samuel López, Seth Meisel, Deborah Pacini Hernández, Peter Manuel, Melanie Morgan, Sonia Pérez Cassola, Josephine Powell, César Salgado, John Santos, Sonia Seeman, Médar and Rebeca Serrano, Angelina Tallaj, and Elio Villafranca. I am indebted to Daniel Piper for his sharing of expertise on traditional Dominican music generally, the detailed suggestions and additions to my text on that subject he provided, and the transcriptions of Dominican *salve* music he contributed in Chapter 3. Special thanks are due to the series editors, Bonnie Wade and Pat Campbell, who have read draft chapters and offered countless suggestions for improvement. I am especially indebted to Bonnie Wade for her invitation to write this volume in the first place and contribute to the Global Music Series and to my wife Lorraine for her endless support and thoughtful contributions.

Thank you to the staff of Oxford University Press: Jan Beatty, Executive Editor; Cory Schneider, Assistant Editor; and Brian Black, Production Editor. Thanks also to those who reviewed this text: David F. Garcia, University of North Carolina at Chapel Hill; Peter Manuel, John Jay College and the CUNY Graduate Center; Tina K. Ramnarine, Royal Holloway University of London; and Suzel Ana Reily, Queen's University, Belfast.

Finally, thanks are also due to the musicians who contributed their talents to the musical recordings that accompany this book. A number of commercially available recordings appear on our CD, but other didactic tracks are based on recordings made by musicians Samuel López, Roberto Rodríguez, Dennis Rathnaw, Sidra Lawrence, and Mark Lomanno. Thanks also to Héctor Delgado, José Ruiz Elcoro, Carlos Flores, Daniel Piper, and Josephine Powell, as well as others who offered their photographs to me for reproduction.

CD Track List

∞

1. *"Tratado* for Elegguá, Oggún, Ochosi, and Inle" (4:43). Traditional Afro-Cuban *güiro* music. From *Sacred Rhythms of Cuban Santería.* Washington D.C.: Smithsonian-Folkways CD SFW40419, 1995.

2. "La comparsa" (1:59). Piano composition written and performed by Ernesto Lecuona From *Homenaje a Lecuona.* New York: RCA International/Sony CD, 1989.

3. "Una viagra que camine" (2:43). Puerto Rican *seis chorreo* written by Hipólito Ríos and sung by José Ortiz. From the uncopyrighted CD *El Huracán Georges.*

4. "Controversia" (4:09). Cuban *punto* sung by Adolfo Alfonso and Justo Vega and accompanied by the Orquesta Palmas y Cañas. From *The JVC Video Anthology of World Music and Dance.* Tokyo: NHK International, 1988.

5. *Güiro* ensemble rhythms (2:10). Demonstration of Afro-Cuban percussion recorded by Sidra Lawrence, Samuel López, Dennis Rathnaw, Roberto Rodríguez, and the author.

6. "India del agua" excerpt (3:07). Afro-Dominican folkloric *salve* recorded by Enerolisa Núñez y el Grupo de Salve de Mata los Indios. From *Música Raiz 1.* Santo Domingo: Fundación Cultural Bayahonda CD, 1998.

7. *Salve* rhythms (1:49). Demonstration of Afro-Dominican percussion recorded Daniel Piper and members of Enerolisa y el Grupo de Salve de Mata los Indios: Argentina Ferrand, Fredi Ferrand González, Barbina Núñez (Yili), Irene Núñez (Yeni), Fulgenio Núñez (Vichán), and Pío Núñez (Osvaldo).

8. *Bomba sicá* rhythms (1:42). Demonstration of Afro-Puerto Rican percussion recorded by Samuel López, Dennis Rathnaw, Roberto Rodríguez, and the author.

9. *Merengue* rhythms (1:18). Demonstration of Afro-Dominican percussion recorded by Samuel López, Dennis Rathnaw, and Roberto Rodríguez.

10. "Amores de colores" (4:39). Commercial *merengue* written and performed by Kinito Méndez. From *Merengue Frenzy/Frenesí de Merengue, vol. 3*. Discos Fuentes/Miami Records CD, 2001.

11. *Son* example 1: bongo drum and *clave* (0:56). Demonstration of traditional Afro-Cuban percussion recorded by Samuel López and the author.

12. *Son* example 2: bass, *clave*, and *maracas* (0:48). Demonstration of traditional Afro-Cuban rhythms recorded by Samuel López, Dennis Rathnaw, and the author.

13. *Son* example 3: conga patterns (1:00). Demonstration of traditional Afro-Cuban percussion recorded by Samuel López and the author.

14. *Plena* rhythms (1:21). Demonstration of traditional Afro-Puerto Rican percussion recorded by Samuel López, Dennis Rathnaw, and Roberto Rodríguez.

15. "Patria borinqueña" (5:15). *Plena* written by Juan Antonio "Toñín" Romero and recorded by Los Pleneros de la 21. *Para Todos Ustedes*. Washington D.C.: Smithsonian-Folkways CD SFW40519, 2005.

16. "Anacaona" (7:16). Salsa composition written by Tite Curet Alonso and performed by Cheo Feliciano and the Fania All-Stars. From *Fania All Stars Live at the Cheetah, Vol. 1*. New York: Fania Records, 1971. Licensed by Red Planet Music.

17. Traditional *cáscara* pattern as performed in "Anacaona," with *clave* (0:59). Demonstration of traditional Afro-Cuban percussion recorded by Samuel López and the author.

18. Salsa bell patterns, with *clave* (1:04). Demonstration of traditional Afro-Cuban percussion recorded by Samuel López, Roberto Rodríguez, and the author.

19. Piano *montuno* pattern from "Anacaona" (0:56) as performed by Larry Harlow, with *clave*. Recorded by Mark Lomanno and the author.

20. "La tarde" (2:05). Early *bolero* from 1907 written by Sindo Garay and performed by Pablo Milanés and Luis Peña. From *Años III*. Havana: PM Records, 1996. Used by Permission of Peermusic III, Ltd. All Rights Reserved.

21. "Que vuelva" (4:46). *Bachata* written by Alberto "Tico" Mercado and performed by Alex Bueno. *Bachata Hits 2001*. Miami: J&N Records CD JNK 83754, 2001.

22. "Oye mi canto" (4:05). *Reggaeton* written and performed by Victor Santiago (N.O.R.E.), Rolphy Ramirez, Edwin Almonte, Leonardo

Vaszquez, Ramón Ayala, Victor Santiago, Nicole and Natalie Albino. From the CD single *Oye mi canto*. Def Jam Records, 2004. Licensed by Universal Music, Miami.

23. "Libertad y soberanía" (3:40). Puerto Rican *nueva canción* written and performed by Andrés Jiménez. From *En la última trinchera*. San Juan: Producciones Cuarto Menguante CD DCM-85, 1992.

24. "La llaman puta" (3:52). Cuban *rap consciente* performed by the duo Obsesión (Magia López and Alexy Rodríguez). Released as part of *La Fabri-K: The Cuban Hip Hop Factory*, produced by Lisandro Pérez-Rey. Havana: Miami Light Project, 2005.

25. "La negra monguita" (3:38). Blackface comic dialogue written and performed by Sergio Acebal with pianist Sergio Pita. RCA Victor 78 #46073-1. Havana, 1928.

26. "Alabí Oyó" (5:19). A Latin jazz composition based on traditional Yoruba praise songs written by John Santos and performed by the John Santos Quintet. From *Papa Mambo*. Machete Records CD M206. Berkeley, CA: Machete Records, 2007.

CHAPTER 1

Introduction

∞

One week each March, a central section of Miami transforms itself into a massive Latin festival. The Calle Ocho (SW 8th Street), a main thoroughfare running from downtown toward the suburbs to the west, becomes the scene of carnival revelry as over a million spectators gather to celebrate in one of the country's largest street parties. For approximately twenty-three blocks on thirty separate stages, bands from across the hemisphere play Caribbean and Latin American music of virtually all sorts: *merengue* (CD track 10) and salsa (CD track 16), Spanish-language hip-hop and *reggaeton* (CD track 22), folkloric drumming (CD tracks 1 and 6), Latin jazz (CD track 26), and countless others. Despite the cultural differences, a certain pan-Latino sense of identity, of shared values and heritage, is evident. The tropical heat is stifling, and the crowd packs the street in such density that it is often difficult to move. This is not a place for those uncomfortable with the human touch.

The public consists mostly of working-class immigrants from Latin America and their children. Adolescents come in large numbers, but a surprising number of middle-aged couples and older residents attend as well. Their dress and appearance vary wildly: bikinied women with sequins; beefy and tattooed construction workers; voluptuous housewives in tightly stretched spandex; older reserved men in *guayaberas* and perma-press; ostentatious dressers in gold chains, rings, and pendants; inscrutable hipsters in oversized wraparound sunglasses. Skin shades of all colors are represented, making clear that "Hispanic" and "Latino" are not terms that correspond to a single look. Here, a man of 70 dressed in red from head to foot dances with a life-sized mannequin; nearby, a dreadlocked vendor beckons the crowd over to buy bandanas fashioned after the flags of Latin American countries. Children pass on shoulders and in strollers, and men lean along shady storefronts. Many revelers are clearly more than a little drunk. Hundreds of food stands jam the five-lane road; grills smoke, fryers pop, green coconuts are opened for their sweet and cool juice, rum is poured into shot glasses.

Signs advertise a barrage of traditional street foods: *pasteles* (meat pastries) and *morcillas* (sausages) found in various countries of the Spanish Caribbean, *arroz con gandules* (rice with pigeon peas), *pernil* (roast pork), and *bacalaítos* (cod fritters) from Puerto Rico, Cuban *ropa vieja* and *yuca con mojo* (a potato-like tuber with garlic sauce), Argentine *choripán* (a sandwich of sausage and crusty bread), Colombian *arepa de choclo* (a snack made of ground sweet corn and cheese), baby goat meat from the Anglophone Caribbean, and Dominican *sancocho* (stew). Paper and plastic trash cover the street underfoot.

To help revelers navigate the mayhem, organizers divide the festival into areas: an alcohol-free family zone, where kids can have their faces painted; a *parranda* space, in which strolling drummers perform repertoire from a number of countries; and a third big zone with the stages where most of the headline artists will appear. Wandering in the third area among the musicians, amplification from one sound system pulses into that of another. Younger Puerto Rican *salseros* Jerry Rivera and Frankie Negrón perform alongside older groups such as El Gran Combo. Venezuelan veteran Oscar D'León appears nearby with his orchestra. Cuban Americans Arturo Sandoval and Albita make an appearance, the former with a Latin jazz band from Florida International University, the latter singing traditional dance music. Cuban American rappers Pitbull and Don Dinero dominate a nearby stage. Several North American rappers appear as well, singing in English. Dominican bands led by Wilfrido Vargas and Los Hermanos Rosario lay down driving *merengue* grooves. Young *reggaeton* artists are perhaps the most numerous, with countless aspiring performers represented from the Spanish-speaking Caribbean: Puerto Ricans Julio Voltio, Edwin "Dynasty" Veras, and Zion Y Lenox; Dominican American Giovanni "El Padrino" Surez; and others.

The Calle Ocho festival has changed a great deal since its beginnings in the late 1970s. At first, only a handful of twenty-something Cuban Americans organized the street fair, using it as a form of entertainment for themselves and of introducing their non-Hispanic neighbors to Latin culture. It was a relatively calm middle-class event featuring golf and cooking competitions as a central component. What began as exclusively Cuban now represents the complex constellation of Latin and Latino cultures and classes in the Miami area, attracting curious visitors from near and far. And emphasis has shifted noticeably to the working-class experience. Spanish-language television covers the event heavily, and local politicians jockey for the chance to address the crowd between performances. Corporate sponsors such as Budweiser, Univisión, Bacardi, and ESPN support the musical acts, vying for market share among the Latino population. They cater both to the longer-term residents of the area as well as to the increasing numbers of Mexicans and Central and South Americans in Miami.

The emergence of festivals such as Calle Ocho are indicative of changing demographics within the United States. By the year 2000, Latinos and Latin American immigrants collectively became the nation's largest minority group, comprising approximately 13.3% of the overall U.S. population; they remain the largest as of 2009, and their ranks have grown to 14.5%. Nearly half of U.S. Hispanics are under age 25, suggesting that their numbers relative to others will continue to grow substantially. One could make the case that areas such as southern Florida—many parts of it predominantly Spanish-speaking—are a harbinger of changes to come as ever larger segments of the population claim Latin American heritage. Another indication of such changes within the United States: Any guess as to what the first and second largest Spanish-speaking cities in the world are? The largest: Mexico City. The second largest: not Madrid, not Buenos Aires, but Los Angeles! Of course, Caribbean and Latin American history has intersected with that of North America for centuries, and cultures from the Spanish Americas have influenced musical styles in the United States since at least the nineteenth century, as well as absorbing influences. But it is increasingly evident in the new millennium that Latin American culture must be recognized as a vital component of North American culture, a central rather than a peripheral voice.

Though all parts of the Americas have unique music, the Caribbean represents an especially vibrant area. An enormous spectrum of expression has developed there, particularly from Spanish-, French-, and English-speaking areas. This relatively small region in geographic and economic terms, whose total population does not exceed 40 million, has proven to be a cultural force rivaling or even surpassing large nations of the developed world. Phenomenally popular commercial music has developed there—*merengue*, reggae, salsa, etc.—that is listened to around the world. The Caribbean supports fascinating but decidedly noncommercial forms of folklore as well. Some of this expression perpetuates elements of music and dance brought to the region hundreds of years ago from Africa, Spain, and elsewhere; some blend these elements together or fuse them with more recent influences. The islands also boast vibrant classical music traditions, everything from vocal music for the Catholic mass to nineteenth-century piano repertoire to avant-garde electronic composition. In terms of literary figures (Nobel Prize winners Derek Walcott, Alexis Leger, V. S. Naipaul), political activists (Toussaint L'Ouverture, Marcus Garvey, Stokely Carmichael), and in other ways that extend far beyond music, the Caribbean has much to offer.

ACTIVITY 1.1 *Do some outside research on the individuals mentioned here. Find out more information about them, who they are, why they are important, and how exactly they have contributed to Caribbean culture.*

From the perspective of those living in the United States, the Caribbean represents an interesting area study for various reasons. Perhaps most importantly, its history is closely linked to ours. Both regions developed through a process of European colonialism, domination, and settlement of foreign territory. Both regions had substantial native populations that suffered brutal treatment at the hands of European immigrants. Both developed plantation economies that generated substantial wealth for landowners and elites. The importance of the Caribbean in generating profits through the sale of coffee, tobacco, and sugar, among the first products associated with international economic trade, can hardly be overemphasized. Some suggest that Caribbean plantations helped to drive the rapid expansion of the Industrial Revolution in Europe and in the United States (Benítez Rojo 1996, 5). Both the Caribbean and the United States continue to deal with the social repercussions of slavery. And finally, musical forms in both areas have developed through a similar process involving the fusion of elements from Europe, Africa, and elsewhere. It is instructive to think about the ways that Caribbean music is similar to or distinct from music of the United States and what has contributed to the divergences in musical styles. Music in both regions can be thought of as telling stories about the places where it developed, stories involving issues of dominance, cultural contact, resistance, and adaptation.

DEFINING THE CARIBBEAN

As a cultural or even a geographic region, the Caribbean is difficult to define. Relative to other parts of Latin America it is less homogeneous, with half a dozen distinct colonial languages (English, French, Dutch, Spanish, various forms of Patois) spoken by the inhabitants. The inhabitants of one island do not always identify strongly with others nearby or have much direct contact with them. Martinicans, for instance, may identify more closely with the French than with Jamaicans or Puerto Ricans. Dominicans may not identify with Haitians, even though they share the same island. Clearly, language differences and colonial history have fractured the Caribbean into many pieces.

In geographic terms, too, one soon realizes that the boundaries of the region are far from apparent. Scholars of Caribbean culture and history tend to refer both to the Caribbean and to the "circum-Caribbean" as a closely interrelated whole. Atlantic coastal regions of South and Central America, and arguably even cities such as New Orleans, have a great deal in common culturally with the islands of the Caribbean. The climate, architecture, and lifestyle of the residents of Cartagena, Colombia, resemble those of Havana or Santo Domingo much more than they do those of Bogotá. One could make a case for describing the Afro-Costa Rican residents of Limón as "Caribbean" rather than Central American as well; the same could be said of north-eastern regions of Brazil. In addition, the massive numbers of inhab-itants from Caribbean islands moving abroad to London, New York, Miami, and elsewhere further complicate the notion of Caribbean geography. Nevertheless, because the Hispanic Caribbean has much in common with certain regions of Spanish- and Portuguese-speaking Latin America, I will occasionally refer to "the Caribbean and Latin America" as a unit.

This book focuses on several islands of the Greater Antilles—the larger islands lying to the northwest beginning with Cuba and end-ing with Puerto Rico—as opposed to the smaller islands of the Lesser Antilles.

ACTIVITY 1.2 *Examine the empty map of the Caribbean and surrounding areas (Fig. 1.1). Consult other maps as necessary in order to add in the names of all islands and countries pictured. Investigate and identify the greater and lesser Antilles.*

Several factors do tie Caribbean islands together, however, related to their common experience of domination by foreign powers and the gradual emergence of new cultural forms in the context of forced slave labor. Does this shared history translate into a shared musical style? In a general sense, yes, though musical forms exist on each island that have no counterpart elsewhere. Most of these genres blend particular elements from European traditions with other elements of African der-ivation or the music of other groups. Common families of instruments (string instruments, drums, hand percussion) are found throughout the Caribbean on virtually every island. Certain commercial genres (reggae, salsa, *merengue*) have found enthusiastic supporters on every

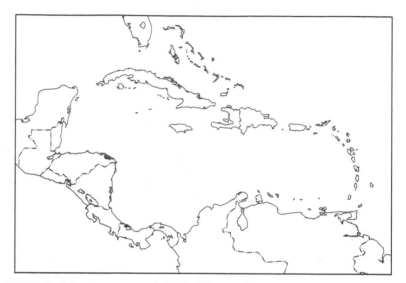

FIGURE 1.1   *Empty map of the Caribbean region.*

island. Catholic music traditions are common to all three islands of the Hispanic Caribbean, as are certain manifestations of African-derived religious music.

Additionally, particular rhythmic cells or building blocks believed to be of Kongo origin (Bantu-Kongo tribes represent a particular ethnic group originating in present-day Angola and Democratic Republic of Congo) appear in the music of different islands and in the music of circum-Caribbean countries. The *tresillo, cinquillo,* and so-called *habanera* rhythms are all extremely common, for instance, tying the region together to an extent. These rhythms appear in Cuban *son* and *rumba* *guaguancó,* in the *danza* and *danzón,* in Puerto Rican *bomba* (CD track 8), in the *bolero* (CD track 20), in Dominican drumming genres such as the *salve* (CD track 6), and in Dominican *merengue* (CD track 10), to mention only a few examples from the Spanish-speaking islands. We should also note that the same rhythms (*tresillo, cinquillo,* and *habanera*) are found in early jazz and ragtime music, again demonstrating the links of the area to North American traditions and in coastal areas of South America. Each of the three beats might be considered a variation of the others. *Tresillo* means "little group of three" and *cinquillo* "little group of five." Both are typically found in duple-meter music and create cross-rhythms or "jumped" rhythms in particular ways. For a basic explanation of rhythm and meter, see Wade (2004).

ACTIVITY 1.3 *The* tresillo *rhythm is notated in Figure 1.2 in both Western rhythmic notation and another notation (known as time unit box system, or TUBS) that is commonly used by ethnomusicologists to analyze rhythm. To feel the* tresillo, *establish a pulse and count to eight out loud in time with the pulse. This grouping, in Western rhythmic notation, fits within one measure. The repeat signs in Figure 1.2—the dark lines with dots before and after them—tell you to repeat what is between the vertical bars, so count out the eight-pulse grouping several times.*

If you don't read Western notation, think of the rectangle simply as an x–y graph that plots pitch against time, with movement up and down representing changes in pitch and movement from left to right representing time. You should be able to glean useful information in that way, and you will also be able to hear many of the rhythms discussed in recorded examples.

Follow the notation to tap on the proper pulses for the tresillo: *The first tap is on the downbeat, the second on the fourth pulse, and the third on the seventh. This marks off subgroups within the eight-pulse grouping: three, three, and two. To experience how the second tap creates a "jumped sound" against the basic pulse, team up with a friend. One of you tap on every other pulse, to mark off the eight-pulse grouping into four straight beats, and the other tap out the* tresillo *against it. By doing this, you have created measures of four beats—that is, duple meter. The* tresillo *rhythm is a cross-rhythm, or "jumped rhythm," within it (Fig. 1.3).*

The cinquillo *represents a slightly more elaborate version of the* tresillo. *In the final example, all three pulses of the* tresillo *are still evident but the second and third pulses are anticipated by an additional pickup note. Try tapping out this rhythm by itself and against a straight beat as well (Fig. 1.4).*

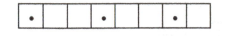

FIGURE 1.2 Tresillo.

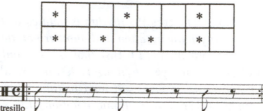

FIGURE 1.3   Tresillo *and pulse.*

FIGURE 1.4   Cinquillo.

If the *tresillo* rhythm is played together with a straight beat, as you may have attempted in Activity 1.3, the resulting aggregate represents another common pattern: the *habanera* rhythm. Readers may recognize this as the basic pulse of modern *reggaeton* music, perhaps the most popular Hispanic Caribbean genre among younger listeners since the late 1990s. It is also evident in certain older forms of African-derived music found in the Caribbean.

The roots of *reggaeton* are complex and transnational, as will be discussed in Chapter 5; the style that most directly contributed to its development is the Jamaican Dem Bow rhythm, a studio-generated groove that served as a basis for improvised "toasting" (speaking over a backtrack) before gaining popularity in Panama, Puerto Rico, and elsewhere. However, the roots of the rhythm are much older. As noted, nearly identical rhythms are found throughout the Caribbean, often in drumming traditions that have existed for centuries. In all likelihood the *habanera* rhythm in all its variations derives from sub-Saharan Africa, though it also bears a great deal of similarity to North African/Arabic dance music rhythms. Of course, Arabic culture itself has been influenced by sub-Saharan African and Spanish rhythms for centuries and has influenced them in turn. Thinking about musical commonalities within the Caribbean and speculating as to the origins of particular elements is a complicated matter and underscores the tremendous diversity of influences that have contributed to modern musical tastes.

MUSIC AND RACE IN THE CARIBBEAN

Before proceeding further with musical details, definitions of a few terms and concepts, such as "race," "ethnicity," and "creolization" would be useful; ideas such as these should help ground discussion on related issues in the chapters to come. One of the central concerns of this book is to explore the ways in which music expresses the perspective of particular racial and ethnic groups.

The cultural influences of Africa are of special interest in the Caribbean for various reasons. First, large segments of the population—a sizeable majority on most islands—are of African or mixed African descent, so a focus on this repertoire becomes central in any conversation. Second, creolized music—that is, music that fuses distinct cultural elements from Europe, Africa, or elsewhere—has been accepted by the entire populations of most countries over time and has come to symbolize their national spirit or character in everyday discourse. This idea is explored in greater detail later in this chapter. Third, repertoire containing African influences has dominated all forms of commercial music making in the Caribbean for at least a century and a half, much as is the case in the United States. For all of these reasons, it deserves our attention.

What is "African-derived music" or "European-derived music"? Are there distinct styles or genres that we can associate with particular racial or ethnic groups? How do ideas about race manifest themselves in the Caribbean and affect music making? It is important to recognize that there are many types of music associated with particular social and racial groups, not just one. Some have strong, nearly exclusive associations with particular communities, others much less so.

One particular style of African-derived music performed in the Caribbean can serve as an example of the sorts of music associated with the region before returning to these issues.

ACTIVITY 1.4 *Listen to a recording associated with African-derived religions in the Caribbean (CD track 1), discussed at greater length in Chapter 3. This is a devotional song to Yoruba sacred beings called* orichas *in Cuba and Puerto Rico, music associated*

with the African-influenced religion Santería. In order to orient yourself, listen first for the bell pattern (Fig. 1.5). The sound of the metal bell should stand out from the other instruments. This rhythm derives from West Africa and is still found there. Try tapping it out along with the recording; it begins after about four seconds, together with the first entrance of a group of chorus singers (vocals are notated along with the bell in Figs. 1.6 and 1.7). Don't worry about the other percussion instruments in the background for the moment. A transcription of the bell pattern is provided below in both TUBS notation and Western notation.

Now try learning to sing a couple of the short melodies that begin this piece (the words are transcribed in Figs. 1.6 and 1.7). Sing them on their own at first, then see if you can sing them against the bell. Learn to clap the bell rhythm and sing the melodies at the same time if you can in order to see how the rhythms and melodies correspond in particular ways. If you read staff notation or have someone available who can help you do so, look now at the transcriptions of what you just tried below. You will see that in this melodic transcription, in cases where the song melodies are divided between a lead singer and chorus, smaller notes in the transcription below indicate the part sung by the lead voice and full-sized notes with lyrics in capital letters indicate the group response. Note that the lead singer improvises and changes the melody constantly, so the transcription below represents only one way he or she might sing it.

The melodies in Figures 1.6 and 1.7 are sung in fragmented Yoruba dialects; similar pieces have been performed in Cuba by enslaved Africans and their descendants for centuries and more recently in other

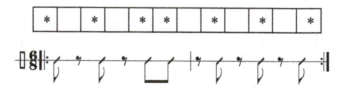

FIGURE 1.5 *Santería bell pattern.*

FIGURE 1.6 *The first responsorial song in the* tratado *dedicated to the* orichas *Elegguá, Oggún, Ochosi, and Inle (CD track 1). This segment is heard from 0:00 to 0:16.*

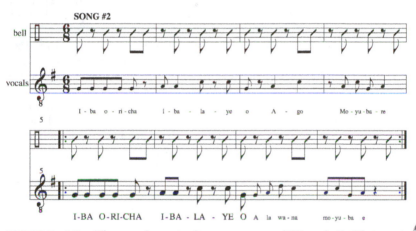

FIGURE 1.7 *The second song in the same sequence (CD track 1). The song is heard from 0:17 to 0:29.*

countries including Puerto Rico and the United States. Similar pieces are heard in the Dominican Republic as well. The music exists largely in oral tradition, with individual religious communities performing songs somewhat differently. Over time, melodies and texts have changed and performers have adapted the ceremonies of which they are a part to reflect new social realities. Most practitioners no longer speak African languages fluently, and they may not know how to translate all of the words they sing exactly. Yet the general meanings are clear. In the example, the words *"moyuba"* and *"iba laye o"* are expressions of homage and devotion. The lyrics of the songs might be translated roughly as "praise to the *orichas*," the deities/ancestor spirits/forces of nature of the religion known as Santería, or *Regla de Ocha*.

It would be difficult to characterize this music as unproblematically "African" because of how different its particular melodies, rhythms, and contexts are in the Caribbean when compared to African traditions, past or present. Yet few would take issue with describing it as African-derived. These songs are associated closely with particular communities of African descendants, performed largely by them, and modeled after African as opposed to European repertoire.

Most examples of Caribbean music, however, are more ambiguous in this sense. The many songs recorded by Afro-Puerto Rican musicians who have distinguished themselves as performers of *música jíbara* are a case in point. *Música jíbara* (roughly "country music") is a tradition examined at greater length in Chapter 2. It is derived from Spanish models, performed on string instruments such as guitars of Spanish derivation, and perpetuated in large part by Puerto Ricans of European descent. How then do we characterize performances by Patricio "Toribio" Rijos, Felipe "Don Felo" Rosario Goyco, Elidio "Pródigio" Claudio, and other prominent Puerto Ricans of color (i.e., those of African or mixed African and European heritage) who have made a name for themselves in this style? Similar examples abound throughout the Americas of African descendants (not to mention indigenous peoples) creating music whose origins lie in places other than Africa, including classical pieces. Conversely, many European descendants perform music in styles derived from African American and Afro-Caribbean communities.

Another important case to consider is that of the fundamentally creolized or hybrid musics that abound in the Caribbean. Consider the folkloric *merengue* discussed in Chapter 4. Dominican *merengue* has a long history, dating back to at least the 1840s. It incorporates numerous instruments and stylistic elements derived from Afro-Dominican folklore; these include the *güira* metallic scraper and the double-headed *tambora* drum. Some ensembles use a large *marímbula* ("thumb piano") as a bass instrument as well, derived directly from Shona and other central African practices (Fig. 1.8). Yet the music demonstrates the influences of European traditions just as prominently. Its primarily melodic instrument is the accordion, first played in Germany and Italy. Lyrics are sung in Spanish, and the scales and melodies used also have European origins. The *merengue* is danced in couples, something almost unheard of in traditional sub-Saharan Africa, apparently in imitation of European dances in vogue in the nineteenth century such as the polka. Clearly, this genre has no single association with European or African heritage.

Perhaps it is best if we take a step back from our focus on music and consider the definition of "race" more broadly, then address its implications for the arts. In an influential work, sociologists Michael Omi and Howard Winant (1986) define "race" as a construct that categorizes physical difference in various, somewhat arbitrary ways. They note that notions of race are not determined exclusively on the basis of appearance

FIGURE 1.8   *The* marímbula, *an African-derived instrument used in various forms of traditional music in Cuba, Puerto Rico, the Dominican Republic, and elsewhere. It consists of a wooden box to which metal strips are attached; performers pluck the strips to produce different pitches.   (Photo by the author).*

or exclusively on the basis of culture-specific categories, yet they are influenced by both. In other words, racial categories derive from the ways particular groups of people make sense of physical difference and the categories they create to do this. Omi and Winant emphasize that racial terms and definitions vary widely by country and region. Thus, they have no fixed, empirical meaning but instead change and develop in response to particular social conditions.

The same authors go on to provide definitions of other useful concepts. They use the term *racial formation* to describe the historical frames within which racial categories are created, experienced, and ultimately transformed over time. Racial formations refer to the broader ways in which societies are organized and experienced racially; the Atlantic slave trade, which contributed fundamentally to the development of Caribbean music, for instance, and the institution of plantation slavery constitute components of particular racial formations, along with the many misguided attitudes about Africa that justified such practices from the perspective of the colonizers.

Finally, Omi and Winant propose the concept of a *racial project*, defining it as an interpretation or representation of race that aims to alter existing racial dynamics (p. 56). This term relates to activism within an existing racial formation. The civil rights movement and the Black Power movement represent examples of particular racial projects in the United States that have both affected notions of race and led to particular kinds of music making. One might also mention artists such as Jamaican Bob Marley and his identification with the oppression of African peoples as inspired by a particular racial project. More problematically, protagonists of blackface minstrelsy in the United States, such as Thomas Rice (1808–1860) ascribed to notions of white/European superiority common in the mid-nineteenth century; their racist views of Africans and black music presented on stage derived from the realities of life in the United States at the time and specifically from debates about whether to end slavery. Clearly, this music also relates to a racial project. Similar examples are found frequently in the Hispanic Caribbean of artists who have used music to comment on racial realities or to attempt to change them.

When thinking about music of the African diaspora and of the creolized cultures of the Caribbean, the important point is that music's racialized associations derive their meanings from the societies of which they are a part and from ongoing notions of and debates about race. It does not matter whether one examines Caribbean drumming styles influenced strongly by traditional West African music, European-derived string traditions, or overtly hybrid music; their overall development, the ways they have been categorized, the meanings attributed to them, and the reasons for their perpetuation in particular communities relate to particular racial formations and projects. Musical performances speak to the values, experiences, and aspirations of Caribbean peoples. Music contributes to ongoing debates about race and ultimately shapes racial attitudes over time.

The notion of "ethnicity" deserves brief mention here as well, especially since Latin America is frequently described as a region with a "triethnic" heritage. The three ethnic groups referred to in this way are Europeans, Africans, and native/indigenous peoples, as you may have guessed. Certainly, all contributed to the development of the Spanish Americas and often figure prominently in political discourse. But authors who extol the virtues of Latin America's triethnic heritage often fail to mention that many there consider non-European cultures less valuable, interesting, and deserving of study than European culture. Ambiguity toward non-European ethnicity abounds in the region.

The concept of "ethnicity" as opposed to "race" deserves clarification. Gerhard Kubik (1994) reminds us that "ethnicity" refers primarily to cultural heritage rather than to physical appearance. He notes that the term dates only from the 1970s and is used primarily to characterize social dynamics in modern, urban, multicultural societies. Ethnicity implies processes of cultural contact, assimilation, and fusion. It also implies cultural loss and an attempt to reassert difference on the part of minorities. Culturally distinct groups under normal circumstances have no need to assert their ethnicity or even to be aware of it. Only when their cultural orientation is threatened or in crisis does the importance of maintaining it become a pressing matter. The Caribbean has certainly been a site of ethnic conflict and one in which we might expect questions of ethnic tension to emerge. For centuries, the European powers not only enslaved and subjugated African and indigenous peoples in the Caribbean but belittled or even outlawed their cultural expression as well.

Kubik (1994, 23) notes that a person suddenly transplanted into another linguistic and cultural world "learns painfully that his or her language, ideas about god, modes of behavior, and values are not universally valid, but rather are relative and often culture-specific." In this context—one typical of slavery—various strategies tend to emerge. One reaction has been described as *reinterpretation,* in which Africans and others come to view the European cultures they encounter through the lens of their own culture. We might view the emergence of African-derived religions and religious music in the New World from this perspective. Santería and related traditions seem to have developed as the result of reinterpretations of European Catholicism on the part of Africans as they learned to reconcile distinct cultural and religious worlds. Similarly, many forms of hybridized dance music described in Chapter 4 might be conceived of as a reinterpretation of European musical practices through the lens of West African aesthetics.

Another cultural strategy common to displaced peoples is that of *adaptation,* forsaking one's (frequently maligned) ethnic expression for that of the dominant ethnic group in one's new society. There are many instances of African and indigenous populations embracing musical styles from Europe, even learning to compose professionally in that style or to perform virtuosic renditions of European repertoire. Music can serve in this way as a means of asserting cultural distinction in particular contexts and allows for upward social mobility. Of course, as time passes people of non-European heritage in the Caribbean may increasingly view themselves as "Western" in outlook and their own heritage as inherently European, at least in part.

Other common strategies adopted by minority ethnic groups include *oppositionality,* an assertion of cultural difference as a political statement or as a means of maintaining a unique identity. The importance of the Puerto Rican *cuatro* (a folkloric string instrument heard on CD tracks 3 and 15 and seen in Fig. 2.3) as a national symbol, for instance, derives in large part from the fact that during the early twentieth century U.S. authorities in control of the island actively suppressed local cultural expression, attempting to "whiten" and anglicize the population. This will be discussed in Chapter 6. The strong influence of North American culture in Puerto Rico—in large part the result of the latter's political influence—threatens the future of many forms of traditional music and has led some individuals to fight to maintain Spanish-language heritage at all cost.

Dominant groups in the Western Hemisphere, for their part, have taken various positions vis-à-vis local forms of minority expression. One early tendency was to parody or belittle such music, as in the case of U.S. minstrelsy or Cuban and Puerto Rican blackface comedy (Fig. 7.1). Alternatively, dominant groups have simply ignored minority expression, refusing it a space in the commercial market or in the mass media. An increasingly common tendency since the mid-twentieth century has been for them to embrace certain forms of more accessible minority music, claiming it as "everyone's." Traditional Puerto Rican *bomba* drumming and dance or Dominican *palo* may rarely, if ever, be heard on the radio, for instance; nevertheless, other Afro-Caribbean music discussed in this volume (*bachata, plena, son*) more overtly influenced by European aesthetics has been accepted without reservation.

These tendencies deserve greater critical attention. Most popular music in the Western hemisphere has developed in relatively marginal communities, with those of African descent especially influential. While many such creolized genres have become widely influential, others are known only locally, and the folkloric genres that gave rise to them are even less known. Music historians have tended not to examine the dynamics of these processes, despite the fact that Afro-Caribbean and Afro-North American music could arguably be described as being at the heart of an emerging global pop sound.

The complex histories of racial blending in the Caribbean have led, perhaps understandably, to different ways of thinking about race from those that exist in the United States. It is very common, for instance, to meet people who recognize that they are of mixed African and European heritage in some measure; they may also note the influence of Chinese, indigenous peoples, East Indians, or others. This blending results from various factors such as the relatively high ratio of non-European inhabitants to Europeans compared to the United States. In part it is due to plantation work in the Caribbean that for many years was supported by large numbers of enslaved peoples and/or indentured laborers.

Additionally, fewer European families settled the Caribbean, leading individuals stationed there (soldiers, merchants, colonial bureaucrats), primarily men, to intermarry with the local population more quickly. Thus, the "black/white" or "black/white/brown" paradigm that has been used to define racial categories in the United States tends not to work as well. Local residents create more racial subdivisions. Much of the population of partially African heritage may not identify as "black"; they may refer to themselves as "mulatto" and consider this a distinct category, or they may use other terms. Interestingly, at the same time that racial categories are more complex, they are also important. References to racial attributes appear frequently in everyday conversations, in popular song lyrics, and in other forms of popular culture.

Consider Figure 1.9. It is a nineteenth-century oil painting by a Spaniard, Víctor Landaluze, who lived in Cuba for many years. Landaluze had a penchant for choosing local character types as the subjects of his work, even to the extent of presenting subjects that Cuban-born painters tended to avoid as embarrassing. Although blacks and mulattos figure prominently in this artist's work, many of his images disparaged black and mixed-race people; he clearly disapproved of their

FIGURE 1.9 *Víctor Landaluze*, Preparing for the Dance, *1880s.* *(Museo de Bellas Artes, Havana, Cuba).*

attempts to climb socially and to integrate into Spanish colonial society. Figure 1.9 features a *mulata*, a woman of mixed race, along with a darker black man. *Mulatas* appear frequently in Caribbean prose and culture; Spanish men tended to view them as beautiful, hypersexual beings. They sought them out for romantic liaisons yet for the most part did not consider them worthy of marriage given contemporary notions of European racial superiority.

Many details in the Landaluze painting give indications of Spanish colonial attitudes toward race. The *mulata* is the center of attention, framed in the light of the candle. Both she and her partner are dressed in fine clothing, yet their postures seem inappropriate. The woman leans forward, displaying her voluptuous body in a manner that probably seemed risqué or even lewd in colonial Havana. Her companion also leans to one side, somewhat awkwardly and ineptly, as he pulls on white gloves for a dance. One notices a marked contrast between the modest dwelling these individuals share, its state of disarray, and the elegant clothes they wear. This contrast is made even more striking by the presence of a broom in the foreground of the image, a marker of manual labor much more commonly associated with Afro-Cubans at the time than formal dress. Landaluze seems to be mocking these individuals, portraying them as inept social climbers with pretensions of grandeur beyond their status. Dances did represent an important site of interaction between those of Spanish descent and Cubans of color, so it is no accident that the artist chose such a theme. Performing in a successful dance band represented one of the most prestigious jobs that Cubans of color could aspire to in the nineteenth century, given that they were barred from many other professions. Additionally, dances created opportunities for women of color (black and mixed-race) to meet Spanish men who might help them economically in various ways.

Racial difference in Latin America today has become a source of both pride and embarrassment to residents. Whether one speaks of indigenous heritage (especially in the case of Mexico, Central America, and the Andes) or of African heritage (most prominent in the Caribbean and Brazil), non-European roots have complex meanings. They represent a marker of distinction, something unique about local character, and yet they signify that Latin American culture will never be synonymous with elite European-derived culture such as the Western symphonic tradition. The latter is often perceived as highly sophisticated, whereas cultures of non-European derivation even today may be (inappropriately) viewed as less important, even "primitive" or "backward." Of the three countries that concern us in this volume, Dominican views toward African heritage have tended in the recent past to be the most negative, for reasons to be addressed later. Because of this ambivalence, the state of research on Afro-Dominican heritage is also the most rudimentary. Puerto Ricans discursively embrace African-influenced heritage to a greater extent but do not necessarily study it or afford it the attention it deserves. The degree of engagement with African-influenced heritage within Cuba also varies widely, from serious academic research on the part of some to total disinterest and even disdain on the part of others.

CREOLIZATION AND DIASPORA

The concept of "creolization" is a central element of Caribbean culture. Appearing originally in the writings of French Caribbean authors of the 1950s, the term has experienced a revival in recent years and is discussed in a number of recent publications (e.g., Buisseret 2000, Chaudenson 2001, Stewart 2007). It refers to the fusion or blending of different racial and cultural groups over time—in the Caribbean, primarily African and European groups—and the creation of something new and different out of those components. Anthropologists have developed a wealth of terms that describe various aspects of this process and its dynamics: "acculturation," "transculturation," "syncretism," "deculturization," etc. Creolization is evident in the varied color of people's skin and in their physical appearance more generally. It is apparent in local vocabularies that often incorporate non-European terms, in ways of speaking and pronouncing, in cuisines that blend various influences, in religious expression, even in grammatical structures (especially in the case of Haiti) that have combined in fascinating ways. Creolization is also evident in musical forms that combine elements from Europe, Africa, and elsewhere. To reiterate, national popular music in this region—commercial music of the twentieth century derived from the working classes but embraced by nearly everyone—tends to demonstrate cultural mixture. Consciously or unconsciously, residents understand that music of this sort best represents their history and identity in symbolic form.

Most scholars agree that Caribbean identity is neither European nor African but, rather, "in-between." Paul Gilroy (1993, 3) refers to it as a "stereophonic" region, one in which African and European sensibilities have been fundamentally interpenetrated. In the same way, ethnographer and author Fernando Ortiz (1947) referred to sugar and tobacco as metaphors for the European and African poles of Caribbean heritage, respectively, suggesting that local culture resulted from a complex "counterpoint" of both. Polyrhythm is a dominant symbol for the Caribbean in the writings of Antonio Benítez-Rojo, who describes individual rhythms cut through by others and the composite in turn cut through by still others (1996, 18). Perhaps this description is one of the most apt since it not only underscores the complexity of the region culturally but also allows for external influences, whether from immigrant communities abroad or from entirely different groups.

Of course, creolized music frequently exists side by side with other forms that may not be as creolized, for instance, music that continues to employ African languages (such as on CD track 1) or that sounds decidedly European, such as music for the Catholic mass. Different degrees of creolization may also appear when examining the same genre, such as the *salve* in the Dominican Republic, some styles of which are very similar to what might have been sung in Spain at a particular moment in history, others much more African-sounding. Ultimately, one must think of Caribbean musical traditions as a continuum in this sense, with certain kinds of music more culturally blended than others. Music from abroad continues to influence the islands constantly as well; this repertoire may be appropriated and performed exactly as it was abroad or in a newly creolized fashion of its own. Various islands also influence each other musically and thus lead to localized sorts of creolization. Residents of the Caribbean move with ease between a dizzying array of different styles of music—local, regional, and international, creole and otherwise. As Kenneth Bilby (1985) notes, they have become "polymusical" in a way that reflects their unique environment.

Notions of creolization are related to broader discussions of cultural hybridity within the Spanish-speaking Americas. Perhaps the most prominent advocate of this sort of inquiry is the Argentine author Néstor García Canclini. In his book *Hybrid Cultures* (1995) he describes the region as inherently fractured, caught between various tendencies and in an ongoing ideological exchange with currents from Europe, the United States, and elsewhere. The author suggests that modern, postindustrial lifestyles and experiences coexist in the region with elements of traditional indigenous- or African-derived beliefs as well as influences from international commercial media. He notes that musicians such as Panamanian-Cuban Rubén Blades, Argentine Astor Piazzola, and Brazilian Caetano Veloso incorporate a vast array of elements (i.e., jazz, local folklore, international classical repertoire) into their compositions that manifest a fundamentally hybridized sensibility. The author suggests that Eurocentric attitudes and practices have been challenged increasingly in the region by artists of all sorts. They have created greater heterogeneity of expression, a "more complex articulation of traditions and modernities" (p. 9), often expressed through music.

Most countries in the Caribbean now embrace their hybridized or creolized roots. In general, this is a decidedly positive trend, one that was not as apparent in past decades. Of course, embracing such heritage does not necessarily help residents appreciate the uglier aspects of the history that gave rise to it. Creolized cultures developed in many cases out of open warfare against indigenous populations. On many islands, the societies that developed thereafter formed stark social divisions: One group consisted primarily of Africans from diverse regions, heterogeneous, fragmented, living in bondage; the other European, relatively homogeneous, in total political control. Historian Gordon Lewis has discussed these issues. Discourse about creolization today often presents a softened or "whitewashed" version of the past, a discourse of unity obscuring a history of conflict. Viewed from this perspective, the development of hybridized culture takes on potentially new meanings. It may be that musical fusion has represented a "weapon of the weak" (Scott 1985), a way of mainstreaming practices that suffered persecution under European domination and needed to be disguised. Certainly, much creole culture contains hidden references for those in the know. These may include Kongo, Yoruba, or other verbal phrases unintelligible to large segments of society or musical references to drumming traditions recognized only by practitioners. Ivor Miller (2000, 10) has documented "double performance" of this sort, in which creolized song encodes multiple meanings for various constituencies rather than presenting a single message.

Creolized Caribbean culture is simultaneously innovative and traditional, dynamically fresh yet grounded in local experiences. While written in the language of the colonizer and often incorporating other aspects of European music, it is also unique. Creole music is usually quite improvisational, incorporating new rhythmic schemes or inventing new ways of playing European instruments. Songs often "signify" in particular ways, making references to common melodies from the past but using them to say something new through changes in context, in accompaniment, in other musical elements, or in lyrics. The meanings of particular songs are far from static; they can change radically from one rendition to the next depending on the wishes of the performer and the readings of the public.

As a way of illustrating such transformation and the complexity of the cultural "in-betweenness" represented in much Caribbean music making, consider the example of "La comparsa" by Ernesto Lecuona (CD track 2). Lecuona (1895–1963) was arguably one of the most famous and commercially successful composers of all time from the Spanish-speaking Caribbean. He was a white or "Hispano-Cuban," born into a middle-class family outside of Havana, who soon became known as a child prodigy on the piano. Lecuona's compositions represent a sophisticated fusion of classical and popular elements. Often, his works take inspiration from folkloric sources; he was one of the first classically trained performers to create works based on Afro-Caribbean themes.

The piano piece "La comparsa" (CD track 2) serves as a good introduction to Lecuona's music. This song dates from 1912, when the

FIGURE 1.10 *Ernesto Lecuona in 1943, standing alongside one of the most well-known vocal interpreters of his compositions, Ester Borja.* (Photo courtesy of Jose Ruiz Elcoro).

composer was only 16. It might be considered an example of *program music*, an instrumental composition inspired loosely by an image, event, or idea. The term *"comparsa"* refers to a carnival or street processional band, traditionally comprised of Afro-Cuban performers who play a variety of drums and other percussion. For centuries, the Spanish governors of Cuba allowed enslaved and free blacks to play such music in the street once a year as part of extended Christmas celebrations (see Fig. 3.1). Lecuona may have taken inspiration from these groups of the past or from others playing in carnival events at the turn of the twentieth century. Authorities banned their participation in street celebrations between 1916 and 1937, believing them too rowdy and too "African," but later reversed policy and invited them to take part once again.

One prominent element in "La comparsa" is the left-hand part, a repeated ostinato or underlying rhythmic figure consisting of four syncopated notes followed by four straight quarter notes (Fig. 1.11).

FIGURE 1.11 *Left-hand ostinato in Lecuona's "La comparsa."*

Lecuona based his composition on this repeating two-measure rhythmic cell, something common to many kinds of Afro-Caribbean music. Note that the first half of the figure appears to be a variation of the *cinquillo* rhythm discussed previously (Fig. 1.4). The phrase is also very close to something known as *danzón clave*, a topic that will appear in Chapter 5. "La comparsa" begins softly in a minor key, evoking an image of a street band playing far off in the distance. Gradually, the sound becomes louder, and the music finally reaches a crescendo after switching to a major mode as the imaginary band passes right in front of the listener, only to gradually fade away again in the distance. Of course, Lecuona has created a highly stylized piece rather than incorporating rhythms or melodies that actual *comparsas* are known to have played. His commercial genius consisted of an ability to draw loosely from folklore and to transform it into light classical fare appealing to concertgoers.

This piece, a semiclassical composition by a white Cuban based on Afro-Cuban folklore, could be interpreted in various ways. Some might view it negatively as a parody of drumming traditions that Lecuona may not have understood fully or may not have been inclined to valorize in their original form because of his European training. Others might view the piece positively as a tribute to African heritage at a time when very little concert music of any sort made reference to black folklore. It is quite possible that various individuals came to both conclusions about the song. One might avoid such polarized readings and simply conclude that the piece reflected the tastes and preferences of a middle-class public at a certain moment in Cuba's history, a specific racial formation in Omi and Winant's (1986) terms. The music fundamentally is neither African nor European. It is creole, and its significance even for specific audiences at a particular moment is difficult to determine. These issues, while complex, help to underscore the importance of understanding not only the musical sounds of a particular song or repertoire but their local uses, meanings, and modes of circulation.

ACTIVITY 1.5 *Listen closely to CD track 2, "La comparsa"*
by Ernesto Lecuona, using the partial guide below and the complete

guide found on the Oxford University Press Web site (www.oup. com/us.moore). It should help you identify the sectional changes in the music as well as other features described in the text.

Partial Listening Guide to CD Track 2

"La comparsa"

0:00–0:05

Initial solo statement of the repeated left-hand figure that serves as the structural basis of the composition. It is played softly, as if the music were at a distance. As mentioned, the left-hand figure is a *"claved"* rhythm consisting of an initial syncopated half over one measure and a straighter half over the next. It outlines an F#–minor chord initially but changes notes (not rhythm) to adapt to different harmonies.

0:06–0:57

First statement of the main theme in the right hand, against the left-hand ostinato. It repeats with minor variations at 0:33 and begins getting louder.

Another interesting aspect of "La comparsa" is that the song has remained in circulation since 1912 and has been performed by white and black performers in many renditions through the years, often with very different relations to Afro-Caribbean heritage. One of the more striking cover versions from the 1970s was recorded by the jazz fusion group Irakere under the direction of Afro-Cuban pianist and composer Jesús ("Chucho") Valdés (Fig. 1.12). *"Irakere"* is a Yoruba term meaning "jungle" or "lush place." The band at that time included a surprising number of virtuosic musicians, many of whom have since gone on to successful solo careers, many abroad: saxophonist Paquito D'Rivera, trumpeter Arturo Sandoval, bassist Carlos del Puerto, percussionist Enrique Pla, etc.

The moment that gave rise to this remake of "La comparsa" was quite different from 1912. Many performers since the revolution of 1959 had been searching for ways of incorporating local Afro-Cuban folklore into

FIGURE 1.12 a *Composer and pianist Jesús ("Chucho") Valdés (b. 1941), director of the jazz fusion ensemble Irakere, pictured here about 1980.* b *Members of Irakere perform. Arturo Sandoval solos on the trumpet accompanied by bassist Carlos del Puerto. Saxophonist Paquito D'Rivera stands behind him.* (Archives, Cuban Ministry of Culture).

popular music and of valorizing such traditions generally. The government may have not actively supported this initiative but, for the most part, did not oppose it. You will notice in Figure 1.12 that a drum appears in the bottom left corner of the image; this is an *Abakuá* instrument, an *enkomo*, a Cuban drum derived from similar percussion in the Calabar delta region on the border between present-day Nigeria and Cameroon. It is indicative of the sorts of experiments with African-influenced heritage undertaken by Irakere. The 1970s was a moment of heightened racial consciousness in North America as well as Cuba, of course; the civil rights and Black Power movements had considerable influence in the Hispanic Caribbean. Individuals such as Angela Davis and Stokely Carmichael visited Cuba during these years; similar activism led Puerto Ricans to found the Young Lords movement in New York and Chicago and to cultural activism in Santo Domingo (see Chapter 6). One might suggest that the spirit of the times inspired a number of groups such as Irakere to "re-Africanize" their repertoire as part of a racial project that attempted to situate this heritage more prominently.

Irakere's version of "La comparsa" can be previewed for free on iTunes, for instance on their *1978 World Tour* album. Listening to it, various aspects of the piece strike the listener as different from the original version. It is much more raucous and modern-sounding, leading off with drum set, electric guitar, and other instruments. Additionally,

FIGURE 1.13 *Bell pattern ostinato in Valdés' arrangement of "La comparsa."*

percussionists perform a bell pattern virtually from beginning to end without a pause. This rhythm is heard in many *comparsa* street bands even today; its presence lends a sense of folkloric grounding to the piece that Lecuona's original lacked. The pattern when notated is shown in Figure 1.13; higher and lower pitches represent two different bells.

Relatively traditional elements such as the bell pattern described above coexist somewhat uneasily with others. These include the drum set, incorporating beats reminiscent of U.S. rock and funk, and the electric guitar with its distortion and wah-wah pedal, bringing to mind groups such as Chicago and Earth, Wind, and Fire. Chucho Valdés plays the initial iteration of Lecuona's melody on a Fender Rhodes piano, its sound also referencing a host of international rather than local repertoire. The saxophone solo toward the end of the song has elements of atonal free jazz in the style of John Coltrane as well as others derived from jazz–rock fusion.

How are we to interpret a rendition like this, and what might it suggest about overall trends in music of the Hispanic Caribbean? First, it should be clear that local conceptions of musical taste are determined by forms based not only in the region but also in the hemisphere and beyond. Caribbean culture since at least the fifteenth century has involved movement, cultural interactions, and assimilation of foreign elements. Additionally, a great deal of pan-diasporic identification takes place in the Hispanic Caribbean, with local populations of all ethnic and racial backgrounds attracted to music of African American communities in other countries (Brazil, Colombia, Jamaica, etc.). The dynamics of both tendencies deserve further investigation.

Consider also that the meanings of internationally disseminated popular culture may not be the same locally as they are in their country of origin. Extremely tense relations between the Cuban and U.S. governments in the early 1970s, for instance, resulted in a de facto ban on most North American and British popular music in the Cuban media; Valdés' decision to perform "Americanized" renditions of Cuban pop for local consumption thus had charged and rather polemical associations. Finally, this remake of "La comparsa" helps us realize that the meanings of popular culture are rarely static. Musical performance dialogues with tradition but is not subservient to it. Individuals make conscious choices in ever-emergent contexts that resignify the past, comment on it, shape it to their liking. Music's messages can change radically, even as new works retain certain associations with those that have come before them.

The notion of diaspora deserves commentary here since it relates to one of this book's central themes. "Diaspora" is a term that has been used increasingly in studies of African-influenced cultures of the Americas since the 1980s (Brubaker 2005). It implies three core elements: (1) the movement or displacement of populations, (2) notions of a shared homeland that displaced groups recognize as having left behind, and (3) a degree of boundary maintenance that they retain in social and cultural terms from others. The Caribbean affords an especially interesting space for thinking about issues related to the African diaspora. On the one hand, it is a region that became home to over 4 million displaced Africans during the Atlantic slave trade and whose residents continue to perform countless forms of African-influenced music. On the other, the Caribbean is known for fundamentally creolized expression, as we have seen; in many instances, European influences arguably predominate within creolized music, and it is performed widely by many social groups. Thus, determinations as to exactly what constitutes Afro-diasporic expression are not always easy. Additionally, not all Afro-Caribbean residents identify as a distinct group—they may feel more "Puerto Rican" than "Afro-Puerto Rican," for instance—or may not conceive of Africa as their homeland. Yet in spite of all this, the term "diaspora" continues to be useful because many Afro-descendant groups do conceive of themselves as a unique group and identify strongly with the music and dance of other Afro-descendant communities, as demonstrated in the discussion of Irakere's music.

While it is beyond the scope of this book to delve deeply into the history of writing about music in the Hispanic Caribbean, it is useful to have a feeling for how substantially scholarship has changed in recent decades. Prior to the 1940s, evolutionist attitudes toward culture influenced a majority of authors. Evolutionists tended to judge all culture from the perspective of elite or middle-class Europeans; they believed essentially that people all around the world were progressing slowly from a state of barbarism toward a particular kind of sophistication represented ultimately by the culture of industrialized European nations. These authors generally could not appreciate non-European aesthetics, nor could they imagine that certain kinds of non-European music could be sophisticated in ways (e.g., in terms of rhythm, the incorporation of microtones, the use of complex melodic modes, improvisation, or any other number of factors) that differed from European music. For this reason, little serious work on African and other non-European contributions to Caribbean music took place in the Hispanic Caribbean for some time. Most authors in the early twentieth century considered African-derived and creolized music "noise" rather than "culture"; they did not believe it deserved study. A few notable exceptions began to emerge beginning in the 1920s, as evident in the writings of figures such as Alejo Carpentier in Cuba and Mário de Andrade in Brazil.

Atrocities committed against Jews, Roma (gypsies), African peoples, and other minorities in World War II and the horrendously racist doctrine of the Nazis gradually led to a questioning of evolutionist beliefs among wider segments of the intelligentsia internationally. The discrediting of the notion of Aryan superiority in the 1930s and 1940s eventually created space for discussion about ways in which non-European peoples might have been portrayed inaccurately. Progressive authors began to recognize the extent to which earlier generations had been influenced by ethnocentric attitudes. Similarly, the end of colonialism as a political practice created more space in the developing world for the voices of others to be heard.

Thus, the mid-twentieth century gave rise to new generations of scholarship and to more progressive attitudes toward non-Western culture. In the Caribbean and Latin America, a number of pioneering individuals at this time began to study local cultures; they included Roger Bastide, Harold Courlander, Melville Herskovits, Alfred Métraux, Fernando Ortiz, Pierre Verger, and others. These authors have been characterized by some as "retentionists" because they devoted much of their efforts to documenting the many elements of sub-Saharan African culture—song melodies, instruments, dances, costumes, religious practices, etc.—that managed to survive and flourish in the Americas, albeit often in modified form. They attempted to document where particular influences had come from in Africa, largely to refute the notion that Africa had no culture or heritage deserving of study.

Since the 1970s, the focus of African diaspora scholarship in the Americas has changed substantially once again. Many younger authors have criticized the retentionist generation, arguing that their work is problematic in various senses. They suggest that it too often characterizes African-influenced cultures as static and unchanging. Beyond this, they believe that the most important issues that music and other expressive forms raise about the human experience derive from *how* culture is used by particular groups and *why* they have chosen to embrace or perpetuate it and not merely the fact that it exists in the first place. Emphasis has shifted, then, from the description and documentation of cultural forms (a necessary first step) toward a greater focus on change, process, agency, and the dynamics of cultural formation. Music is more often studied at particular moments in history with an eye toward its significance for individual groups and the ways that they recreate

and/or alter music through performance. Additionally, musical scholarship (and most other work in the humanities) has tended to become
more politically aware in recent decades. Authors are now sensitized
to broader problems facing the groups they study and often link music
making to issues of social inequality, poverty, racism, political subjugation, gender inequality, and the like.

These, then, are a few recent trends that will be reflected in this volume. My goal is to give you some feeling for the amazing variety of
music making in the Hispanic Caribbean, particular styles of performance associated with various islands, the sorts of groups that perform
them, the meanings they convey locally, and the broader tendencies that
have given rise to them. The Caribbean provides fascinating insights
into how unique cultural forms are created, how diverse elements slowly
converge into synthesis, and how individual communities continue to
create cohesive musical lives out of fractured and disjunct experiences.

CHAPTER 2

Music and Spanish Colonization

∞

This chapter begins with a brief history of the Hispanic Caribbean, describing the native inhabitants living on the islands at the time of first European contact and the process of colonization itself. It then focuses on one of two broad categories of music that have had the strongest influence on musical performance in the region since that time: Spanish-derived heritage. Chapter 3 continues by exploring the other major category, African-influenced heritage. The juxtaposition of these traditions underscores the diversity of music making in the Hispanic Caribbean and the many styles that demonstrate strong ties to the past. Though all music in the Caribbean has been creolized, the music discussed in Chapters 2 and 3 demonstrates the strongest direct ties to the Iberian Peninsula and to West Africa, respectively. My intent is to help you think of music in the Hispanic Caribbean as a continuum of musical styles extending from string instruments and poetic forms derived from medieval Spain and the Arab world, on the one hand, to a vast array of drumming, dance, and vocal styles influenced by Yoruba and Kongo traditions, on the other, in addition to those of other West African groups. Later chapters shift emphasis, first by examining fundamentally creolized music in detail and then by charting the histories of musical forms that have developed more recently through constant processes of international cultural exchange.

A BRIEF HISTORY OF COLONIZATION

Early travel accounts tell us that various indigenous groups lived on Caribbean islands in the late fifteenth century when Christopher Columbus first sailed blindly into the area, believing he was in Asia. Native peoples there included the Arawaks, Caribs, Siboneys, and Taínos. Though most greeted the newcomers as friends, it quickly became apparent that the Europeans cared little for their welfare; they planned to plunder and dominate the entire region, enslaving native people in the process. During the first decades of settlement, Spaniards ruled the Caribbean from the island known today as Hispaniola (now divided into the Dominican Republic and Haiti). Within a period of 150 years they managed to kill off all but a handful of the original inhabitants of the region, who by some accounts numbered in the millions. This genocide occurred as the result of various factors including open warfare, disease, starvation, and overwork. An article in *U.S. News* suggested that the years immediately after Columbus' arrival appear to have brought a toll on human life in this hemisphere comparable to all the world's losses in World War II (Lord 1997, 68).

Regrettably little information remains about the culture and music of most Caribbean indigenous groups. Some native foods like cassava are still eaten, and practices such as sleeping in hammocks and, of course, smoking tobacco remain. The names of many Caribbean islands derive from indigenous languages (e.g., Haiti, Arawak for "mountainous land"; Borinquen, the Taíno name for Puerto Rico; and Cuba from "Cubanacan," Taíno for "central place"). The *areíto* (also spelled *areyto*) is mentioned in some early missionary accounts, however. These were large, communal music-and-dance events involving as many as a thousand participants who moved in circles around a group of musicians. Some *areítos* had religious origins, while others took place after the death of a community member or in preparation for warfare. Performances could last several days, with songs serving to chronicle the history and collective memory of the community. The dancers are said to have sung in call–response style, following the cues of a lead singer and accompanied by various percussion instruments. These included a slit drum known as a *mayohuacán* (Fig. 2.1), *maraca*-like shakers, conch shell trumpets, and notched gourds similar to the modern *güiro*. Indigenous influences on present-day Caribbean music making are relatively minimal; only small hand percussion such as the *güiro* or *maraca*s (Figs. 2.2, 2.5) may have persisted as an influence.

For the first century and a half of the colonial period, Spain alone controlled the entire Caribbean region. Those countries that continue to speak Spanish today—the focus of our interest—thus reflect the initial phase of European settlement. Beginning in the seventeenth century, latecomers to Latin American colonization, including Britain, France, and the Netherlands, began to challenge Spanish authority in the region and to attack its settlements. They proved easy to invade since the majority of Spain's troops had moved to Mexico and the Andes where gold and other valuables had been discovered. In 1650, the British succeeded in taking the island of Jamaica; France controlled much of Hispaniola by

FIGURE 2.1 *A* mayohuacán-*like slit drum instrument found by archeologists in* *Puerto Rico.* *(Music Museum of Ponce. Photo by the author).*

1664 and eventually renamed their territory Saint-Domingue; Trinidad and Tobago passed hands at various times between the British, French, and Dutch.

SPANISH-DERIVED MUSIC

Spanish-derived music has had a strong influence on music throughout the Americas. Musicians from the Iberian Peninsula are known to have accompanied European explorers from their very first visits to the area. Likewise, Catholic priests performed religious music on expeditions and incorporated music into their efforts to "civilize" and convert both indigenous groups and later Africans. Catholicism of

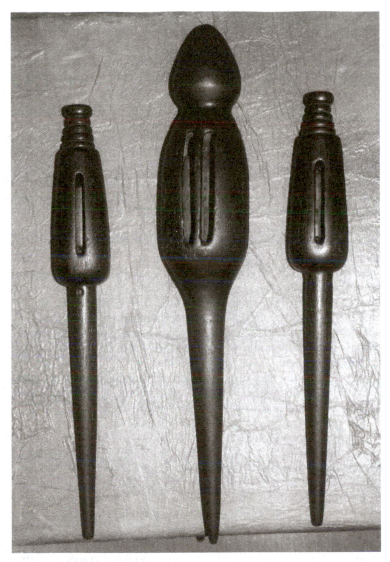

FIGURE 2.2 *Rattles used by indigenous residents of Puerto Rico at the time of the European conquest. (Music Museum of Ponce. Photo by the author).*

many sorts continues to be practiced in the Caribbean, a direct result of the Spanish presence. In secular music today, the legacy of Spain is also evident in myriad forms, from *romances* (epic narrative ballads) and *seguidillas* (strophic songs) to poetic forms such as the couplet and quatrain. European-derived instruments abound as well, particularly the guitar, the accordion, the violin, and the piano. Virtually all string and keyboard instruments in the Caribbean come from Europe or were based on European models. Popular dances stretching back centuries—the waltz, contradance, schottische, even modern-day dances such as salsa—either derive directly from Europe or incorporate many features from it. Despite the fact that they represented a demographic minority in most Caribbean countries, Europeans controlled local societies and influenced them profoundly. They brought "cultivated" musical traditions—that is, classical music of various sorts performed by conservatory-trained instrumentalists—as well as folk traditions. This split reflects the social divisions between the poorer agriculturalists and tradesmen who emigrated from Spain and the smaller circle of elites who controlled political and business interests.

At the time of the conquest of the Americas, especially, Spain was far from a unified cultural entity; thus, speaking of "Spanish music" can be problematic. The region had been dominated during various periods by Greeks, Romans, Phoenicians, Arabs, and others and had its own population of African slaves beginning in the fifteenth century, who contributed significantly to musical development. Thus, when we speak of Hispanic traditions in the Americas, we are actually referring to culture that is itself fundamentally hybridized, with Arab contributions being especially prominent.

Puerto Rico is the island of the Hispanic Caribbean where Spanish-derived folk traditions are arguably the strongest and most widely practiced, so perhaps it would be appropriate to discuss *música jíbara* first. The term *"jíbaro"* in Puerto Rico means *campesino*, a rural farmer or laborer. Thus, *música jíbara* can roughly be translated as "Puerto Rican country music." It is a style that prominently features the voice supported by a number of string instruments, especially the *cuatro*, a small folk guitar with ten metal strings in double courses (Fig. 2.3). Its typical tuning from low to high is B–E–A–D–G. The doubling of strings produces a bright, piercing sound; many *cuatro* performers are known for their fast, virtuosic melody playing and improvisation. The name *"cuatro"* (literally "four") apparently derives from earlier versions of the instrument that were built with only four doubled courses of strings and without the addition of two lower bass strings common today. Other string instruments common in Spanish-derived folk music in the Caribbean include the *bandurria*, a mandolin-like instrument with six pairs of doubled strings; the *laúd* (Fig. 2.4), also with six doubled strings; and the guitar. *Música jíbara* singers are famous for beginning songs with something known as a *lalaleo*, an improvised melody incorporating

FIGURE 2.3 *The* cuatro, *Puerto Rico's best-known instrument and one that has become emblematic of the nation.* *(Music Museum of Ponce. Photo by the author).*

the syllables such as la, le, lo, and lai. This repertoire in earlier times was most popular in the countryside and still has strong rural associations, yet it can be heard in urban areas today. The music of the *jíbaro* and the *jíbaro* himself have become emblematic of Puerto Rican identity.

FIGURE 2.4 *A display of the many sorts of string instruments used by Puerto Ricans during colonial times. The instrument on the far right is a* laúd. *(Music Museum of Ponce. Photo by the author).*

PUERTO RICAN *SEIS*

The most common style of *música jíbara* performance is *seis*, a general term for string-based music incorporating sung poetry, largely derived from Spanish antecedents. It may be played for listening or for dancing. This tradition is hundreds of years old; through the early twentieth century it represented the mainstream of secular entertainment on the island. Folklorist Francisco López Cruz (1967) tells us that the term *seis* (literally "six") derives from Seville, Spain, and specifically groups of six children who danced in religious activities in front of the church altar during celebrations of Corpus Christi and the Immaculate Virgin. Although the genre may have had close religious associations originally, much of it is secular today. Many variants exist; some are defined by the dance movements that accompany the music (*seis chorreao, seis zapateao, seis amarrao, seis valseao*, etc.) but also by the region in which they developed (*seis fajardeño* from the city of Fajardo, *seis llanero* from coastal plains, *seis bayamonés* from Bayamón) or by the name of the composer of the particular melodies or rhythmic styles associated with them (*seis Andino, seis Pepe Orné, seis Portalatín, seis Villarán*). Many subgenres incorporate unique, repeated melodies that make them immediately recognizable to local listeners.

Seis dance styles in earlier times involved a stiff torso and movement primarily of the waist and feet, sometimes with rhythmic striking of shoes against the ground. This style is related to what is known as *zapateado* (or *zapateo*) in much of the Spanish-speaking Americas, taking its name from *zapato*, the word for shoe. It is similar in this sense to flamenco and Mexican folkloric dancing. Various forms of *seis* choreography such as line dancing are discussed in historical documents, but today it tends to be performed in couples, ballroom style. *Seis chorreao*, or "flowing *seis*," is by far the most common. It involves couples in a loose embrace who alternately take one step forward and one back, turning a bit to the right and left as they do so. The dancers' feet are said to slide low against the floor so that they look like they're "*chorreando*," or "flowing."

Instruments most commonly featured in *seis* include voices, the *cuatro*, the guitar, and the Puerto Rican–style *güiro*. The latter is a thin, dried, and varnished gourd with small grooves cut into the outside that are scraped with a metal pick called a *puya* (Fig. 2.5). The *güiro* performs half a dozen common rhythmic patterns that help to define various subgenres, as well as improvising flourishes and variations. The latter practice is known as *hacer piquetes* ("to pick at") or *flirtear* ("flirt") with the *güiro*. In modern recordings, electric or acoustic bass may be added to *seises*, as well as other string or percussion. The music is typically in a major key with relatively simple harmonies (tonic-dominant, I–IV–V, etc.) and consists of short phrases of four to eight measures. So-called Andalucian cadences (I–bVII–bVI–V) taken from southern Spanish and related music are also common. Instrumentalists complicate the *seis'* brisk duple meter by performing syncopations and hemiola figures against its straight pulse.

A brief instrumental introduction begins most pieces, followed by vocals. In some cases, singers improvise verses on the spot; in fact, high-profile competitions exist for improvisers of *música jíbara* that often involve cash prizes. Subgenres are too numerous to describe at length, but a few examples will suffice. *Seis bombeao* derives its name from bawdy, jokey interjections or "*bombas*" heard in interludes between instrumental segments. After playing dance music for a while, the band stops and a member of the public shouts out a rhymed couplet, often making oblique reference to someone at the gathering.

FIGURE 2.5 *Puerto Rico–style* güiros. *The gourd on the left is unfinished; the others are finished* güiros *that have been cut with small grooves so that they can be scraped with a metal* puya. *In the background on the left you can see conch shell trumpets used by Taíno Indians.* (*Music Museum of Ponce. Photo by the author*).

Aguinaldos constitute another well-known style of *seis*. The *aguinaldo* derives from religious events and is often sung during the Christmas season (December 24–January 15); it is common in the Dominican Republic as well. One might think of the *aguinaldo* as a type of Christmas carol, though many variants exist; some are heard all year and are performed by individuals rather than groups. The religious variety is most typically performed between Thanksgiving and Epiphany, January 6. They may be sung in churches or individual houses but also in street processions by singers who move from house to house as part of events known as *parrandas* (parties) or *asaltos navideños* ("Christmas assaults"). Singers enter the homes of friends and acquaintances, sing *aguinaldos* or other seasonal repertoire for them, then demand copious amounts of food and drink before heading on to perform for their next "victims." Another format of *seis* is the *seis de controversia*, a sung poetic duel between two singers similar to the Cuban *música guajira* example discussed later.

All rural, Spanish-derived music in the Caribbean places considerable emphasis on poetry, with music often in a secondary or supportive role. Singers and instrumentalists may even use previously composed melodic lines rather than creating entirely new ones. Lyrics are expected to follow strict rhyme sequences; one common approach uses a four-line "internal" pattern in which line one rhymes with line four and line two with line three (i.e., an *abba* rhyme scheme). This is different from most popular verse in the United States, which employs an *abcb* rhyming structure. A more extended variant of the internal rhyme idea is called *espinela* form, named after its inventor, fifteenth-century Spanish poet Vicente Espinel. *Espinela* form consists of two five-line units, the first half in the pattern *abbaa* and the second in the same pattern but with different rhymes: *ccddc*. This is the most common rhyme scheme found in *décima* poetry, ten-line stanzas found in Spanish-derived music throughout the Americas.

In the box are song lyrics that provide a good example both of the sound of Puerto Rican *seis chorreao* and of *décima* lyrics in *espinela* form (CD track 3). This song is precomposed rather than improvised. It is rather amusing since it takes as a theme the erectile-dysfunction medication Viagra. The example was written by Polito Ríos and performed in the late 1990s by José Ortiz. It exemplifies the way many Caribbean musicians incorporate topical themes and issues of the day into their songs. Note the instrumental introduction featuring the *cuatro*, the instrumental interludes between each verse, and the *cuatro* solo after verse two. Harmonies for the most part are quite simple, consisting exclusively of the following four-measure repeated pattern: I–IV–V–V (in this case, D–G–A–A). Only the introduction and instrumental sections include somewhat complex harmonies, perhaps to keep the focus on the lyrics.

Be aware that CD track 3 includes a *pie forzado* or "forced foot," a poetic line the composer is obliged to work into every *décima* as a final phrase. In this case, the author chooses his own *pie forzado*, but such lines may also be given to singers in competitions to see how effectively they can work with them spontaneously. Composers of *décimas* with a *pie forzado* must ensure that the fifth and sixth lines of each *décima* rhyme with this final (tenth) phrase. In the lyrics of CD track 3, the bold letters beginning each line correspond to the *décima*'s rhyme scheme.

Partial Listening Guide to CD Track 3

"Una Viagra que camine" ("A Viagra Pill that Walks")

A complete listening guide of the entire piece can be accessed at www.oup.com/us.moore.

0:00–0:12

Instrumental introduction featuring the *cuatro*, electric bass, and percussion. The section begins with strings only; percussion enters about 0:07.

0:13–0:40 Verse 1

A	Un nuevo medicamento	A new medicine
B	Conocido por el Viagra	Known as Viagra
B	En el mundo se consagra	In the whole world it's glorified
A	Como el gran descubrimiento	As a great new discovery
A	Ese formidable invento	This formidable invention
C	No hay duda que me fascine	There's no doubt that it fascinates me
C	Mas si me deja que opine	Yet if you let me share my opinion
D	Voy a decir en voz alta	I'll say out loud
D	A mí sólo me hace falta	What I really need
C	Una Viagra que camine	Is a Viagra pill that walks

0:40–0:46

An instrumental interlude, similar to the second half of the introduction.

0:47–1:14 Verse 2

A	Una joven elegante	A young elegant woman
B	Que al amar con interés	Who gets serious about loving
B	No cabe duda que es	There's no doubt that that is
A	El mejor estimulate	The very best stimulant
A	Resultaría fascinante	It would be quite fascinating
C	Que sus caricias combine	If her tender touch would combine with
C	Aunque al final las domine	And even come to be dominated by
D	Con mordiscos o cosquillas	Little bites and tickling
D	Quiero en lugar de pastillas	I want instead of taking pills
C	Una viagra que camine	A Viagra pill that walks

ACTIVITY 2.1 *Compose a few quatrains in English using an internal rhyme scheme (abba). Next, try to do the same using a ten-line décima structure. Choose a* pie forzado *that everyone in the class will use in his or her own fashion, then compare the results. The* pie forzado *should be approximately eight syllables in length. It could be something as simple as "My sunny tropical holiday" or "Across the Caribbean Sea."*

CUBAN *PUNTO*

The term *"música guajira"* in Cuba is the equivalent to *"música jíbara"* in Puerto Rico; it is used to denote any sort of folk music associated with rural farmers, called *guajiros*. Many *guajiros* are of Spanish origin whose ancestors emigrated from Galicia, Andalusia, Asturias, and the Canary Islands. *Música guajira* is most commonly heard in Pinar del Río, to the west of Cuba (known for its tobacco farms), and in the center, specifically the area stretching from Santa Clara to Camagüey.

As one might expect, string instruments predominate in *música guajira* traditions as well. They include the *laúd* and *bandurria* (instruments also played in Puerto Rico), the *tres* (a folk guitar with three double courses of strings), and other local instruments. These days, some Afro-Cuban percussion (*maracas, clave*, even *conga* drums) may be used by *música guajira* groups as well. The most famous piece influenced by this body of song—especially its lyrical style—is "La guajira guantanamera" ("The Country Girl from Guantánamo"), written by Joseíto Fernández in the 1940s and covered by U.S. folk singer Pete Seeger, among others. *Música guajira* is usually performed in a major key but in triple meter as opposed to the duple meter of *seis*. In the past it was also often intended for dancing. The music can be vocal or instrumental. *"Punto"* is the term used in Cuba (rather than *"seis"*) to refer to sung *décima* poetry accompanied by guitars or other instruments. This name comes from the verb *"puntear,"* the plucking or picking out of melodies on strings. As in the case of Puerto Rican *seis*, the melodies used in Cuban *punto* often consist of relatively short, repeated stock phrases. They are used to support and foreground sung poetry rather than to serve as the primary focus of musical interest themselves.

Singers of Spanish-derived folk music often improvise the words they sing on the spot, similar to what freestyle rappers in the United States might do. All three islands of the Hispanic Caribbean have multiple traditions that involve improvising lyrics in the act of performance. The *punto* example on CD track 4 features two lead singers rather than one. It is common for performers of improvised poetry to sing together and to compete in a friendly fashion against one another. Dueling between two or more performers is referred to as *controversia* or *desafío*. In some cases, while one singer is in the process of creating a verse, the other (if he or she is thinking quickly enough) may actually jump in and "snatch away" the initiative, inventing a different line from what his or her opponent was planning but that nevertheless rhymes appropriately within the *décima*. This sort of intervention, a tug-of-war over ownership of the verse, is referred to as *controversia candente* ("burning controversy") or *tira tira*

("shootout," "gunfight"). In the full text transcription of the lyrics to CD track 4, available online, these moments of "snatching" between singers are marked with double asterisks.

The *controversia* on your CD is performed in a style known as *punto libre*, or free *punto*. This means that the pulse of the song is not strict but instead slows down and speeds up at various points. Musicians accompanying the singer play in a slow *rubato* while he or she recites improvised verses. At the conclusion of a given couplet or *décima*, however, they suddenly break into a livelier tempo in triple meter, playing repeated stock phrases in variation until one of the singers has invented a new rhyme and is ready to begin singing again. As in the previous *seis* example, a major key is used and the harmonies are simple, with no modulation.

The following example of *controversia*-style *punto* music (CD track 4) is taken from the *JVC Video Anthology of World Music and Dance*. Its improvisatory nature is especially evident when we consider the subject they have chosen to discuss: Japan and Japanese culture. The JVC crew that came to film this event was from Japan, and though they never appear in the video, the two singers seem to have adopted their ethnicity as a central theme. It is quite likely that the camera crew had no idea they were becoming the butt of various jokes! In the full transcription on line, "JV" refers to the older singer (Justo Vega) who performs first and "AA" to the younger singer (Adolfo Alfonso, Figure 2.6). Both sang for years on the Cuban television show *Palmas y cañas* (*Palm Trees and Sugarcane*) beginning in the 1960s.

The text begins with several complete *décimas*; more heated exchanges that come later include a few shorter two- and four-line stanzas as well. These apparently represent "failed" *décimas*, verses that could not be extended to the full ten-line form because of the difficulties presented by spontaneously improvised competition. One could also analyze the poetry as consisting of two four-line *cuartetas* in *abba* and *cddc* form, respectively, hooked together by two bridge lines with an *ac* rhyme scheme. The occasional repetition of a single line of text seems to

FIGURE 2.6 *Adolfo Alfonso at home in Havana, as interviewed by the author in 2008. In the background you can see the many national awards he has won through the years in* repentista *competitions. (Photo by the author).*

indicate that the singer could not formulate a new rhyme fast enough and thus was forced to repeat himself while he considered what to say next. Finally, at the end of the segment Vega and Alfonso recite a final full ten-line segment together, this one possibly conceived ahead of time in light of its carefully crafted nature. Bold letters beginning each line indicate the overall rhyme scheme.

ACTIVITY 2.2 *Listen closely to CD track 4 on your own and see if you can identify the poetic form and rhyme schemes used. Note the* controversia candente *exchanges in the second half. Next, download the complete listening guide to CD track 4 at www.oup. com/us.moore and compare your findings to the analysis provided.*

Partial Listening Guide to CD Track 4

"Controversia"

0:00–0:06

The background musical group plays a brief introduction in C major. The pulse is triple meter. Various string instruments can be heard (*laúd*, guitars) in addition to percussion (conga and bongo drums, *güiro*). The accompaniment suddenly stops and continues more sparsely, out of time, as Justo Vega begins to sing.

0:06–0:30

Vega intones his first two lines (0:06–0:13), then apparently can't decide how to proceed. The backup band enters in time again, covering for him until he continues at 0:19, repeating the first two lines (0:19–0:24) and singing two more. Note the stock chord sequence that the band uses behind the singer as they improvise, something like I–ii–IV–V–III–VI–II–V. It invariably ends on the dominant chord.

A [JV] Donde el zéfiro que gira	[JV] Where the zephyr that circles	
B Mueve la palma real	Sways the royal palm tree	
B Columnata tropical	Tropical column	
A Que por la lluvia suspira	That longs for the rain	

0:31–0:34

A brief fill by the band in time as Vega invents his next line of poetry.

0:34–0:41

Vega finishes the first half of his *décima* and begins the second half.

A Se eleva la voz guajira	The voice of our countryside
C De nuestra revolución	Of our revolution is lifted

0:41–0:44

Another brief instrumental interlude, lending credence to the idea that the singer may be thinking of the poetry here as two four-line segments (*abba* and *cddc*) hooked together by a two-line *ac* segment.

0:46–0:58

Vega finishes a complete *décima* in this segment; an impressed audience gives him a round of applause.

C Dándole de corazón	Giving from the heart
D Con amistad y con nombre	With friendship and with renown
D La bienvenida a los hombres	A greeting to the men
C Progresistas del Japón	Progressive [leftists] from Japan

FOLK CATHOLICISM AND
THE DOMINICAN *SALVE*

A final example of Spanish-influenced folklore comes from religious traditions in the Dominican Republic. As mentioned, Catholicism is one of the influences that binds the Hispanic Caribbean together, as well as linking it to Latin America more generally. Missionaries accompanied the earliest expeditions of the conquistadors, and churches represented a prominent part of the very first colonial enclaves. In most Spanish-speaking countries, Catholicism remains a prominent force;

however, orthodox traditions derived from Rome exist side by side with less orthodox local practices known as "folk Catholicism." In the latter, ceremonies and rites brought to the Caribbean by Spanish immigrants centuries ago have changed over time, developing unique characteristics and in some cases adopting influences from West African and other cultures. On the three islands discussed here, religious folk traditions derived directly from Spain arguably have remained strongest in Puerto Rico, owing in large part to the greater proportion of European immigrants who settled there. Folk Catholicism is also very prominent in the Dominican Republic but less so in Cuba, where government policy after the socialist revolution of 1959 discouraged participation in religious events. This policy derived from Marx's notion that religion represented an "opiate of the masses," a form of false consciousness.

One common manifestation of folk Catholicism on all three islands are *fiestas patronales*, or patron saint festivals. These are annual events held in honor of Catholic saints who hold a special place in the history of a particular town or city or are of importance to an individual patron who sponsors them. Many sorts of festivals exist, some on more than one island. For instance, the *Fiestas de la Cruz de Mayo* (Fiestas of the May Cross) in Puerto Rico have a long tradition dating back at least to the seventeenth century and are quite similar to *Altares de la Cruz* (Altar to the Cross) celebrations from Cuba and the *Fiestas de la Santísima Cruz* (Fiestas of the Saintly Cross) in the Dominican Republic. Patron saint festivals often take place over nine-day celebratory periods called *novenas*. They involve activities including the creation of an ornate altar, often with nine tiers, the singing of devotional songs, as well as the preparation of large communal meals and participation in secular music and dance during lighter moments. It is typical for the final night of the *novena* to be reserved for the most important events, and this often falls on the specific day associated with the patron saint in question. While clearly tied to religious practice, *fiestas patronales* have become more secular in recent decades and often showcase local folklore or other music in addition to, or even instead of, sacred repertoire. More focused religious events in the Dominican Republic are commonly associated with small rural churches or devotional events in private homes.

The rites of folk Catholicism may involve street processions, often with a statue of a saint carried aloft by participants (Fig. 2.7). In the Dominican Republic such processions take various forms. They can be associated with *fiestas patronales*, they can represent part of a *velación* devotional event (discussed later in this chapter) organized by a small church community, or they can be part of longer pilgrimages to holy

FIGURE 2.7 *A rural religious procession for a* velación *in the town of Najallo al Medio in the south-central region of the Dominican Republic, December 2008. Processions of this sort represent one of many forms of folk Catholicism. The saint being honored is Santa Lucía; worshippers began and ended their trek at a small family-owned church, stopping at the houses of devotees along the way to pray and sing.* (Photo by Daniel Piper).

sites in various parts of the island. In the Dominican Republic, the latter events are known as *penitencias*, while in Puerto Rico they are referred to as *rogativas*.

The *salve* may well be the genre of Dominican religious music most widely performed by the population at large, yet very little work has been conducted on it beyond Martha Ellen Davis' groundbreaking study from the early 1980s (Davis, 1981). Since it has rarely been recorded or disseminated in the media, it is virtually unknown abroad. *Salves* take their name from a Catholic chant known as the *Salve Regina*, which dates from the Middle Ages and was often used in conjunction with recitations of the rosary. The name *"Salve Regina"* literally means "Save the Queen," referring to the Virgin Mary. Though the Vatican no longer incorporates *salve* prayers into its standard services, they remain prominent in Dominican worship. Residents perform them in a variety of different formats that vary by region, some closely linked to their

Spanish roots and others only tangentially related in a musical or lyrical sense. I discuss the Spanish-influenced form in the Dominican Republic here, then consider more strongly African-influenced or creolized *salves* in Chapter 3.

The communal *velación* (literally "vigil") is the principal context of the *salve*. These devotional activities typically take place in a private home in front of an altar, or on the grounds of a community church, and last from about 10:00 a.m. to 6:00 p.m. (Fig. 2.8). The more European-influenced *salves* to the Virgin tend to be sung in lines facing the altar, while the creole *salves* examined in Chapter 3 are performed more often in circles, typical of West African practice. The *velación* represents a relatively "free," unregulated space for the expression of devotion associated with folk Catholicism; some rites, despite their significance for local communities, may not have the official blessing of the Church because they are considered too unorthodox. *Velaciones* thus allow for a wide variety of religious activity, from Catholic to creolized. Note that in addition to the aforementioned altar, Dominican *velaciones* often require the creation of a thatch-covered outdoor area known as an *enramada*.

FIGURE 2.8 *A private altar in Pueblo Nuevo, a neighborhood of San Cristóbal city, also in the south-central region of the Dominican Republic, 2008. Shrines such as this one, dedicated to San Carlos de Borroméo, serve as a setting for extended salve chants and sung prayers. In many cases the Catholic saints addressed are syncretized with African deities as well.* (Photo by Daniel Piper).

This serves as a place for secular dancing and recreation later in the evening and in the early morning, after formal devotional commitments have been fulfilled.

Dominican liturgical *salves* more strongly influenced by the original Spanish traditions are sometimes called *salves de la Virgen* (*salves* to the Virgin Mary). Devotees often repeat *salves* various times during the evening as they face an altar. In many instances a paid lead singer will initiate and guide a singing of the rosary, followed by one or more *salves*. The lyrics of the original European-derived *"Salve Regina"* chant are printed here. "Aimless wandering" references the experience of Jews in the Old Testament, who spent years in the desert after their escape from bondage in Egypt.

Salve Regina

Dios te salve	May Our Lord save you
Reina y Madre de Misericordia	Queen and Mother of Mercy
A tí llamamos	We call out to you
Los desterrados hijos de Eva	The displaced, homeless children of Eve
A tí suspiramos	We long for you
Gimiendo y llorando	Moaning and crying
En este valle de lágrimas	In this valley of tears
Ea, pues, Señora, abogada nuestra	Hear our plea, our Lady, our advocate
Vuelve a nosotros	Return to us
Esos tus ojos misericordiosos	Your gaze filled with mercy
Y después de este destierro	And after this wandering in exile
Muéstranos a Jesús	Show us Jesus
Fruto bendito de tu vientre	The blessed fruit of your womb
O clemente, o piedosa	Oh beneficent, merciful
O dulce Virgen María	Oh sweet Virgin Mary
Ruega por nosotros	Pray for us
Santa Madre de Dios	Holy Mother of God
Para que seamos dignos	So that we may be worthy
De alcanzar las promesas	Of achieving the promises
De nuestro señor Jesuscristo, Amén	Of our lord Jesus Christ, Amen

European-style *salves* to the Virgin have no definite pulse and are performed in a loose *rubato*. The tempo remains fairly slow, despite minor fluctuations. Often, singers recite the same text multiple times with different melodies in distinct modes. In this sense the pieces are more complex harmonically than most other forms of Spanish-influenced folklore. *Salve* chants are antiphonal; that is, they consist of two different groups of singers who intone lines of the prayer to Mary and respond to each other in alternation. Most singers' vocal production is rather tense and nasal; they sing in a high register, which also reflects southern Spanish folk traditions. Though a majority of pieces are performed a cappella (without instruments), hand clapping or African-derived percussion can accompany singers in some cases. If you would like to listen to Dominican chants to the Virgin of this sort, including *salves* and rosary songs, they can be found on the following CDs: Verna Gillis and Ramón Daniel Pérez Martínez, prod., *Music from the Dominican Republic. Songs from the North*, Vol. 4 (Smithsonian Folkways CD FW 4284, 1976), and *Fiesta en Banica* (Earth Partners CD, Magnetic Art Productions, 2005, www.earthcds.com).

An iteration of some of the basic characteristics of European- and Spanish-derived folk music in the Americas concludes this chapter. Such repertoire tends to be sung in a European language, and the poetic forms it employs are also European. If performers play instruments, they are most often fretted strings of various kinds (guitar, lute, etc.) similar to those used in Spain. With some exceptions, the melodies of this repertoire are diatonic, that is, simple major or minor scales in standard European tunings; and (in the case of songs and chants) the form of the music is often strophic, with musical segments closely paralleling the text. Poetry represents a prominent part of Spanish-derived repertoire; music often serves a secondary or supporting role to the lyrics. Songs may incorporate a certain amount of syncopation, but they have a single basic pulse that is readily discernible every two, three, or four beats. Duple and triple meters are both common. Spanish-derived folk music often has a certain number of sections performed in sequence—verses or strophe, for instance—that predetermine its length and duration.

ACTIVITY 2.3 *To review this section, reorganize your notes around this final summary and find illustrations of them in the various genres discussed.*

The Spanish colonial legacy has left its imprint on music making of the Caribbean in many ways. Its influence can hardly be overestimated since a majority of folk, popular, and classical traditions from the islands incorporate the Spanish language and manifest many other influences from Spain in terms of overall structure, the use of European harmonies, and so on. However, Spanish political dominance for so many years has also led to an overemphasis on the importance of Hispanic heritage to the region in some publications to the exclusion of others. Folklorists, musicians, and critics of years past often failed to appreciate African-derived musical forms; many expressed embarrassment at their presence or simply ignored them. Chapter 3 attempts to rectify this imbalance by exploring African-derived traditions in the region and the ways in which they too have left an imprint on the Hispanic Caribbean, in some cases even stronger than that of Spanish-derived influences.

Cultural Legacies of
the Slave Trade

∞

HISTORY OF THE SLAVE TRADE

The Atlantic slave trade is arguably the historical event that has had the greatest influence on modern Caribbean history and culture. In all, from the beginnings of the colonial period through the late nineteenth century, approximately 12 million Africans were brought under horrific conditions to the Americas as laborers; the vast majority who survived the experience lived and died in South America and in the Caribbean. For centuries the Atlantic slave trade represented the center of all commerce in the Western Hemisphere. Slaving ships sailed a "middle passage" as part of a triangular trading route. The first leg involved travel from Europe to the West African coast with manufactured goods including weapons, textiles, and metal hardware. These items would be sold to African slavers in exchange for human captives. Next, the ships sailed across the Atlantic, trading their slaves in the Americas for tobacco, rum, coffee, sugar, and other goods. Finally, the ships returned to Europe, turning a profit a third time on the sale of plantation goods to British merchants before beginning the whole process again. It must be noted that slavery had existed for some time in Africa prior to the trans-Atlantic trade. But the new European colonies created such tremendous demand that they increased the practice exponentially, destabilizing large areas of West Africa as tribes attacked each other to provide captives.

The colonization of the Americas is usually discussed as a European phenomenon, but in fact the population of most settlements consisted primarily of Africans through about 1800 and in some cases well into the mid-nineteenth century. This is especially true in Brazil and the Caribbean. Brazil received more slaves than any other single country, approximately 39% of all Africans brought to the Western Hemisphere. The Caribbean as a collective region imported slightly more, approximately 40% of the total, with the remaining 21% distributed throughout Central, North, and South America. Only about 5% of the total were taken to the United States. Needless to say, these sizeable differences in the numbers of Africans brought to various regions had a strong impact on the sorts of music that would develop in particular areas.

Within the Caribbean as well, significant demographic differences are found in African- and European-derived populations as some colonies imported many more slaves than others. Islands such as Puerto Rico, where smaller rural plantations flourished and farmers required less manual labor, imported far fewer slaves. For this reason, Puerto Rico has remained demographically "whiter" than other islands such as Hispaniola. Cuba falls somewhere in between demographically; large numbers of Africans arrived well into the 1860s and 1870s, yet shortly thereafter large numbers of immigrants from Spain and the Canary Islands settled the island as well. Thus, one finds strongly African-influenced music and strongly Spanish-influenced music there, together with creolized forms.

The Caribbean slave trade began in the early 1600s but intensified in the next century as colonial powers began to establish farms, primarily to cultivate sugarcane. French-controlled Saint-Domingue on the western side of Hispaniola led the way initially, by the 1780s having imported nearly 800,000 slaves. It became the region's wealthiest colony, producing 40% of the sugar consumed in Europe and generating tremendous revenues for landowners. Following massive slave revolts there in the 1790s and the breakdown of its export economy, other countries, including Brazil, Cuba, and Santo Domingo, began importing slaves in larger numbers to meet the insatiable European demand for sugar. In Cuba the slave trade intensified through the 1840s and ended definitively only in 1886. In Santo Domingo slavery ended earlier, in the 1820s. This resulted from conflicts with Haitian armies (consisting of freed slaves) and their control of all Hispaniola for about twenty years, through 1844. By the time slavery had finally been abolished in all of Latin America in 1888, 3 or 4 million Africans and African descendants lived in the region. About that time colonial authorities began to bring indentured laborers from China, India, and elsewhere to meet the ongoing demand for plantation labor, further diversifying local populations.

Three major West African cultural groups figure most prominently in the trans-Atlantic slave trade: (1) Muslim-influenced cultures of the savannah regions such as the Ashanti, Mandinga, and Wolof associated with Guinea, the Sudan, northern Nigeria, the Gambia, and Sierra Leone; (2) Bantu-Kongo tribes from the area that now comprises Angola, the Central African Republic, and the Democratic Republic of Congo; and (3) groups associated with the rain forest or coastal littoral regions of present-day Cameroon, Nigeria, and Benin, especially the Yoruba, Ewe, Ashante, Fon, and Ibo. The colonial powers of various countries purchased their slaves in different areas. For this reason, slaves from the first group listed tend to be most heavily represented in former British colonies which controlled the African Gold Coast area. Bantu groups, taken from areas controlled by Portuguese slave traffickers, are especially prominent in Portuguese and Spanish colonies. This was the area in which slave trafficking resulted in the largest numbers of captives sold into bondage in the New World overall. Finally, Yoruba-derived traditions are most prominent in countries such as Cuba and Brazil, whose slave trade reached its peak in the final decades before abolition. In the mid-nineteenth century, a series of political conflicts in what is now Nigeria and Benin resulted in large numbers of prisoners being sold into slavery from that region.

> **ACTIVITY 3.1** *Download a blank map of Africa from the Global Music Web site (www.oup.com/us.moore). Fill in all of the African countries mentioned, and note where the particular ethnicities are located. Identify the three larger regions mentioned above as well.*

Many African captives and their descendants maintained distinct ethnic identities through the early nineteenth century. In British colonies and in the United States, however, authorities stopped bringing new slaves from Africa by 1807; many outlawed the practice of slavery entirely in the 1830s. All of this occurred much earlier than in the Hispanic Caribbean. By the early twentieth century, as a result, few African descendants in English-speaking areas knew much about their specific ancestry and ethnicity. This is also true of islands with smaller numbers of African descendants, such as Puerto Rico and the Dominican Republic, where the institution of slavery ended relatively early. By contrast, on islands where the slave trade lasted much longer (such as Cuba) or where slaves successfully revolted early on (Haiti), communities retained a clearer sense of such heritage and continued to speak African languages well into the twentieth century. Musical practices in these locations also remained more closely tied to specific forms of African heritage.

FIGURE 3.1 *An oil painting,* Día de Reyes *by Frédéric Miahle of African music and dance that took place annually on the streets of Havana through the 1880s. It is demonstrative of the extent of West African cultural influences in much of the Caribbean and Latin America.* (Museo de Bellas Artes, Havana, Cuba. c. 1855).

Most slaves arrived in the New World young, between the ages of 9 and 20, and did not necessarily represent the most knowledgeable culture bearers of their respective ethnic groups. Plantation slaves worked exhausting sixteen-hour days of intense manual exertion that resulted in a very low life expectancy; nearly half died within a decade or so. Men predominated as laborers, meaning that they often could not marry or could not establish normal community relations. The creolization of African traditions thus began very early; African-derived genres of music and dance blended with each other at least as much as with European forms. Landowners often consciously mixed ethnic groups together so that slaves could not easily communicate with one another. They also set strict limits on permissible times and places for cultural activities. In virtually every Caribbean country, colonial authorities passed laws that suppressed African heritage in various ways.

Given all this, it is nothing short of amazing that music and dance influenced by Africa have flourished to this day in the Caribbean and elsewhere! They clearly served an important purpose for particular communities, establishing a sense of common heritage and providing refuge against the harsh realities of everyday life. Note that the primary sites for the maintenance of African cultures in early years included rural slave barracks (known as *barracones*), *cabildos* in the cities (discussed later), and encampments of maroons or runaway slaves, usually referred to as *palenques* in the Hispanic Americas.

AFRO-CUBAN *TOQUES DE GÜIROS*

The scope and diversity of Afro-Caribbean musical traditions are nearly overwhelming, and much research remains to be done on them. Each island has many types of performance with its own unique rhythms, dances, performance contexts, and local meanings. This discussion of African-influenced culture will necessarily be introductory, focusing on three examples. The first is Yoruba religious music from Cuba, the same piece you began to learn about in Chapter 1 (CD track 1). The second is a creolized *salve* from the Dominican Republic, to which drums and other percussion have been added (CD track 6). The third is secular *bomba sicá* drumming and dance from Puerto Rico (CD track 8). The latter two are sung in Spanish and demonstrate other European-derived influences yet clearly incorporate African characteristics as well.

The Caribbean repertoire in which African musical retentions have been strongest is religious; on various islands, African slaves and their descendants managed to reconstruct ancestral religious beliefs and used them as a means of retaining their unique heritage. They did so in many cases by forming mutual aid societies organized along ethnic lines. Colonial authorities in the Spanish Americas actually encouraged the creation of such institutions, known as *cofradías, cabildos,* or *hermandades* (literally, "councils" or "brotherhoods"). They hoped slaves would maintain distinct ethnic identities and the rivalries many harbored, making them less likely to revolt en masse. *Cabildos* and related institutions were commonplace from the sixteenth through the early nineteenth centuries in countries including Cuba and the Dominican Republic. With the abolition of slavery, authorities dismantled the *cabildo* system, yet African descendants have continued to perpetuate religious beliefs in much the same way. Afro-Caribbean community worship today often takes place informally, in private homes, and may fuse the practices of various African ethnicities together with European or other influences to a greater extent than in earlier periods, but the principle is the same.

The example of Afro-Cuban religious music on CD track 1 comes from the Yoruba-influenced religion known as Santería; this name implies worship of "saints" or deities. Traditional West African religion revolves around ancestor veneration, including the spirits of deceased parents and family members. The most powerful deities (*orichas*) of Santería are believed to be ancestors as well, kings or other historical figures who lived centuries ago but who still influence the physical world. They are archetypes with unique personality traits who simultaneously represent

FIGURE 3.2 *Two distinct African-derived instrument sets from Cuba.* Left: *These hourglass-shaped instruments are* batá *drums, reflecting Yoruba heritage.* Right: *These tall drums are used in* yuka *drumming, part of Kongo traditions. They give some sense of the tremendous variety of African influences in the Caribbean and beyond.* (National Music Museum, Havana, Cuba. Photo by the author).

fundamental aspects of human existence: wisdom, motherhood, beauty, skill in warfare, etc. Perhaps most importantly for our purposes, the *orichas* love music and dance; and as a result, both are fundamental to Santería. Each deity is associated with many specific praise songs, rhythms, and dance movements, all of which correspond to legends told about them in their various incarnations on earth. Santería involves spirit possession; the gods want to communicate with devotees and will take over the body of an initiate in specific ritual contexts in order to speak through them and interact with the community for a time.

Toques de güiros, literally "the playing of gourds," may be organized to thank an *oricha* for divine intervention in daily life (such as the healing of a sick person), to celebrate the anniversary of becoming an initiate, or for other reasons. Instruments used in the ensemble include one or two conga drums, a metal bell or hoe blade, and three roundish dried gourds of different sizes surrounded by a net of beads. The latter are known as *güiros* or *chéqueres* and are significantly larger than the *güiros* used in Puerto Rican *seis*. Musicians play the *chéqueres* by shaking them so that the body rubs against the beads in various ways or by using the

FIGURE 3.3 *Chéquere instruments such as those played in Cuba. The small end of each dried gourd has been cut off and the seeds taken out of the inside; around the outside, a net filled with beads or seeds has been strung. Practitioners refer to the smallest* chéquere *as "uno" or "primero," the middle-sized instrument as "dos" or "segundo," and the largest as the "caja" (literally, "box").* (Photo by the author).

palm of the hand to strike the bottom of the gourd so that a resonant tone comes out the hole at the top.

Chéquere performance may have developed in Cuba at the turn of the twentieth century as a result of prohibitions against the use of African drums. Similar instruments exist in Africa, in any case; the Yoruba term for them is *abwe*. A lead singer, a chorus, a bell, and one or two conga drums (*tumbadoras*) complete the *chéquere* ensemble.

Drumming in the Hispanic Caribbean is generally performed by men; women participate in worship as dancers and singers and constitute a sizable majority of the initiates, but they rarely play drums themselves. In the case of the *batás*, religious norms specifically prohibit women from performing for ceremonies; in other styles, no overt prohibitions exist but local custom discourages women from playing percussion all the same. Greater interest in African-derived culture in recent years and the creation of folkloric drumming workshops have helped spread Afro-Caribbean music of this sort beyond its original communities and have created more opportunities for women to play it, Cuban and foreign.

The recorded example of *chéquere* music on CD track 1 begins with a series of songs praising all the *orichas*, then continues with a sequence devoted to Elegguá and other specific *orichas*. Elegguá is a messenger deity, a "guardian of the crossroads" or important moments involving choice, and an opener and closer of doorways, spiritual and otherwise. He is always recognized first in any Santería event in order to facilitate communication between the sacred and secular realms. As is typical of Santería repertoire, most chants in this selection repeat in variation a few times before a new one is heard and are performed in call–response format. This is typical of Santería repertoire. As in most Afro-Cuban religious music, the basic pulse is in triple meter, though instruments such as the bell often create complex cross-rhythms.

Each *chéquere* has a particular rhythm to play (see Fig. 3.4). The smallest (*primero*) marks groupings of three eighth notes with its open tone; if played alone this part makes a sharp "pop" as the palm strikes the bottom, then a less precise sound as the net of beads bounces up and then back into the player's hands. The second *chéquere* (*segundo*) plays a pattern similar to that of the bell but filling in every eighth note. The lowest (*caja*) typically marks the third eighth note of every other measure strongly with an open fundamental tone. The *caja* improvises a great deal, deviating more than the other *güiros* from its basic pattern. The conga drum in this example serves a supporting role, repeating a relatively short pattern with strong open tones on the final two eighth notes of each measure. The bell also plays a constant pattern.

Figure 3.4 is a graphic representation of common *chéquere* parts in Western notation, together with the conga drum and bell. A D under a note indicates that the player makes a sound by letting the instrument fall downward into his or her hands. A U means that sound is made by tossing the *güiro* upward into the other hand. An accent over a note with a round head means that the player emphasizes that particular beat, striking the bottom of the *güiro* with one hand and letting its fundamental tone sound.

In this and other conga drum transcriptions throughout the book, letters above the note heads refer to various ways of playing on the drum: B = bass tone, a heavy hit with the full palm of the hand against the center of the head; M = muff, a stronger hit with the full length of the fingers against the edge of the skin but one that "chokes" the sound by leaving the fingers pressed against it; P = palm, a light stroke of the palm against the head, similar to a touch; Sl = slap, a light but quick whip of the hand against the edge of the head that produces a high-pitched noise; T = touch, a barely audible stroke of the fingertips against the

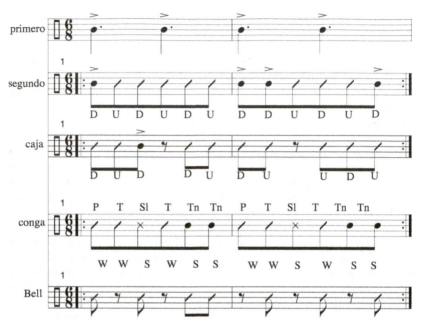

FIGURE 3.4 *Transcription of individual instrumental parts in the* toque de guiros.

head, used primarily for time-keeping purposes; Tn = tone, a loud open tone involving a stroke with the fingers in which they bounce quickly off the skin, letting the entire head resonate freely; an S below means the note is played with the strong hand, with W indicating the weak hand. Muffs and slaps are not played in the transcription here, but they appear in the *bomba sicá* transcription in the following pages.

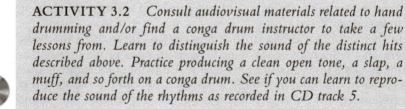

ACTIVITY 3.2 *Consult audiovisual materials related to hand drumming and/or find a conga drum instructor to take a few lessons from. Learn to distinguish the sound of the distinct hits described above. Practice producing a clean open tone, a slap, a muff, and so forth on a conga drum. See if you can learn to reproduce the sound of the rhythms as recorded in CD track 5.*

CD track 5 provides examples of what individual instruments play in a *güiro* piece so that you can more readily hear each one. First, you will hear the bell enter, playing two complete patterns. Then, the the conga drum enters, playing its rhythm against the bell for four *clave* lengths. Next, the conga falls silent and the bell continues along for two full patterns before being joined by the *güiro primero*. This instrument also plays for four full bell patterns, then drops out. The bell continues alone for two cycles and is then joined by the *güiro segundo* for four cycles. After it drops out, the bell continues and is joined by the *caja* for four cycles; note that in actual performance this instrument would improvise, deviating from this rhythm and returning to it at will. Finally, the bell again begins alone but is joined successively by all the other instruments mentioned in the same order. Each continues playing, however, so that by the time the *caja* enters the rhythmic texture is rich and complex.

ACTIVITY 3.3 *Tap or clap out the* güiro *primero part against the bell pattern as heard on CD track 5. If you have drums and other percussion available, try performing each individual part. If not, try imitating each subsequent line against the bell with your voice. Eventually, see if you can work with other students to perform all the parts together, either on actual instruments or by singing. Listen to the end of CD track 5 for the combined melodies of the open tones on all three* güiros *and on the conga drum; these instruments provide the characteristic sound of the* güiro *genre.*

Songs heard in these events are sung most often in a fragmented, antiquated form of Yoruba. Hundreds of short liturgical melodies exist to accompany Santería worship. They are chosen spontaneously in the moment of performance by the lead singer and strung together in sequences called *tratados* (literally "treatments") dedicated to particular *orichas*.

ACTIVITY 3.4 *Try learning two more of the melodies that appear in this* tratado. *Transcriptions of the additional chants are supplied, written against the bell. An optional harmony line has been added to some of the choruses in the second example as short choruses are often sung in parallel thirds.*

Learn the melodies first by themselves, then try to perform them against the bell and other rhythm instruments. You can divide into two groups at first, with half of you singing the melody and half tapping or clapping out the bell. Ultimately, see if you can learn to clap the bell rhythm and sing the chants at the same time. It's difficult, but it is the best way to understand the close relationship between the two parts and to keep from getting rhythmically lost in the performance.

As in Chapter 1, be aware that the part transcribed represents only the "simple" version of each chant as the chorus performs it. The lead vocalist, a more experienced singer, varies his or her performance substantially, and these variations are not represented.

SONG #3, to Elegguá

I- ba - ra go____ mo - yu - ba____

I - ba - ra - go____ a - go mo-yu - ba-ra o - mo-de ko - ni-

ko-si ba ra go__ a - go mo-yu - ba-ra, E-le-gguá E - chu/o-lo - na__

FIGURE 3.5 *The third song in the Santería* tratado *from CD track 1 and the first dedicated specifically to Elegguá. The chant is heard from 0:30 to 0:59. Note its relatively extended length, spanning six clave patterns.*

SONG #4, to Elegguá

I-chon chon a - be_____ I-chon chon A-

be   o - da - ra   ko - ro ni   le - yo ba - ba e - mi   I - CHON CHON A-

BE o - da - ra ko - ro - ni le - yo a - la - ro - ye I - CHONCHON A - BE

O - da - ra ko - ro - ni - le o_____ I-chon chon a

Chorus repeats full chant

FIGURE 3.6 *The fourth song in the Santería* tratado *from CD track 1, also dedicated to Elegguá. The chant is heard from 0:59 to 1:27. The chorus must learn two different responses to the* akpwon *in this chant. The first is the short, harmonized chorus notated in measure 12. The second is the entire chant, cued by the* akpwon's *singing of the higher melody in measures 13–15.*

A little more information about the other *orichas* whose songs are performed on CD track 1 is needed here; their names are Oggún, Ochosi, and Inle. These three deities, as well as Elegguá mentioned earlier, represent only a few of approximately twenty-four *orichas* who are recognized in most Santería ceremonies. Oggún is a deity of iron, the forge, and demanding physical labor. He is a fierce warrior known for his dogged determination and lives alone in the jungle. Oggún's symbol is the machete, and he is syncretized with the Catholic saint San Pedro. This means that a devotee of Santería will assume an image of San Pedro represents both the Catholic saint and the *oricha* Oggún at the same time. *Syncretism* represents a particular type of creolization; it implies fusion of two distinct sets of cultural practices into a single whole. Both sets of beliefs persist, but they are perceived as a single unit by local residents. Ochosi, the third deity praised in the *tratado*, is a deity of the hunt, a woodsman, and, along with Elegguá and Oggún, one of the three primary warrior *oricha*. His symbols are the bow and arrow and birds of prey. He is syncretized with the Catholic archangel Santiago. Inle is a less prominent deity in the Santería pantheon, who is a hunter, fisherman, and doctor. He symbolizes health and abundance and is represented by the image of a fish. He is syncretized with the Catholic archangel Rafael.

Preparations for a *toque* or *tambor*—a "touching" or "drumming," generic terms for an Afro-Cuban religious event—involve the creation of an altar to a particular deity and the cooking of ritual foods. Animal sacrifices may also be made for the *orichas* or for the drums themselves in order to feed the divine force some are believed to contain. Animals offered up in this manner are usually cooked and eaten by participants after the ceremony has ended. After the guests arrive, ceremonies begin in earnest with a series of songs accompanied by drumming and dance that salute all the *orichas* in a set order. As each is recognized, initiates whose lives have been dedicated to that *oricha* are required to come forward to dance and salute the drums, prostrating themselves before the instruments in homage.

In later sections of the *toque*, participants dance and sing faster and with greater intensity, inviting spirit possession. At this time, the lead singer chooses which songs to sing with greater freedom and may intone dozens of pieces to the same *oricha* (often for as long as twenty to thirty minutes per *oricha*), varying them in order to "bring down" that deity. Ceremonies typically last at least five or six hours, as long as is necessary in order to induce possession. Participants possessed by an *oricha* are usually dressed in special ritual clothing and proceed to interact with the community in trance. They may offer advice to those in attendance, call for particular sacrifices to be made, or request music or dance of various kinds. Ceremonies end with a section consisting of yet more ritual actions. Any devotees still in trance are coaxed out of this state by the head of the religious community. Usually, they remember nothing of what has transpired during their possession.

Many similar yet distinct African-derived musical/religious traditions exist in Cuba as well aside from Yoruba-influenced styles, such as Kongo-derived *cajón* events (Fig. 3.7).

ACTIVITY 3.5 *Listen to the entire recording of CD track 1. Try to identify the rhythmic parts that you have been practicing individually, especially the bell, conga drum, and the open*

FIGURE 3.7 *Performers in an Afro-Cuban religious event held in Havana in July 2008 organized by religious leader Rodolfo Almeida. This ceremony was Kongo-derived, a so-called* cajón para los muertos *in honor of spirits of the dead. Instruments used here include the* cajón *itself, a resonant wooden box (far left), a woodblock and bells on a stand, conga drum, and* maracas *(not pictured), in addition to vocals.* (Photo by the author).

fundamental tones on the güiros. Later, follow the complete listening guide (www.oup.com/us.moore) and see if you can identify all the different responsorial songs as they enter. Make a note of chants dedicated to individual orichas.

Partial Listening Guide to CD Track 1

Afro-Cuban *Güiro* Music

0:00–0:03

The lead singer enters alone, introducing song 1, "*Moyuba, moyuba oricha.*" This song is general, addressing all the *orichas*, as noted in Chapter 1.

0:04–0:06

The chorus sings an antiphonal response to the first song; the bell enters simultaneously. Both the lead section and the choral response section last one full *clave* length (what we might think of as two measures); thus, the song overall lasts for two *claves* (or four measures).

0:06–0:12

The leader repeats the initial solo melody of song 1 in variation, followed by the same choral response. During the leader's second entrance, the full percussion battery, including *chéqueres* and conga drum, begin playing. At 0:12–0:16 we hear the third call–response repetition of song 1.

0:17–0:22

Song 2 begins, the other song to all *orichas* learned in Chapter 1. The leader sings the full iteration: "*Iba oricha, iba layeo, ago moyuba.*"

0:22–0:29

The chorus enters, singing their response to song 2. They in turn are answered by the leader and respond again with the same melody at 0:27.

0:30–0:59

At 0:30 the lead voice introduces song 3, specifically dedicated to Elegguá. He initially sings a very free, embellished version. Note that this song is longer than the previous two, extending over six *claves*. The chorus enters with a simpler and more standard version of the same song at 0:44, which corresponds to the transcription in Figure 3.5. Its lyrics: "*Ibara ago moyuba, ibara ago, ago moyubara omo ode koni kosi bara ago, ago moyubara, Elegguá Esu alona.*"

Before continuing, it is important to consider the concept of *clave* since the word can be used in different ways. "*Clave*" in Spanish can be used by musicians like "clef" in English when referring to written music. In addition, "*clave*" or "*claves*" can refer to an instrument, a pair of rounded, resonant wooden sticks used in *rumba*, *son*, salsa, and other music. However, when people talk about "playing *clave*" or "being in *clave,"* they are referring to constantly repeated rhythmic figures found in much Caribbean folkloric and popular music and in West African music. The rhythms are short, usually two measures in length, and serve as the structural basis for the rest of a piece's rhythms and melodies. They can be performed on the *claves* themselves or on other objects. The rhythms typically consist of two "sides" or halves that contrast a more syncopated pattern with a relatively straight one. It is understood that the rhythm should be synchronized to an extent with the other rhythms in the song. If such a synchronization does not occur, the musicians will describe the song as being "out of *clave*" or having a "crossed *clave.*"

Distinct rhythmic patterns of this nature exist for the *son, rumba, danzón,* Yoruba-derived religious music, and other genres, including Dominican and Puerto Rican music. The bell pattern in the *toque de güiros* represents the fundamental rhythm of that genre; other such rhythms will be presented later, including in the following section. You will find as you learn the first few songs of CD track 1 that its melodies have been conceived "in *clave.*" That is, the melodies emphasize and conform in large part to the rhythms in the bell pattern.

ACTIVITY 3.6   *Look again at the transcriptions of the melodies from the* güiro *piece provided in Chapters 1 and 3 (Figs. 1.6, 1.7, 3.5, 3.6). Consider how the rhythms in the melodies of the vocals reflect and conform to the bell pattern. As a way of investigating this relationship further, try singing the melodies against the bell but "out of* clave," *that is, against a flipped bell pattern that puts the songs' rhythms against the other side of the bell's repeated figure. The "in-clave" singing should feel easier and more natural than the "out-of-clave" singing. The latter creates more rhythmic tension against the bell, fighting its rhythm rather than matching it.*

AFRO-DOMINICAN *SALVES*

Music of the Dominican Republic contains many African influences, some more creolized than music of Santería in Cuba. Because the Dominican slave trade ended in the early rather than the late nineteenth century, African-derived elements have fused to a significant extent with European forms in many cases. That said, overtly African-influenced traditions remain a more central feature of Dominican culture than in Puerto Rico. This is due in part to the overall demographics of the Dominican Republic, with its higher percentage of individuals of black or racially mixed heritage; to the prominence of Afro-Dominican *cofradías* and *cabildos* and their role in perpetuating cultural traditions; and to ongoing cultural interactions with Haiti, a country with very strong Afro-Caribbean heritage. As in other parts of the Caribbean, of course, one finds a gamut of musical forms existing side by side in the Dominican Republic, some more creolized than others.

Cofradías and *cabildos*, the community-based, religious social and cultural groups mentioned earlier, are more prominent in the Dominican Republic today than they are in either Cuba or Puerto Rico. Of special note are the Afro-Dominican *cofradías* of Espíritu Santo in Villa Mella, San Juan de la Maguana, and Cotuí and San Juan Bautista in Baní. The histories of these institutions are not terribly well researched, but they appear to be of Kongo derivation, as evident in the instruments many of them perform on such as *palo* long drums (see Fig. 3.8), very similar to the instruments depicted in Figure 3.2. Many different kinds of religious brotherhood exist, some larger or smaller, some closely tied to the institutions and beliefs of Catholicism, and others like the Afro-Dominican *cofradías* almost entirely distinct. Most promote musical traditions with African influences, though the kinds and degrees of influence may vary. All are of importance in a discussion of creole *salve* performance, however, since their events frequently incorporate such music.

We should note that in activities associated with some *cofradías*, folk Catholicism is fused not only with Kongo cultural forms but also with others derived from Haitian religions, the latter with roots in present-day Benin and Dahomey. In the Dominican Republic, this Haitian–Dominican religious system is known as Vodú. As in the case of Santería, Vodú involves the veneration of ancestor spirits, African deities, and indigenous leaders of the past. The deities are known as *luás* (from the Fon/Dahomeyan term for "saint") or *misterios*, from the French *mystère* ("mystery" or supernatural force). Vodú ceremonies involve possession of particular initiates by the *misterios*, much as in the case of Santería; they are said to "rise up upon" the initiate and take control of his or her body and mind for a time.

Of the many Afro-Dominican folkloric styles performed today, I have chosen to concentrate on the African-influenced *salve* in this chapter. It is one of the most popular and widespread musical forms on the island and one that illustrates the process of creolization to which countless originally European musical forms have been subject in the Caribbean. As mentioned in Chapter 2, some *salve* variants differ little from the music cultivated by European immigrants centuries ago. Others are virtually unrecognizable as European, sounding decidedly African to the outside observer. Thus, a wide spectrum exists, beginning with Spanish-style *salves* to the Virgin discussed toward the end of Chapter 2, continuing through *salves con versos* (songs incorporating some or all of the original Catholic chant but adding additional lyrics or verses of local origin), and ending with Afro-Dominican *salves*. The latter exist in a variety of regional forms; they may use little or none of the original *Salve Regina* text and tend to foreground African-derived instruments and other musical elements. In *salves* more influenced by European traditions lyrics constitute the most important part of the performance, while in African-influenced *salves* the accompanying music and percussive improvisation tend to be emphasized.

Musicians play Afro-Dominican *salves* at a brisk tempo with a strongly marked beat. Call–response singing predominates between a lead singer and chorus, often alternating between them after each phrase, as in our example (CD track 6). Alternatively, the lead singer may sing longer, European-derived couplets or quatrains. Instruments accompanying the creole *salve* vary; in the east and in northern Cibao, performers employ round frame drums known as *panderetas* or *panderos* (see Fig. 3.8) similar to a tambourine, along with a small drum held between the knees known as a *mongó* or *tamborita* (little drum). In the Peravia area, especially, a wide variety of *panderos* are used, some quite large, while in the east and in the Cibao area smaller *panderetas* with jingles are preferred. In regions such as the south and southwest, *palo* drums (see Fig. 3.8) may provide *salve* accompaniment. Other percussion typically associated with the creolized genre include the *balsié* (a medium-sized drum that can be played horizontally on the ground using special foot-dampening and finger-gliding techniques, as depicted in Fig. 3.8, or upright), the *tambora* (a double-headed drum played horizontally on the lap with one hand and one stick; see Fig. 4.1), and the *güira* scraper (Fig. 4.1). Younger, more experimentally inclined performers may accompany *salves* with all of the instruments mentioned. The Afro-Dominican *salve* on CD track 6 features *panderos*, *balsié*, *mongó*, and *güira*. Though *palo* drums, *balsié*, and *mongó* are found only in regional folkloric music, the *tambora* and *güira* have become prominent components of *merengue* bands as well.

Traditional contexts for the performance of Afro-Dominican *salves* are essentially the same as those described for *salves de la Virgen* in Chapter 2: *velaciones* in small churches or private homes, brief street processions, pilgrimages to sacred locations, and so on. Events may be organized by individuals to offer thanks for answered prayers such as the curing of an illness or the resolution of financial problems. Activities

FIGURE 3.8 *Dominican musicians at a folk festival in 2008. The seated figure is playing a* balsié *drum, using both his hands and the foot dampening technique. The standing performers to the left are playing* palo *long drums, while in the upper right-hand corner a* pandero *player is striking his instrument.* (Photo by Daniel Piper).

surrounding performance are festive; they typically involve periods of prayer and ritual activity but also socializing, drinking, and dancing. Other kinds of music such as folkloric *merengue* or brass band pieces, often performed live, may alternate with *salves* in any given event. Creolized *salves* may even be danced by couples as the evening progresses. Women often predominate in creolized *salve* groups, both as singers and as *pandero* players. Note that if a town organized a *fiesta patronal*, officials would be unlikely to include creole *salves* since many do not view such strongly African-influenced traditions favorably. At best, they might permit a controlled period of such performance in the Catholic church after official ceremonies were finished or perhaps a staged presentation of drumming that separated the music from its original religious context.

Attempts to achieve a heightened religious state constitute an important part of Afro-Dominican *salve* performance. As opposed to the relatively short and restrained verses of the European-derived *salves*, creole *salves* involve prolonged music making that often leads to feelings of transcendence. The state is referred to as *subido* (literally, a "raising" or "heightening"). "Hotter" *subido* moments of an evening's performance involve a combination of fast rhythms, a greater degree of rhythmic syncopation, increased volume, virtuosic improvisational drumming, and often a raised vocal pitch. The aesthetic surrounding Afro-Dominican *salves* is similar in many ways to that of music in African American church services. As opposed to Santería events, ritual possession is not necessarily a part of *velaciones*; possession does occur at times but is more common in *salve* traditions that have fused with influences from Vodú.

Salves have typically been a rural phenomenon, but performances increasingly take place in urban areas as well. They are presented on stage at arts festivals and recorded for commercial release in sound studios. Daniel Piper (in press) notes that some *palo* ensembles are invited to perform at neighborhood bars and secular parties and that DJs increasingly play recordings of Afro-Dominican *salves* at dance clubs. *Merengue* superstar Kinito Méndez, the author of CD track 10, has fused commercial and folkloric sounds together in his popular release *A palo limpio* (2001) by mixing Afro-Dominican *salve* rhythms with a contemporary dance band format.

CD track 6, "India del agua" ("Indian of the Water") was recorded by Enerolisa Núñez (b. 1952), a semiprofessional performer of traditional repertoire whose family is known for its involvement in Afro-Dominican arts. Núñez's great grandmother, Baí Minier, served as head of a Kongo *cofradía* in the Mata de Indios area on the northern outskirts of Santo Domingo; and her mother and aunt were both well-known vocalists. This area has a sizable Afro-Dominican population. The *cabildos* and *cofradías* mentioned earlier played an important role there historically, and some continue to exist. Núñez established her own *salve* group in the 1990s and has made recordings as part of nonprofit initiatives. While the performers often play for community-based events, CD track 6 was recorded in a studio and released on the CD *Enerolisa y el grupo de salve de Mata los Indios. Música raiz*, Vol. 2. Her son Osvaldo plays *güira* on this release, and her daughter Yeni sings lead on some songs and in the chorus.

The lyrics to CD track 6 discuss a supernatural spirit associated with native Taíno groups who is believed to live under the water, the "India del agua" or Indian of the water. As in the case of other countries in the region—Colombia, Venezuela, Mexico, Brazil—the practices of folk Catholicism have fused not only with elements from Europe and Africa but also with native cultures and/or reinterpretations of them on the part of others. It is not uncommon in Latin America to find statuettes of Indian spirits adorning altars alongside those of Catholic saints and

FIGURE 3.9 *Enerolisa Núñez (left) performing with Jomayra Moreno of her salve ensemble at the Académica Dominicana de Ciencias for the public inauguration of the Red Dominicana de Culturas Locales, February 19th, 2009.* (Photo courtesy of La Red Cultural).

to find that the ceremonies used to worship both involve drumming, dance, and song practices with strong ties to West Africa. Such is the case here, lending yet another layer of complexity to the processes of creolization discussed earlier. *Indios* in Dominican folk Catholicism are spirits associated with nature and the countryside, often with particular locations such as rivers, natural springs, or caves. Devotees often make pilgrimages to sites associated with a particular deity in order to pray or to request divine intervention in their lives.

Partial Listening Guide for CD Track 6, by Daniel Piper

The *Salve* "India del agua"

Download the complete listening guide at www.oup.com/us.moore

0:00–0:06

Enerolisa Núñez begins to sing unaccompanied, introducing the first song with the phrase *"Lo' marinero' son del agua"* ("Sailors come from the water"), followed by the choral response *"marinero', ay ombe, marinero'"* (*ay ombe* is a common affective exclamation in the Dominican Republic and in Colombia). Notice how the soloist starts singing on the same pulse on which the chorus responsorial ends. This type of overlap is common in the singing of some ethnic groups from West Africa.

0:06–0:12

Núñez sings another line, *"Ay, eso no se le hace, ay ombe"* ("Ay, you shouldn't do that"), and the chorus repeats its antiphonal response.

0:12–0:18

Núñez continues with the line *"Ay, a ningún hermano, ahora"* ("Ay, to any brother, now"), followed by the chorus. A single *pandero* enters with what might be considered the central *clave* pattern of this *salve* (see the "Pandero 1" and "Pandero 1 variation" lines in Fig. 3.10). The 6/8 rhythm sounds similar to the bell part heard in CD track 1 and stretches over a two-measure phrase but contains fewer notes. The *pandero* rhythm might be thought of as a five-stroke variant of the seven-stroke bell pattern found in CD track 1; it is certainly related to other forms of "*claved*" music from Africa and the Caribbean. The *pandero's* pattern repeats four times as the soloist and chorus complete one full melodic cycle. Listen closely for the muted yet resonant sound of the thumb hitting the drum surface "on the rebound" as it turns. This is represented by the open tone in the "Pandero 1 variation" line.

0:19–0:24

A second *pandero* enters with an interlocking pattern ("Pandero 2" line in Fig. 3.10), over which Núñez continues with the line *"Ay, marinero' somo' ahora*" ("We're all sailors now"), to which the chorus responds. The second *pandero* rhythm is mixed in the opposite stereo track from that of the first, so you may be able to hear it more clearly using headphones by panning the balance back and forth on your stereo.

0:25–0:30

Núñez sings "*Ay, y en el mar andamo', ay ombe*" ("Ay, into the ocean we go"). A third *pandero* enters doubling the initial *clave* rhythm.

0:31–1:06

Yet another *pandero* enters. This thickens the rhythmic texture further as the soloist continues with new verses, in alternation with the chorus. While the sequence of *pandero* entrances was specially arranged for this recording, it is typical for traditional *salve* musicians to stagger their entrances one after another. Accompanying the text segment below, the singers perform six full cycles of the eight-measure melody. The lead lyrics sung by Núñez in this section are the following.

Ay, ven que te lo doy ahora	Come, I'll give it to you now
Ay, que uste' 'ta presente, ay ombe	Ay, now that you are here
Ay, ampara y socorre ahora	Ay, offer help and protection now
Ay, a toda esta gente, ay ombe	Ay, to all these people
Ay, no me deje sola, ay ombe	Ay, don't leave me alone
Ay que el barco me da mareo	Ay, that boat makes me sea sick

Figure 3.10 provides a transcription of rhythms heard on CD track 6. Note that the *güira* strokes on the first and fourth eighth notes of each measure differ from the others; at these moments the performer lets the metal *gancho* or striker come to rest on the instrument momentarily, resulting in a "closed" sound, rather than letting it slide off. Typical *salve* ensembles include multiple *pandero* players, at least three; often, the *pandero* lines transcribed here would be performed by more than one player. Slaps on the *panderos* are indicated by an *x* and open tones with a round head, as in the case of earlier transcriptions.

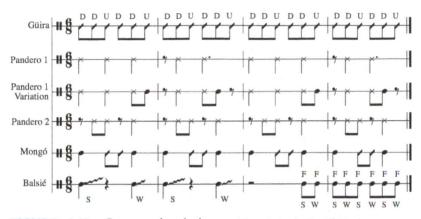

FIGURE 3.10 *Common* salve *rhythms.* *(Transcription by Daniel Piper).*

Panderos play many rhythmic variations; only the basic patterns are provided in the transcription. The *balsié* drum is especially difficult to represent as it improvises frequently and there is no "standard" pattern that all performers use. Both of the two-measure phrases notated on the *balsié* line represent common riffs played in order to fill in the percussive sound of the group as necessary, in dialogue with the singers and other percussionists. Two idiosyncratic sounds heard on the *balsié* include a friction-based sound created by gliding a finger lightly over the head of the drum (this is indicated by the squiggly glissando line). Another is a raised pitch when the musician applies pressure with the heel of the foot during performance (notated with an F).

ACTIVITY 3.7 *Listen to CD track 7, a didactic recording of individual* salve *percussion instruments and the rhythms they play. The* güira *enters first, followed by individual* pandero *parts against the güira's pulse one at a time. Following this, the* mongó *and* balsié *enter individually against the* güira, *and finally all percussion instruments stack against each other and play together. Listen to this short recording several times until you can recognize all the different parts, then try performing them yourself individually on any percussion instrument you have available, using Figure 3.10 as a guide. Eventually, see if you and others can perform all the parts together.*

PUERTO RICAN *BOMBA*

Many African-influenced musical forms exist in Puerto Rico, but they tend to be highly creolized, integrally blended with European musical forms rather than sounding as overtly "African" as Santería music, for instance. The most common Afro-Puerto Rican genre featuring percussion and voice that continues to be played today is *bomba*. This term translates roughly as "drum" in the Akan and Ashanti languages of West Africa. *Bomba* is a secular dance music form, intended for recreation rather than devotion. It developed in coastal areas of the island in the 1600s and reached a peak in popularity in the late 1700s. Some researchers believe it may have been influenced by the arrival of Francophone immigrants fleeing the Haitian revolution. In *bomba's* peak years, many variants existed in cities such as Ponce, Guayama, Mayagüez, Santurce, and Loíza Aldea with their own unique rhythms and dance steps. Documents suggest that the music played a prominent role in slave uprisings of the mid-1820s as well. After the abolition of slavery in Puerto Rico in 1873, the center of *bomba* performance shifted decisively to marginal urban areas as rural laborers migrated to the cities in search of better jobs. Try not to confuse the use of *"bomba"* here (a distinct musical genre) with that of the *"bombas"* in *seis bombeao* discussed in Chapter 2 (meaning a joke).

These days, despite a notable resurgence in interest in the style among Puerto Rican youth, *bomba* music is often confined to staged performances by folklore troupes or community centers. Residents of Loíza Aldea outside of San Juan (a predominantly Afro-Puerto Rican town) represent an exception to this rule; they continue to perform the music as part of community festivals, especially the *fiesta patronal* of the apostle Santiago (St. James), held in July. It features dancing and costumed street processions, among other activities. National and international critics recognize the Cepeda family from Santurce and the Hermanos Ayala from Loíza as virtuosic performers of *bomba*. Ponce remains a home of traditional *bomba* as well, reflected by folkloric groups such as Babalué and Paracumbé. Both Loíza and Ponce have retained their own styles of *bomba*, but the distinct music and dance of many other areas have been lost.

ACTIVITY 3.8 *Search for a map of Puerto Rico, and identify all the major cities and regions discussed in the paragraph above.*

In the 1970s and 1980s, *bomba* everywhere seemed to be dying out, though its rhythms continued to influence arrangements of commercial dance music. Since the late 1990s, however, this folkloric music has attracted new enthusiasts among Puerto Rican youth. They attend so-called *bombazos* in urban areas that blend *bomba* drumming with influences from rap, hip-hop, break dancing, and other styles. A certain tension exists between older performers, who disapprove of this sort of musical mixing and assert that the *bomba* should be performed in a "traditional" manner, and the youth. But ultimately the resurgence of interest would appear to be a positive change, ensuring greater public involvement in this music in the future.

Bomba incorporates at least two drums, wider and shorter than conga drums and more resonant (Fig. 3.11). The lower drum, called the *buleador* (plural *buleadores*), plays a relatively static pattern. A *bomba* ensemble may have only one *buleador* drum or may include two or more. However, only one player improvises on the more prominent lead drum, known as the *bomba* or *primo*, at a time. Musicians hold their instruments upright in Loíza, but in Ponce the drums are laid on the ground and straddled by the performer. A pair of sticks known as *cuá* or *fuá* provide a supporting rhythm, usually a repeated *cinquillo* pattern or a variant; it is similar

FIGURE 3.11 *Early twentieth-century* buleador *drums used in* bomba *music. Note the pegs used to tighten the skin head, a technique apparently derived from Dahomeyan cultures in present-day Benin and Dahomey and that may have been influenced by Haitian immigrants.* (*Music Museum of Ponce. Photo by the author*).

in many respects to the *catá* pattern in Dominican *palo* or the *cáscara* pattern in Cuban *rumba*. The use of the *cuá* apparently derives from southern *bomba* styles, though the instrument has now been adopted across the island. A *maraca* is often played as well, marking a constant eighthnote pulse.

The *bomba* or the *primo* drum plays a role similar to that of the *quinto* (lead conga) in the Cuban *rumba*, soloing prominently over the other instruments; it often attempts to mimic with sound the movements of a particular dancer. Indeed, *bomba* performance in Loíza usually showcases one dancer at a time, who will stand in front of the lead drummer and enter into an extended rhythmic dialogue with him in this sense. Dances are also performed by couples in some cases, especially in Ponce; they flirt and compete with one another in various ways but do not touch, as is typical in West African folkloric traditions. Male dancers often wear white cotton pants and long-sleeved shirts, while women wear full-length skirts, all of this in imitation of nineteenth-century fashion. Colorful scarves are frequently incorporated into the choreography as well. In the south, women predominate as singers, both lead vocals and chorus, while men play percussion. In the north, men most often play all instruments and sing lead while women dance and sing in the chorus.

I will discuss *bomba sicá* here, given that it is one of the variants most often incorporated into modern dance music. Figure 3.12 is a transcription of common patterns in this style; *the buleador* drum plays a constantly repeating figure very similar to a *cinquillo* (Fig. 1.4), and the *cuá* a slightly busier rhythm . Note that the overall phrase is a single measure in length, as opposed to the two-measure pattern played by many instruments in the *chéquere* example. Against the *cuá* and *buleador*, the *primo* or lead drum improvises. As before, open tones have been written in the drum transcription with round heads, as they are especially prominent in the pattern. Thus, *sicá* can be recognized because of its muff tone on "1" of the 4/4 measure and especially by the strong open tones on the "and-of-3" and "4."

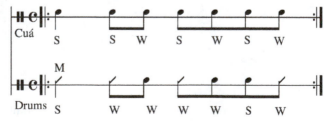

FIGURE 3.12 *A typical* cuá *pattern in* bomba sicá *and the composite rhythm played by the* buleador *drums as performed by Samuel López. See the discussion of drum technique preceding Figure 3.4 as necessary to interpret this transcription.*

CD track 8 provides examples of what rhythms individual instruments play in the *sicá* style. First, you will hear the *cuá* enter, playing four complete patterns. Then, the *maracas* enter against it for four measures or four complete patterns. After a brief interlude, the *buleador* enters. This instrument also plays its part four times, then drops out. Finally, all instruments play together for a time so that you can listen to their parts in tandem, with a *primo* player executing typical solo phrases against the other percussion.

ACTIVITY 3.9 *Together with friends, a pair of* maracas, *drum sticks, and at least one hand drum, try imitating the rhythms transcribed in Figure 3.12 and recorded on CD track 8. Begin with the simpler lines, the* cuá *and* maracas. *Next, add the* buleador *rhythm, making sure to make as much distinction as possible between tones, slaps, touches, and muffs. You can stop there or add a solo drummer to the mix as well if someone in your group has more experience playing hand percussion.*

A number of *bomba* variants exist to this day in both 4/4 and 6/8 time, including *belén, cuembé* (or *güembé*), *cunyá, holandé* (or *holandés*), *leró, sicá, yubá,* and others. *Leró* and *güembé* are most commonly performed in the south. *Cunyá, belén,* and *holandé* appear frequently in folkloric performances throughout the island, while other subgenres such as *calindá* are less common. *Bomba* is much more than a single rhythm, clearly; it is an umbrella term for a broad category of rhythms and is comparable in this sense to *rumba* or *salve*. More information about individual *bomba* rhythms is available on instructional videos, for instance, *Conga Virtuoso Giovanni Hidalgo* (Warner Brothers DVD, 2003), and in the writings of Emanuel Dufrasne-González (1994).

ACTIVITY 3.10 *After you have become familiar with the basic sound of* bomba sicá, *track down some commercial CDs of Puerto Rican folkloric music by groups such as Los Pleneros de la 21 or Paracumbé and see if you can recognize the* bomba sicá *pattern in their recordings. Locate and watch Roberta Singer and Ashley James' documentary on the Cepeda family of Santurce,* Bomba, Dancing the Drum *(Searchlight Films, 2000), which will provide you with examples of the northern dance style as well.*

Concluding this introduction to African-influenced music from the Caribbean, it is constructive to consider what musical characteristics correspond to this sort of repertoire in a general sense. The music usually demonstrates a high level of "rhythmic density" or polyrhythm, with many different beats sounding simultaneously. Pieces may be in duple or triple meter, or (at least as frequently) they may incorporate simultaneous rhythms that emphasize both groupings of two and three. Relationships *between* rhythms are very important; many performers of traditional percussion music do not read Western notation and orient themselves solely on the basis of how their part fits against others. What is more, many of the individual rhythms lock together in certain ways to create aggregate melodies. *Güiros* in the *chéquere* ensemble, for instance, combine to create an overall pattern of open tones that is perceived as a single pattern even though it consists of multiple parts. Afro-Caribbean aggregate rhythms are melodic as well in the sense that various percussion instruments play open tones at different pitches, though the melody may not sound like melodies in European-derived music.

In terms of form, much West African and Afro-Caribbean music is based on cycles and loops; in fact, it might be described structurally as adopting an open-ended form that lasts as long as the performance event requires. There is often a hierarchy of instruments in African-influenced repertoire, and some instruments like the *clave, maraca,* or bell play a more or less static, unchanging line that serves to keep the pulse. Others vary their parts a bit more, while still others feature prominently as solo instruments, fighting the relatively constant rhythms laid down by the rest. Call-and-response singing is an African-derived characteristic in much of this repertoire, as is a preference for a wide variety of timbres, often nonpitched, in any given ensemble. Many Afro-Latin musics incorporate a vast array of such sounds from metal, wood, animal skin, plant material, and other sources.

These comments may serve as a starting point for thinking about what makes Caribbean music distinct. However, it is also worth considering how the musical "Africanisms" mentioned here may have affected performance traditions in the United States as well. Listening to traditional black gospel music, for instance, one hears call-and-response singing, open-ended cyclical form, improvisation, polyrhythmic accents, and considerable room for variation or embellishment of musical lines and individual expression. Consider Aretha Franklin's award-winning song "Spirit in the Dark" as one example. The piece begins in a moderate tempo with a more or less strophic verse section. Later on, when the call-and-response section begins, the pace accelerates; the concluding section increases in tempo again with a shortened chorus and becomes a vehicle for ecstatic communal expression and vocal improvisation.

Listening to the repeating riffs or melodies played by the piano, bass, and other instruments and the overall slow-to-fast progression, one is struck with the similarities to traditional African-influenced ensembles of the Hispanic Caribbean such as those we have been discussing. One might suggest that the organization of this kind of North American music owes as much or more to Africa than to Europe, despite the English lyrics and the prominence of many European-derived instruments. Might we be able to argue that the United States is a creolized nation in particular ways, producing music that is similar to that of the Caribbean?

Art historian Gerardo Mosquera (quoted in Perna 2005, 9) notes that the real feat of African-derived cultures in the Americas is the story of their flexibility, the fact that essential aspects of African heritage have been perpetuated in variation under conditions of extreme dominance and intolerance. His writings speak to the central goals of this chapter, which has attempted to provide a context for thinking about broad patterns of cultural development in the Hispanic Caribbean, the political and economic factors contributing to them, and the specific kinds of people and music thrust together in the region. Chapter 3 also focuses on similarities and differences between various islands, a topic worthy of further discussion. Differences we have touched upon include the extent and duration of the slave trade in particular areas, the overall demographics and ratio of European to African immigrants, and differences in local musical terms, in instrument construction, in performance contexts, and in the specific styles of music derived from Africa and from Spain that have come to influence local expression most strongly over time. Similarities are found in general contexts, in patterns of development, in the aesthetics of music and dance performance, and in particular rhythms and musical structures shared throughout the region.

On each island of the Caribbean we can observe musical styles that demonstrate the fusion of elements from Africa, Europe, and elsewhere, as well as others that demonstrate much less fusion. It is striking that varying degrees of creolization exist side by side and that such differences can appear even in substyles of the very same genre, as in the case of the Dominican *salve*. Little research has been undertaken on the reasons for such differences in the process of cultural blending. This "incomplete creolization" speaks to distinct local uses and meanings of culture in particular communities and perhaps even more directly to a lack of complete social/racial integration in the Caribbean, even in the twenty-first century. When discussing the region, it is important to consider not only fusion and reconciliation but also ongoing difference and disjuncture.

Chapters 2 and 3 emphasize relatively "pure" Hispanic and African-derived traditions in order to underscore both the extent and variety of such heritage. Most well-known genres from the Caribbean tend to demonstrate greater fusion than these folkloric forms, greater reconciliation of distinct cultural "poles." Even in the music discussed here, however, significant creolization has been evident (e.g., the Afro-Cuban instruments that appear in the *controversia* [CD track 4], the *güiro* and other percussion in the contemporary *seis chorreo* [CD track 3], and the styles of clothing worn in and Spanish-language texts of *bomba* dance). Later chapters will emphasize hybridity to an even greater extent, focusing on popular traditions, on music that has developed in dialogue with influences from other countries, on immigration from the Caribbean and resultant musical change, and on the modification of folkloric genres for the commercial music marketplace.

Creolized Dance Music

∞

Chapter 4 considers the musical characteristics and historical development of three styles of traditional dance music that have become powerful national symbols in the Hispanic Caribbean: Cuban *son*, Puerto Rican *plena*, and Dominican *merengue*. Though rejected for many years by Caribbean elites as crass, lewd, and/or simplistic, these genres ultimately triumphed and gained broad acceptance. Chapter 4 explores issues of creolization, particularly the ways in which the repertoire fuses cultural elements of Spanish and African heritage. Fusion occurs on the levels of text, instrumentation, musical form, and dance choreography. The chapter ends with an overview of the development of New York salsa music, a repertoire that draws from traditions on various islands of the Hispanic Caribbean and fuses them with music from North America and elsewhere. Salsa is a highly creolized dance form as well that has generated interest throughout Latin America as well as among Spanish-speaking immigrants in the United States, resonating with their daily experiences and their multicultural sensibilities. It continues to generate new audiences in North America, Europe, and beyond.

DOMINICAN *MERENGUE*

Merengue has been the most popular form of dance music in the Dominican Republic since the early twentieth century. Its early history is poorly documented, but most agree that it began as a creolized working-class variant of ballroom dances imported from Europe such as the polka. *Merengues* are mentioned in written documents beginning in the 1840s; initially, they were performed on a variety of melodic instruments with accompanying percussion, but by the late 1870s musicians had adopted the diatonic button accordion as their instrument of choice. The *merengue* slowly gained national acceptance in the 1930s, owing in part to the populist cultural policies of the country's leader at that time, Rafael Trujillo. With a tactic that proved increasingly common in later decades throughout the Caribbean and Latin America, he used the promotion of working-class music such as *merengue* as a means of suggesting his identification with the common people. Ñico Lora, Toño Abreu, and Luis Alberti are among the musicians and bandleaders who accompanied Trujillo during his travels across the island. The acceptance of the *merengue* by high society also had to do with a wave of cultural nationalism that swept the island in the wake of U.S. military occupation for eight years (1916–1924), discussed at greater length in Chapter 6. Trujillo's policies effectively marginalized many other folkloric dance styles from the airwaves and catapulted the *merengue* into the national spotlight, where it has largely remained ever since.

One of the first styles of *merengue* heard on the radio was the *merengue típico* from the northern Cibao region, specifically around the city of Santiago de los Caballeros. Trujillo apparently chose to promote the variant because the Cibao is known to have a demographically "whiter" population than most other parts of the country. This obscured the creolized nature of the genre and its many African-derived influences, which in the 1930s still carried significant negative associations among the middle classes and elites, especially in Santo Domingo. Many critics expressed outrage at the appearance of Afro-Dominican percussion in exclusive dance halls nevertheless and refused to accept the *merengue* for some time, preferring the waltz, *danza*, and other genres.

The instrumentation of the *merengue típico*—a folkloric style derived from the rural working class—consists of accordion, a metal scraper known as a *güira*, a bass instrument of some sort (usually an African-derived *marímbula*-like instrument [see Fig. 1.8] or an acoustic bass), a cylindrical double-headed drum played across the knees called a *tambora* (Fig. 4.1), vocalists, and sometimes one or two saxophones. Over the years, the traditional *merengue típico* format has been fused with influences from big band jazz, salsa, and international popular music and the instrumentation of most groups has expanded. In commercial recordings, pianos now take the place of the accordion, an electric bass has replaced the *marímbula*, and conga drums have been added, as well as a large horn section featuring saxophones and trumpets. To a greater extent than most other Latin ensembles, commercial *merengue* orchestras are renowned for their flashy coordinated costumes and the choreographies performed by group members on stage. The use of glittery outfits, elaborate choreography, and slick stage presentations began in the early 1970s; Johnny Ventura represents an important trend setter in this sense and influenced countless other groups in subsequent decades. Another common variant of recent years is the *típico moderno* format, accordion-based as in the earlier *merengue típico* but with conga, saxophone, bass drum, and somewhat more elaborate arrangements.

FIGURE 4.1   Merengue *instruments:* tambora, güira, *button accordion.*   *(Photo by the author).*

ACTIVITY 4.1   *Search for recordings or YouTube clips of merengue típico to familiarize yourself with the sound of this folkloric style. Good examples include songs by accordionist Francisco Ulloa on CDs such as* Ultramerengue *or* Pegaito. *See if you can locate a button accordion player in your area who can explain to you how the instrument is played. Failing that, find information on what makes a button accordion different from keyboard models.*

Most *merengue* compositions have a two-part structure similar to that of the Cuban *son* and of salsa music, discussed later in the chapter: They begin with a short instrumental introduction (often known as the *paseo* or "promenade"), followed by (1) a strophic verse section known as the *cuerpo* ("body") and (2) a faster call-and-response section known as the *jaleo* (literally, a "pulling" or "stretching out"). Typically, the *cuerpo* section precedes the *jaleo* in its entirety, but in some songs the sections will alternate early on, with a segment of the *jaleo* dividing each verse. It is also common for additional "hot" instrumental interludes to be written into the *jaleo* to build intensity. The most characteristic aspects of the *merengue* genre are its accelerated tempo—*merengues* are played in a fast duple meter, often very fast—its unique percussion, and (in larger band formats) its horn lines, especially evident in instrumental breaks within the *jaleo*.

Merengue dance style involves ballroom-style dancing in couples, but these days it also incorporates a great deal of hip movement derived from African traditions. Dancers usually stand very close to one another, stepping on the strong beats (one and three) of each 4/4 measure and at times executing intricate turns and spins derived from salsa music and earlier African American traditions such as lindy and swing.

The *tambora* drum (Fig. 4.1) is probably the most unique instrument in the *merengue* ensemble, both folkloric and commercial versions. Its two heads are traditionally made of goat skin and tied with *bejuco* vine, though these days the drum can be purchased ready-made by companies such as Latin Percussion, with fitted heads and metal tuning lugs. Percussionists place the drum horizontally across their knees and strike one side with their strong hand using a stick (stems up in Figs. 4.2 and 4.3), the other side with the palm and fingers of their weak hand (stems down in the same figures). The hand with the stick sounds more loudly than the other, alternating high, sharp cracks on the rim of the instrument and open-tone flams or rolls against the head. The weak hand dampens the opposite head during the rim shots and releases during the roll to let the drum resonate fully. *Tambora* players have some freedom to vary their basic pattern, embellishing and filling in the overall texture as they see fit. One of the Dominican Republic's best players, Catarey (Angel Miró Andújar), can be seen on YouTube demonstrating the basic rhythm in variation.

A transcription of one basic rhythmic pattern associated with the *tambora* is provided in Figure 4.2. Round note heads designate an open tone on one of the heads of the instrument, slash heads a rim shot with the stick, and an *x* a slap with the weak hand. Note the repeated open tones played on the *tambora* at the end of measure two that roll toward the downbeat. These contrast starkly with the rim shots and slaps, ringing out more loudly and helping to define the characteristic *merengue* sound. This rhythm is associated with older, rural *merengue*; a newer and even more syncopated variant known as the *maco* or "toad" rhythm has been used by many groups since the 1970s (Austerlitz 1997, 94).

The *güira* scraper for its part plays quick eighth-note patterns; common patterns include a downbeat and two upbeats ("*one, two-and three, four-and*" of the 4/4 measure) or strong beats 1 and 3 preceded by a pickup ("*and-one*, and two, *and-three*, and four" of the 4/4 measure). The *güira* also improvises with flourishes and other variations from the basic pulse.

FIGURE 4.2 *Basic* tambora *rhythm.*

In larger dance bands, the congas play a characteristic two-measure pattern against other percussion as well, very similar to the rhythm used in *soca* bands and to back up steel drumming ensembles.

A transcription of characteristic rhythms performed by all of these instruments is provided in Figure 4.3 in relation to one another. In both the *tambora* and conga parts, stems up indicate strokes performed by the strong hand and stems down those performed by the weak hand; notes written on the top line of the conga transcription are played by the higher-pitched drum, while notes toward the middle of the staff are played on the lower drum.

On CD track 9, percussionists briefly perform the rhythms transcribed in Fig. 4.3 so that you can hear clearly what the parts sound like. The *güira* enters first with its constant pulse (remember that this is only one of several common *güira* patterns). Next, the *tambora* and conga drums enter individually against the *güira*, and finally, all three instruments perform together.

ACTIVITY 4.2 *With a few other students, imitate the rhythms recorded on CD track 9 and notated in Figure 4.3, either by singing them or by playing them on actual percussion instruments. Slow them down as much as you need to; begin with single parts; after you have mastered them individually, try combining two at once, and finally add in all three.*

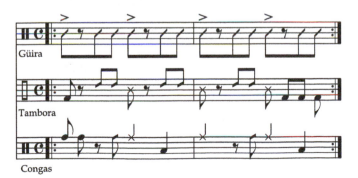

FIGURE 4.3 Merengue *percussion rhythms:* güira, *congas,* and tambora.

ACTIVITY 4.3 *Listen to recorded examples of* merengue *(folkloric or commercial) from your own music collection or that of others and analyze their form, listening for how the music is organized section by section. See if you can discern the rhythm of the conga,* tambora, *and perhaps other instruments in the music.*

ACTIVITY 4.4 *Listen closely to CD track 10, a commercial* merengue *entitled "Love of Colors," written and performed by Kinito Méndez. The complete listening guide available at www. oup.com/us.moore will help you identify major segments and transitions within the piece. Notice how the basic percussion rhythms are varied and embellished at various moments and the breaks the instruments play with the melodic instruments. Notice how the bass rhythm changes in various sections.*

Partial Listening Guide for CD Track 10

"Amores de colores" ("Love of Colors")

0:00–0:23

The *paseo* or instrumental introduction beginning with a break section (0:00–0:05) in which horns, bass, and percussion all play the same rhythm.

0:24–1:01

Verse 1 of the *cuerpo*. Note that the section beginning at 0:37 is sung by the chorus and then at 0:43 the chorus and lead vocalist sing the verse together in alternation. Horns fill in with short figures between the melodic phrases. For the most part, the bass plays a fairly straight rhythm under this and the other verse sections.

Quiero definir con los colores	I want to define with colors
El amor y el cariño de la gente	The love and affection of people
Quiero definir con los colores	I want to define with colors
Las clases de amores diferentes	All the different kinds of love there are
Y VERÁS QUE VAS A ENCONTRAR	YOU'LL SEE THAT YOU'LL FIND
TU COLOR	YOUR COLOR
Será verde SERÁ MORADO	Whether it's green OR BROWN
Será blanco O COLORADO	Whether it's white OR REDDISH
Será negro SERÁ ROSADO	Whether it's black OR PINK
Tu color	Your color
Quiero definir, señores, con colores	I want to define, sirs, with colors
El cariño de la gente	The affection that people have
El amor y la pasión (¡dice!)	Their love and passion (and it says!)

1:02–1:13

An instrumental interlude begins here that features saxes, then trumpets, then a series of rhythmic breaks. This figure repeats in the middle beginning at 1:08. The bass begins to vary its pattern more frequently.

The prominence of saxophone lines in this example is characteristic of both folkloric and commercial *merengue*. Saxophones often play lightning-quick arpeggios, outlining the tonic-dominant harmonies of the song in various ways. However, commercial recordings differ from their folkloric counterparts in other ways. Keyboard parts in larger groups tend to be highly syncopated, bearing little relation to accordion melodies; they are more similar to the salsa keyboard patterns discussed later in the chapter. Bass rhythms vary quite a bit in all sorts of *merengue*. The most common beat is a rather heavy, straight pulse on "one" and "three" of the 4/4 measure. However, in the *jaleo* section, especially, some groups play an *apambichao* style that is more syncopated and in fact similar to the anticipated bass of the Cuban *son*, also discussed later. In the last ten or fifteen years, commercial releases have begun to feature a different sort of bass style; the bass is used less to keep the pulse (this function is often taken over by the floor tom of a drum set) and more to add color or "punch" at various moments. Slides and slaps are prominent, and the performer stops and starts at various times rather than playing consistently. You can hear some of these techniques in "Love of Colors."

Finally, in the hot horn interludes of the *jaleo*, saxophone and trumpet melodies stack on top of one another in interesting ways. The use of overlapping horn melodies is structurally comparable to what the percussion parts do as they combine with one another; the technique derives from traditional West African music, as we have seen. Examining dance genres such as the *merengue*, we can see the fundamental interpenetration of elements from European musical heritage (instruments such as the saxophone or piano, scales and harmonies derived from Europe, Spanish-language texts) and African heritage (instruments such as the *tambora* and congas, cyclical form, combinative melodies). The combinative melodic technique is roughly the same as what happens in the instrumental interludes of much salsa music, though in the case of salsa it is trumpets and trombones that tend to be foregrounded rather than trumpets and saxes. Saxes are apparently preferred in *merengue* because of their ability to play fast lines with relative ease and to repeat them for extended periods without tiring.

As you listen again to the initial section of the *jaleo* of "Amores de colores," you might consider the ways that independent horn lines interact with one another. The transcriptions in Figures 4.4 and 4.5 of sax and trumpet lines provide a good example of how distinct melodies played at the same time often begin and end their phrases at different moments. The saxophone section begins with a repeating phrase at 2:32.

At 2:40, the trumpets enter with an entirely different melody that begins about a measure later, adding to the complexity of the overall musical effect. The first four measures of the trumpet line are

FIGURE   4.4   *Repeating saxophone line in CD track 10, "Amores de colores,"*
at 2:32.

FIGURE 4.5   *Initial segment of the trumpet line in CD track 10, "Amores de colores," at 2:40.*

represented in the transcription in Figure 4.5. Stems up in the first two measures indicate lines played by the first trumpets and stems down, lines played by the second trumpets.

Having now discussed the history and musical characteristics of one style of creolized dance music, it should be instructive to compare it to another from a different island and to think about the similarities and differences between them in terms of rhythm, structure, instrumentation, and other factors.

CUBAN *SON*

The *son*, another influential form of Hispanic Caribbean music, has been heralded as a national symbol in Cuba for years, in large part because it effectively bridges the worlds of African and European aesthetics. Like the *merengue*, *son* is an excellent example of creolized culture. Though sung primarily in Spanish, African-derived terminology appears in some pieces. *Son* instrumentation includes both string instruments derived from Spain and percussion modeled on African heritage. Instruments of all sorts often repeat riffs and thus contribute to a texture based on repeated or layered loops, lending themselves to open-ended improvisation. In many cases, the rhythms performed on melodic instruments are at least as important in this style as the pitches they play, suggesting that they are being utilized in a manner similar to that of the percussion. As in the case of *merengue*, the structure of *son* music is hybrid. It combines a verse section known as the *verso* or *canto* and a cyclic *montuno* finale with call–response vocals, the equivalent of the *merengue*'s *jaleo*. The initial section (the *canto*) derives from European models, the latter (the *montuno*) from African models. Salsa dancing also demonstrates hybrid influences and is similar in many ways to the *merengue* choreography described earlier.

Cuban *son* developed in the nineteenth century in eastern Cuba, the largely mountainous region known as Oriente. It was originally a rural dance music for parties and other informal gatherings, performed by the Afro-Cuban community in the hills surrounding cities such as Santiago, Baracoa, and Guantánamo. Many subgenres of *son* continue to exist there in distinct areas. Accounts from around 1900 suggest that in its earliest manifestations it consisted only of a repeated chorus supported by very simple tonic-dominant chords. Against this background, a lead singer might improvise brief phrases or perhaps insert a longer couplet or quatrain before the group sang the chorus once again. Those who have heard early rural recordings of African American music such as work songs may note a similarity between them and rural *son* subgenres, underscoring again the ties between cultural traditions in North America and Latin America.

The years following the Wars of Independence against Spain (1868–1898) witnessed a great deal of demographic movement in Cuba that disseminated the *son* throughout the country. Rural families whose homes and farms had been destroyed relocated to urban areas. Others found themselves displaced by the development of huge sugar plantations and other commercial farming. The creation of a national army in 1908 and the eventual circulation of soldiers throughout the island also resulted in the movement of many Cubans to new areas. All of these trends led to the gradual spread of the *son* to poorer neighborhoods in Havana and other western cities. Soon the music began to fuse with new forms of music including the *bolero*, North American jazz, and various types of Afro-Cuban folklore. By the 1920s an urban *son* variant had developed with a more elaborate formal structure and instrumentation. The popularization of the genre helped break down many racial barriers, allowing working-class performers of color into the mainstream music industry in significant numbers for the first time. Urban *son* sextets and septets (*sextetos, septetos*) gained widespread popularity on the radio and through the sale of 78 records beginning in the mid-1920s. *Son* was the first genre of popular music to incorporate performance on a drum played with the bare hands, previously considered a "primitive" and unsightly practice by urban audiences.

The most typical instrumentation of urban *son* bands of the 1920s included the guitar, *tres* (a smaller guitar-like instrument with three courses of double strings, usually tuned to a major or minor chord), *maracas, claves,* bongo drum, bass, and often a trumpet (Fig. 4.6). In rural ensembles other instruments substituted for the European acoustic bass. One of these was a ceramic jug called a *botija* that Cubans used to import oil from Spain (jug bands in the United States used similar instruments). Another early bass instrument was the *marímbula*, discussed previously (see Fig. 1.8). But urban groups gradually came to view them as "rustic" or "hick." They adopted the European bass in an attempt to appeal to middle-class tastes and to allow for greater harmonic possibilities.

Various sounds characterize the *son*. One is its unique fundamental rhythm, the *son clave*, usually played on the *claves* themselves. This

FIGURE 4.6 *The Septeto Habanero (Havana Septet), a traditional Cuban* son *group performing in Havana in 2001. Instruments seen in the front row (L–R) are the* güiro, claves, maracas, guitar, *and* tres. *Instruments in the back row are the bass and* bongo *drum, though at this moment the* bongosero *is playing his bell.* *(Photo by the author).*

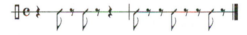

FIGURE 4.7 Son clave.

rhythm is similar to a repeating rhythm found in *rumba* (*rumba clave*) and appears to derive from it. *Son clave* consists of a two-measure repeating pattern with two strokes on one side and three on another. Either side can be played first to begin the phrase. The pattern beginning on the "two side" is written in staff notation in Figure 4.7.

Another characteristic element of *son* is the rhythmic melody played on the *tres*, outlining or implying chords but not actually strumming them. In the final *montuno* section, especially, rhythms on the *tres* often correspond to the *clave* pattern, with a somewhat straighter melodic line played against the "two side" of the *clave* and a more syncopated melody played against the "three side." A typical pattern in a major key is represented in Figure 4.8. You will notice that the first part of the pattern corresponding to the "two side" of the *clave* emphasizes

FIGURE 4.8   *A typical* tres *pattern from the* montuno, *transcribed against* clave.

FIGURE 4.9   *An alternate* tres montuno *pattern for the same implicit chord progression.*

the downbeat of the measure and thus appears a bit less syncopated, whereas the second half of the pattern on the "three side" is entirely syncopated.

There are in fact many different kinds of *montuno* patterns a *tres* might play, even over the rather simple chord progression implied in the example above (I–IV–V–IV or G–C–D–C). Another is shown in Figure 4.9. These *tres* patterns are important to the development of salsa music, influencing the style of keyboardists in commercial dance bands as early as the 1940s.

ACTIVITY 4.5   *Search for recordings or video clips of traditional Cuban* son *and listen to the performance style of the* tres *player. Try to hear the various patterns used to accompany music in the* montuno *section, and then compare them to the typically freer patterns employed in earlier sections. Songs on commercial recordings that might serve as a good point of departure include "Son de la loma" ("They're From the Hills") on the Corason CD collection* Septetos Cubanos; *a slightly different piece in a minor key by the same name on* Routes of

Rhythm. A Carnival of Cuban Music. *Vol. 1 (Rounder Records); or "Adios compay gato" ("Goodbye Mr. Cat") on the Orfeón CD* Cuba: Guajira y son, caña tabaco y ron, *Vol. 2.*

Another rhythm found in *son* music is that played by the bongo drum (Fig. 4.13) during the initial sections, called the *martillo* or "hammer" pattern. The *martillo* in its most basic form consists of constant eighth notes, with accented strokes on the smaller head of the drum on beats one and three of the 4/4 measure and on beat four on the larger drumhead (Fig. 4.10). Bongo players deviate from this basic pattern constantly, however, improvising in order to fill in spaces between the melodic lines and to generate excitement. Careful listening to recordings of traditional *son* will reveal the sorts of variations and sounds generated by the bongos. In the hands of an experienced player, it is a decidedly virtuosic instrument. The improvising is not entirely free, however; the *bongosero* listens and responds to vocals and other instruments, filling in with embellished rhythms at particular times in order to complement rather than overshadow other performers. When the *montuno* begins, the bongo player typically switches to a bell, emphasizing the strong beats of the music in order to drive the tempo forward and generate excitement (as discussed later).

CD track 11 provides a short excerpt of a bongo drum player performing against the *clave*. This combination is not traditional but helps the listener focus on the bongo performance style and its contribution to the overall sound. The bongo performer begins by playing the basic *martillo* pattern but soon begins to vary and elaborate on it, as would be typical in an actual performance.

Probably the most unique aspect of the *son* is the pattern played on the bass. The bass player executes something known as an "anticipated

FIGURE   4.10   *The basic bongo drum pattern in Cuban* son, *known as the* martillo. *Higher notes are played on the smaller drumhead of the bongo and the lower notes, on the lower head. Slash noteheads indicate light touches or notes that are dampened.*

bass" rhythm, meaning that the notes often sound slightly earlier than one might expect. For instance, in many types of music (most rock, country, polka) the bass plays mostly on strong beats—one and three of the 4/4 measure. In the *son*, by contrast, the bass plays on the "and-of-two" (i.e., an eighth note before the "normal" spot on beat three) and on four (a full quarter-note beat before the "normal" spot on beat one), as shown in Figure 4.11. This lends the music an interesting "uneven" syncopated feel that repeats constantly.

CD track 12 provides a brief example of a typical *son* bass pattern played against the *clave* and *maracas*. The percussion enters first to establish the time, then the bass enters shortly thereafter. CD track 12 closely imitates the bass harmonies and rhythms found in the song "Mueve la cintura," discussed in Activity 4.6. Once you have become familiar with the general characteristics of the anticipated bass and its relationship to the *clave*, you may find it instructive to compare this didactic recording with the recording on which it is based.

ACTIVITY 4.6 *"Mueve la cintura" ("Shake Your Hips"), recorded on the Corason CD* Casa de la Trova de Santiago de Cuba, *serves as a good introduction to traditional son bass. If you can, track down a recording of this piece; if not, listen closely to CD track 12, which imitates its bass patterns. Focus first on the* clave *and see if you can clap it out, noting that it begins on the "three side." Focus next on the bass, hearing its pattern in relation to the* clave. *Notice how the* clave *creates constant tension and release with the bass pattern by first lining up with it and then deviating from it in alternating measures. Written against one another, the two lines would look something like the transcription in Figure 4.11.*

FIGURE 4.11 *"Mueve la cintura," clave and bass patterns. These two instruments together with a* maraca *perform the rhythms played on CD track 12. The same pattern can be found in the son "Mueve la cintura," discussed in Activity 4.6.*

ACTIVITY 4.7 *Now that you have some feel for the basic elements of* son, *try performing a repeating vamp in this style with classmates. You will need to imitate the* tres, *bass, and* clave *at the very least. Figure 4.12 adds a* maraca *part for good measure and a chorus to the well-known piece "Son de la loma" from the* Septetos Cubanos CD. *Use your voices or whatever instruments are available to reproduce as many parts as you can. The chorus lyrics translate as "They're from the hills, they sing on the plains."*

The sound of Cuban *son* has changed significantly through the years. From the 1910s through the late 1920s, groups typically consisted only of string instruments, percussion, and voices, more or less in the style of "Son de la loma." About 1930, many groups added a single trumpet player. In this expanded ensemble (a septet instead of a sextet), the *tres* played a slightly less prominent role as soloist, with embellishments between vocal lines and solos often performed on the trumpet instead. In the 1940s and 1950s, a new *son* style became popular in Havana, known as *conjunto.* This format introduced additional changes. For instance, a second and often a third trumpet were added to the bands. This in turn required that written arrangements be created so as to coordinate melodies played by the entire section. Pianos became a standard part of *son* instrumentation at this time, sometimes

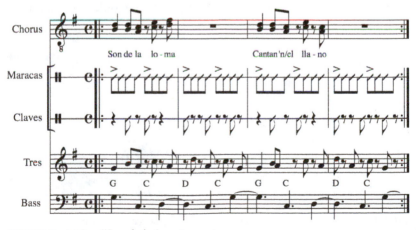

FIGURE 4.12 *"Son de la loma"* montuno *vamp.*

replacing the *tres*, sometimes playing alongside it. As more performers joined *son* bands who had formal training and knew how to read music, the pieces slowly became more elaborate in structural and harmonic terms.

One or two conga drums were incorporated into most ensembles by the 1950s. The *timbales*—an instrument originally from eastern Cuba and formerly used only in styles of dance music such as the *danzón* and *chachachá*—came to be played in some groups as well, for instance, in the Sonora Matancera.

The *timbales* and congas both have an interesting history but were initially used in totally different kinds of ensembles. *Timbales* derive from European-style military percussion instruments such as the snare drum and tom-tom played by black and mulatto soldiers in Cuba during the nineteenth century. Over time, performers seem to have "re-Africanized" these instruments, playing various new rhythms with sticks on the sides of the drums as well as on the heads. They also began pressing on the head of the drum with one hand as they played, dampening the sound in particular ways to change the timbre. *Timbales* performed in this creolized fashion have appeared in dance bands since at least the 1830s. Congas prior to the 1940s were used exclusively in Afro-Cuban folkloric music such as *rumba* or *comparsa* carnival groups. Many middle-class Cubans refused to accept them in dance orchestras for some time, considering the practice of playing percussion with the hands inappropriate, as mentioned. During the early years of the conga's incorporation into *son* bands, dance band leader Antonio Arcaño (interview, July 1992) informed me that representatives of some recreational venues asked the drummers to play behind a curtain so their presence would not offend the guests!

FIGURE   4.13   *From left to right: conga drums, bongo, and timbales.*   *(Photo by the author).*

Figures 4.14 and 4.15 provide transcriptions of two common ways of playing the conga drums to accompany the *conjunto*-style *son*. Both are written out against *son clave* since they are two-sided patterns and need to be heard in relationship to *clave*. Figure 4.15 represents what a percussionist might have played on a single drum in the 1940s or 1950s. *P*s and *T*s (palms and touches) represent light touches with the weak hand; as before, an *x* indicates a slap and a round note, an open tone. Figure 4.15 represents a more elaborate pattern played on two different drums; its melody includes two open-tones on different pitches rather than one. Pattern two is more typical of conga drum performance in dance bands of the late 1950s and 1960s in Cuba and in New York salsa. Some present-day performers begin with a simpler one-conga pattern and then switch to the two-conga pattern during the *montuno* section or other "hot" sections of music.

CD track 13 provides recorded examples of the two conga patterns transcribed. The *clave* enters first, followed by the single-drum style

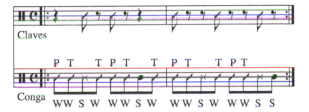

FIGURE 4.14 *A typical conga pattern in early* conjunto-*style* son, *played on a single drum.*

FIGURE 4.15 *A conga pattern more common in the later 1950s, played on two drums.*

represented in Figure 4.14. After a few repetitions, the congas drop out, entering again shortly thereafter with the two-drum pattern transcribed in Figure 4.15. The basic patterns are demonstrated in these recordings, but of course, in an actual performance a percussionist might well vary the rhythms considerably.

ACTIVITY 4.8   *Contact a percussionist who has experience playing hand drums and ask him or her to demonstrate the parts notated. Search the Web for didactic videos of conga drum performance or instruction.*

The 1950s gave rise to scores of influential *conjunto* and other dance bands in Cuba that had a strong influence on dance music throughout Spanish-speaking Latin America and in the United States. Many musicians contributed to these developments, both in Cuba and in cities such as New York with large numbers of Caribbean immigrants. *Tres* player Arsenio Rodríguez (1911–1970) was especially important in defining the early *conjunto* format and the first bandleader to incorporate the conga drums. He experimented in many ways, for instance, developing a *"claved"* style of bass and piano playing that proved very influential.

ACTIVITY 4.9   *Track down a few CDs or Web videos to compare the sound of Cuban son from different periods. You might begin with the Corason CD Septeto Habanero: 75 Years Later in order to hear roughly what son music of the 1930s sounded like. Next, search for footage or recordings of conjunto performers from later decades such as Arsenio Rodríguez or Félix Chappottín. Compare the repertoire in terms of overall form, instrumentation, harmonies, bass lines, and so on. Note how in conjunto style the piano, bass, and tres often perform as a unit and perform two-measure "claved" patterns.*

With the onset of the Cuban Revolution in January 1959, relations between Cuba and the United States began to sour. The new Cuban

FIGURE 4.16 *Singer Miguelito Cuní (left) and trumpeter Félix Chappottín (right). Both performed with Arsenio Rodríguez and helped define the emerging* conjunto *sound of 1950s Cuba that influenced the development of salsa.* *(Archives, Cuban Ministry of Culture).*

leadership, consisting of figures such as Fidel Castro and Ernesto ("Che") Guevara, soon demonstrated its adherence to socialism. The leaders began to nationalize foreign industries and to establish closer trade and military ties with the Soviet Union. In this cold war era, fear of the spread of socialist ideals, among other factors, led the United States to impose an economic embargo on Cuba as well as a travel ban that prohibited most North Americans from visiting the island. The idea was to isolate Cuba economically and to force a change of government. In the latter sense, the U.S. embargo proved decidedly ineffective, but it did isolate the country. Political tensions meant that Cuban artists could no longer travel freely abroad or sell their music to capitalist countries. As a result of all this, the center of music making in the Hispanic Caribbean shifted decisively from Havana to New York, with its predominance of immigrants from Puerto Rico. The following section considers one form of creolized music and dance that developed within Puerto Rico itself before shifting attention to developments in New York.

PUERTO RICAN *PLENA*

The *plena* is a form of Puerto Rican music similar to the *merengue* and *son* in that it incorporates both African- and European-derived elements and exists in both folkloric and commercial forms. *Plena* developed at the turn of the twentieth century in largely Afro-Puerto Rican neighborhoods of Ponce such as Joya de Castillo. It seems to have resulted from musical interactions between residents there and recent immigrants from islands of the British Caribbean such as Barbados, the Virgin Islands, and St. Kitts. *Plena* first attracted attention throughout Puerto Rico and internationally beginning about 1920 and was recorded in stylized form (i.e., with additional instruments, extended harmonies, or in dance-band arrangements) by artists such as Manuel ("El Canario") Jiménez. As in the case of other genres we have discussed, *plena* was the first form of working-class music to emerge in Puerto Rico that became popular among all social classes. As with the other genres, its history also reflects friction between classes and ethnicities. Urban professionals did not embrace *plena* immediately, considering it unrefined and musically uninteresting. Only in the 1940s and beyond, with the dissemination of more elaborated versions of the music by César Concepción (1909–1974, known for his gentrified "salon *plenas*") and other bandleaders, did it manage to attract broader audiences. The *plena* has been important as a sort of chronicle of the lives of the common people, a means of conveying stories and histories, and at times a form of social protest.

The early instrumentation of folkloric *plena* groups was relatively flexible, consisting of frame drums of various sizes derived from Spanish and

FIGURE 4.17 *An ad-hoc ensemble of* plena *musicians performing at the Festival Bacardí in San Juan, Puerto Rico, 1999. Various* pandero *frame drums can be seen in the foreground.* (Photo by the author).

Arab culture known as *panderetas* or *panderos* (Fig. 4.17), as well as instruments such as the button accordion, Puerto Rican *cuatro, güiro,* guitar, and *marímbula* (see Figs. 1.8, 2.3, 2.5). Harmonies tended to be simple, and the structure consisted of an alternation between choruses and brief couplets or quatrains (often improvised) performed by a lead singer, usually four or eight measures in length. Over time, the *plena* has fused with other forms of music including salsa and jazz. If danced by couples, *plena* choreography typically involves a single step forward and back in closed position similar to *merengue* dance but with relatively few turns and spins.

Various rhythms can be performed by *pleneros*, but the most common are transcribed in Figure 4.18. They are quite similar to particular *bomba* genres (specifically the *bomba holandé* mentioned in Chapter 3) and may derive from that source. For the most part, *panderetas* produce only two sounds: an open tone created by hitting the edge of the skin with the thumb and letting it bounce off and a sharp slap produced by letting the full hand hit the center of the skin. The Puerto Rican-style *güiro* and the low *pandereta* (the *seguidor*) provide a basic pulse. Against this, the middle *pandereta* (the *segunda*) plays a slightly more involved pattern. Finally, all three combine with the high *requinto* frame drum and its more syncopated, "jumped" rhythm, as well as its frequent improvisations. A composite rhythm of the high and low *panderetas* can also be imitated on the conga drums by dance bands. You can see in Figure 4.18 that the *requinto* figure extends over two measures and consists of two halves, one more syncopated than the other, similar in structure to *son clave*. It differs from the other parts that consist of shorter repeating figures. In this transcription, a slash note head indicates a slap or closed hit, while a round note head indicates an open tone.

CD track 14 provides a recording of the rhythms transcribed in Figure 4.18. The *güiro* enters first to establish the pulse. Following this, the low *seguidor* pattern is demonstrated by itself, followed by the *segunda* and basic *requinto* patterns. Finally, all three of the *pandereta* parts are heard together against the *güiro*.

ACTIVITY 4.10   *See if you and fellow students can locate a few hand-held frame drums and a Puerto Rican* güiro *or other scraper to use as you attempt to perform the rhythms recorded on CD track 14. Tambourines with their jingles taped or silenced would do in a pinch as* panderos. *Begin with the* güiro *and* seguidor, *then add the* segunda *and* requinto *parts. The* plena *rhythm notated in Figure 4.18 begins at 0:58 on CD track 15. Listen to it as it enters and see if you can recognize the beat.*

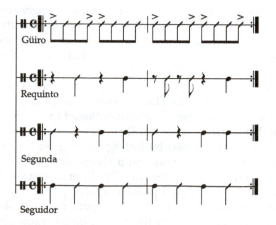

On CD track 15 you have a *plena* recorded by Los Pleneros de la 21 (The Plena Performers from Bus Stop 21) entitled "Patria Borinqueña" or

FIGURE 4.18 Plena *rhythms.*

"Land of Borinquen," the indigenous term for Puerto Rico. The Pleneros group was founded in 1983 in the Bronx, New York, by Juan Gutiérrez Rodríguez. Members take their name from a bus route that used to run through a predominantly Afro-Puerto Rican neighborhood of Santurce, outside of San Juan. They are a professional folklore troupe, dedicated to performing traditional Puerto Rican music, especially *bomba* and *plena*.

Songs such as this one to which bass, piano, and *cuatro* have been added underscore the fact that *plenas* may be played solely on percussion instruments during a rally or street festival or by dance orchestras with melody and harmony instruments. "Patria Borinqueña" represents a hybrid in this sense: It incorporates many additional instruments and was recorded in a studio, yet it retains a self-consciously folkloric sound. The song begins with a nonmetrical introduction featuring voices, piano, and *cuatro*, slow and soulful. The relatively short formal structure of this *plena*, typical of most, consists largely of eight-measure phrases played repeatedly in variation by a lead singer and chorus. The only exception is an instrumental bridge section in a contrasting key and toward the end a shorter call–response coda of sorts—what we might consider the *"montuno"* of the piece—beginning at 3:17.

ACTIVITY 4.11   *Listen closely through CD track 15, making a note of how the piece is organized. See if you can recognize and make a written note of where instrumental interludes occur, when the key changes, when particular instruments are featured as soloists, and so forth. Then consult the full listening guide at www. oup.com/us.moore and check your conclusions against it.*

Partial Listening Guide to CD Track 15

"Patria Borinqueña"

0:00–0:53

Slow, nonmetrical introduction featuring piano, three-part chorus vocals, and *cuatro*.

Patria borinqueña, jardines de rosas	Land of Borinquen, garden of flowers
Déjame cantarte, borinquen hermosa	Let me sing to you, beautiful Borinquen

0:53–1:14

Instrumental introduction, beginning with a prominent *cuatro* melody over a percussion break. The percussion instruments end their break and enter in time at 0:59. The *cuatro* plays the chorus melody twice.

1:15–1:31

Chorus, sung twice in time and with only two-part harmony instead of three.

ACTIVITY 4.12 *Work with someone who reads Western notation and have him or her play each of the three vocal lines in Figure 4.19, taken from the introduction to "Patria Borinqueña." Learn to sing each line by itself, then put them together with classmates to create the harmonies you hear on the recording.*

Now try learning the first and second chorus parts as performed on CD track 15 and notated in Figures 4.20 and 4.21 so that you can sing them along with the recording.

Brief mention should be made of Puerto Ricans Rafael Cortijo (1928–1982) and Ismael Rivera (1931–1987), given that their performances of dance-band *bomba* and *plena* in the 1950s, 1960s, and early

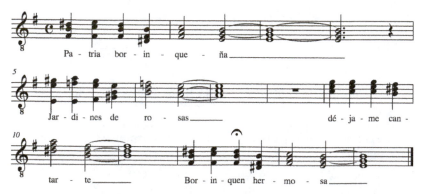

FIGURE 4.19 Rubato *vocals in the introduction to "Patria Borinqueña."*

FIGURE 4.20 *First chorus vocals and sample lead line, "Patria Borinqueña"* *(1:15).*

FIGURE 4.21 *The second chorus to "Patria Borinqueña," beginning at 3:17.*

1970s represented a high point of creativity and effervescence in the history of Puerto Rican dance music. The two also led of one of the first commercially successful groups consisting almost exclusively of Afro-Puerto Ricans. Cortijo and Rivera were born in the impoverished Villa Palmeras neighborhood of Santurce, on the outskirts of San Juan, to working-class parents. The area at the time was 87% black and a center of Afro-Puerto Rican artistic expression. Cortijo and Rivera became fast friends as boys, often playing drums and singing together. By the mid-1950s, they began performing in an ensemble organized by Cortijo that included many of the individuals who would later perform as El Gran Combo, one of Puerto Rico's best-known salsa bands.

Cortijo y su Combo, as the initial group was known, became immensely popular by fusing big-band jazz instrumentation and some Cuban rhythms with their own adaptations of the *bomba sicá* and *plena*. Cortijo, who played *timbales*, established a sound for the band that consisted of up-tempo, driving rhythms and nearly constant interlocking bell patterns

FIGURE 4.22 *Ismael Rivera performing with Los Cachimbos in the Aragon Ballroom, Chicago, Illinois (circa 1970).* (Photo by Carlos Flores).

of various sorts that accompanied the congas and other percussion. For his part, Ismael Rivera gained a reputation as a master of improvised lead vocals known as *soneos* in response to the chorus. Cuban bandleader Benny Moré gave him the nickname "El Sonero Mayor" ("The Greatest *Son* Singer") because of these abilities. Rhythmically, Rivera was one of the first to sing longer improvised vocal phrases that overlapped the chorus, leaving no space between their vocals and his. This technique proved decidedly influential on later salsa performers. Lyrically, the group's compositions dealt with many important social themes (unemployment, poverty, racial pride, longing for one's homeland) that resonated with the public. Cortijo y su Combo are important for having promoted local Puerto Rican musical styles over those from Cuba, North America, or elsewhere; they were one of the first local bands to do so. Despite Rivera's run-ins with the authorities over drug use in the early 1960s, both he and Cortijo have become revered symbols of Puerto Rican music and culture.

NEW YORK SALSA

All of the distinct dance music forms we have been discussing intermingle to a certain extent in salsa music from New York City of the 1970s and 1980s, where performers from all islands of the Hispanic Caribbean lived and worked together. There is some controversy over the term "salsa" and the extent to which it represents a distinct musical genre. We can safely say that it is a commercial label used to describe a style of Latin dance music based largely on the Cuban *son* (and specifically the *conjunto* sound of the 1950s) but that also incorporates elements from jazz and the folkloric music of Puerto Rico and elsewhere. Salsa is thus a decidedly transnational music, having developed as a result of the movement of people and sounds across the Atlantic, within the Caribbean, and to North America. Salsa incorporates the characteristic syncopated bass of the *son*, its bongo and conga drum patterns, the *son clave*, and other elements. Yet its sound is distinct in terms of instrumentation, the prominence of particular instruments such as the *timbales*, its harmonic complexity, and frequently its lyrics. The music began as a community phenomenon promoted by small, independent record labels based in New York such as Tico, Alegre, and Fania. These "mom-and-pop" businesses emerged because major labels at the time refused to record and promote the music of Latino immigrants. Salsa audiences tended to be locally oriented in the early years, and the lyrics of the music frequently spoke to issues relevant to the working class.

ACTIVITY 4.13   *If you can find them, listen to a modern salsa recording of Ruben Blades' "Pablo Pueblo" ("Pablo Everyman") or "Ritmo en el corazón" ("Rhythm in the Heart"), recorded by Ray Barretto and Celia Cruz. These pieces incorporate brief segments of* bomba sicá *into their overall* son-*derived musical structure, marking them as Puerto Rican–influenced. See if you can hear the change from the* son/*salsa beat to the* bomba sicá *rhythm. In "Pablo Pueblo" this occurs at 0:48–0:54 during verse 1 and 2:17–2:23 in verse 2. In "Ritmo en el corazón," the* bomba *section appears at 1:12–1:28.*

The best-known salsa label of the 1970s and 1980s was New York's Fania Records, which rose to prominence during unprecedented growth of Hispanic Caribbean immigrant communities in that city. Initially a small company formed by Dominican flautist and bandleader Johnny Pacheco together with Italian American Jerry Masucci, Fania managed to sign a majority of the most popular salsa artists of the day and became a major artistic force. During the first half of the 1970s, Fania dominated 80% of the commercial salsa market. Virtually all major figures of the era recorded for them: *conguero* Ray Barretto, trombonist and composer Willie Colón, singers Celia Cruz and Héctor Lavoe, pianists Charlie and

Eddie Palmieri, *timbalero* Tito Puente, flautist Johnny Pacheco himself, etc. Salsa became hugely popular both among Latino immigrants of virtually all nationalities and throughout Latin America. In Puerto Rico itself, as well as in Colombia, Venezuela, Costa Rica, and other countries, this music resonated with the spirit of the times. It became a means for individuals throughout the hemisphere to express their Latin American heritage and at the same time urban sophistication and social awareness.

Celia Cruz (1925–2003) figures among the best-known performers of New York salsa during its initial peak of popularity in the 1970s and 1980s and is especially important as one of the few women to have excelled at that time in a male-dominated industry. Born on the outskirts of Havana, Cuba, into a working-class family, Cruz began singing on live local radio broadcasts in the 1940s; in the 1950s a well-known dance band called La Sonora Matancera (The Matanzas Sound) contracted her as their lead vocalist. Following the revolution of 1959, Cruz together with many members of that group left Cuba permanently, eventually settling in the New York area. Tito Puente (see Fig. 7.5) invited her to record her first albums in the United States in the 1960s, but she achieved much more widespread celebrity as part of the Fania All Stars beginning in the mid-1970s. Cruz recorded over seventy albums during her career and performed many different kinds of music including *plena* and *merengue*, though *son* and salsa predominated. Lyrical themes of many sorts are found in her recordings including nostalgia for life in Havana, an attractive topic for the many Cubans who left the country when she did. Several well-known pieces advocate for pan-Latino unity and activism among Hispanic immigrants as well, including "Latinos en Estados Unidos" ("Latinos in the United States") on *Celia y Johnny* (1974) and "Pasaporte latinoamericano" ("Latin American Passport") on *Azúcar negra* (*Black Sugar*, 1993).

Most salsa since the 1970s has been written by men, and the lyrics as well as album cover images reflect a decidedly male perspective. Frances Aparicio (1998) has explored these issues at length, providing numerous examples of songs that objectify women's bodies, represent them stereotypically or superficially, condone male infidelity while criticizing women for the same inclinations, and so forth. Cruz's stage persona and a number of her recordings critiqued male perspectives and created alternate representations of women and gender relations. Songs such as "Usted abusó" ("You Took Advantage of Me," 1974), "Las Divorciadas" ("Divorced Women," 1985), and "Que le den candela" ("Light It on Fire," 1994) aired women's views on heterosexual relationships, for instance. Some recordings of "Bemba colorá" ("African Lips") include commentary on domestic violence as well, largely by means of improvised quatrains sung in alternation with the chorus.

Perhaps even more importantly, Cruz consistently presented herself on stage as an attractive woman but also as a modest and temperate one who did not flaunt her sexuality (Abreu 2007). This represented a significant break with the personae of female performers from the Hispanic Caribbean of earlier decades. Cruz's stage costumes, while flamboyant in the extreme, were not physically revealing. She traveled constantly with her husband, Pedro Knight, making clear by his presence as well

FIGURE 4.23 *Celia Cruz performing with the Tito Puente Orchestra at the Universal Amphitheater in Hollywood, California, 1985.* *(Photo by Josephine Powell archives).*

that she wished to be treated professionally and was unavailable to other men. Rather than presenting herself as a sexual object, she engaged listeners primarily by means of her abilities as a vocalist and an improviser. Cruz's success helped open professional opportunities for new generations of female artists, a number of whom are mentioned in the conclusion of this chapter.

In New York, salsa first gained popularity in the context of social and political activism by Latino immigrants. Many lived deplorably, for instance, in ghettoized neighborhoods of the Bronx and East Harlem. They struggled to get ahead in U.S. society and came to resent the lack of attention to Latin American history and culture and to the Spanish language in most public schools. Salsa thus became an important emblem of cultural identity and frequently made reference to harsh living conditions. It was also associated by many with the independence movement in Puerto Rico, those who wished for complete sovereignty from the United States. The political connotations of salsa repertoire developed in tandem with the African American Black Power movement, protest against the war in Vietnam, and the rise of the Young Lords among Puerto Rican youths in the United States. The latter group formed in the late 1960s in order to protect the integrity of Latino neighborhoods, protest police violence, and educate the population about Puerto Rican heritage and history. Salsa music came to symbolize a valorization of traditions that had been ignored by mainstream society. Salsa's roots in Cuban *son* traditions became less significant to performers over time, and instead they began to consider the music something that reflected the experience of all Latin American immigrants.

ACTIVITY 4.14 *Do some independent research on politicized salsa of the 1970s and 1980s, pieces like "Justicia" by Eddie Palmieri, "La abolición" by Tite Curet Alonso, "Color latino" by Willie Colón, and "Pablo Pueblo" by Rubén Blades. See if you can find translations of the song lyrics and/or the original versions. Also, take a look at the Shanachie video* Salsa: The Rhythm of Latin Music *(1979) in order to see footage of the salsa phenomenon at its peak and its relation to grassroots activism.*

As one might expect, New York salsa music of the 1970s and 1980s has a raw, edgy sound and charged lyrics in many cases. Salsa from this period is often referred to as *"salsa dura,"* literally "hard salsa" in the same way that Anglo-Americans might speak about hard rock. New York salsa tends to be faster than Cuban *conjunto* music, with percussion featured more prominently in the recording mix. Its harmonies are often complex and jazzy. The frequent use of multiple trombones as lead instruments rather than trumpets also makes the sound distinct from *conjunto*. Many New York–based salsa pieces incorporate folk instruments such as the *cuatro* or rhythms from folkloric drumming genres unique to particular Latin American countries.

CD track 16 reproduces the salsa piece "Anacaona" written by Tite Curet Alonso and performed by the Fania All-Stars in 1971. The recording comes from a famous live concert at the Cheetah Club in New York, subsequently popularized on the video *Our Latin Thing.* (Masucci and Gast 2004) The woman referred to in the lyrics, Anacaona, was an indigenous princess in what is now the Dominican Republic at the time of the Spanish conquest (late 1400s). She initially welcomed the Spanish but eventually led an uprising against them when she realized that they planned to enslave her people. Before long the Spanish captured and executed her; nevertheless, over the years she has been transformed into a symbol of bravery, independence, and resistance to foreign domination for residents of the Caribbean. In the context of twentieth- and twenty-first-century politics, Anacaona here represents the island of Puerto Rico and her oppressor in this allegory is the U.S. government.

ACTIVITY 4.15 *As you listen through CD track 16 using the guide below and the full guide at www.oup.com/us.moore, make sure you can identify all of the sectional changes mentioned in this listening example.*

Partial Listening Guide to CD Track 16

"Anacaona"

0:08–0:22

Instrumental introduction, with the melody passing between trumpets and trombones.

0:23–0:32

The chorus enters, with trumpets filling between phrases. Listen for the bell patterns played by the *timbalero* and bongo player.

| Anacaona, india de raza cautiva | Anacaona, Indian of the captive race |
| Anacaona, de la región primitiva | Anacaona, from the primitive region |

0:33–0:56

The lead singer, Cheo Feliciano, is featured here. The *timbales* revert to a *cáscara* pattern, and the bongo player shifts to playing on the drumheads.

Anacaona oí tu voz	Anacaona I heard your voice
Como lloró, como gimió	How it cried, how it moaned
Anacaona oí la voz	Anacaona I heard the voice
De tu angustiado corazón	Of your anguished heart
Tu libertad nunca llegó	Your liberty never came
De de le le le lo lai, ¡Anda!	De de le le le lo lai lai, get to it!

0:56–1:14

The chorus enters with the same phrase as at 0:23, and it is followed with another free variation of the same lyrics by Cheo Feliciano at 1:06.

It is worth considering again how "Anacaona" and similar salsa pieces compare to Cuban *conjunto* music of the 1950s (refer to the earlier section on Cuban *son* as necessary). One striking difference is the driving sound of the *timbales*, a prominent element in New York and Puerto Rican salsa and one adopted by only a few Cuban groups of the 1950s. The *timbales* play unique rhythmic patterns on the shell of the drum during the verse sections, and later a bell pattern that locks together with the bongo player's bell during the chorus sections and the *montuno*. The sound of the interlocking bell patterns in climactic sections of the music is very characteristic. The two-part form of most salsa music—strophic verses and call–response *montuno*—is clearly demarcated in most cases by the *timbales* and the bongo. When you hear the interlocking bells, chances are that you are listening to the *montuno* section or to a choral vocal associated with it. When you hear the more subtle sound of wooden sticks against the side of the *timbales* and the bongo heads being played, chances are that you are listening to the verse or perhaps a solo by a quieter instrument such as a piano or flute.

Figure 4.24 is a transcribed example of one common *cáscara* or shell pattern played with sticks on the sides of the *timbales*, written against the *clave* so you can see the relationship between the two. The rhythm played by the *timbalero*'s strong hand actually represents an elaboration of the stick patterns used in folkloric Cuban *rumba*. Since performers playing the *cáscara* and/or bells can begin their rhythmic patterns on either measure, depending on the song and its particular *clave*, the decision to write the rhythm beginning on the "two side" in the transcription in Figure 4.24 is somewhat arbitrary. Stems up in the *timbales* transcription indicates that the strokes are played by the performer's strong hand (usually right). Stems down indicates strokes played by the weak hand that fill in the *rumba clave* pattern to create a more constant sound.

CD track 17 provides a recording of two common ways of performing the *cáscara* pattern. As before, the *clave* enters first to establish the pulse. From 0:05-0:27, a pattern is demonstrated consisting of the rhythm depicted by the up-stems in Figure 4.24 only (the strong-hand part), against which the performer's weak hand marks beats two and four on a *timbales* drumhead to keep time. Beginning at 0:32, a two-stick *cáscara* is demonstrated corresponding exactly to the transcription in Figure 4.24. Both these patterns appear frequently in salsa music.

Figure 4.25 is a transcription of the typical bell pattern played by the *timbales* and bongo players against chorus phrases and in the *montuno*. As before, the patterns are written beginning on the "two side" of the *clave*. In this transcription, stems down on the bongo bell indicates a stroke on the larger, open end of the bell that creates a lower, somewhat muted tone; strokes up indicates a higher, sharp tone created by striking the smaller closed end of the bell. The *timbalero* plays the rhythm on a single bell using a stick in the dominant hand. CD track 18 briefly

FIGURE 4.24 *The* timbales' cáscara *pattern and* clave *as performed in* "Anacaona" *(CD track 16) and on CD track 17.*

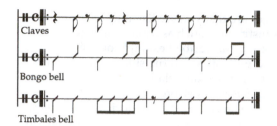

Claves

Bongo bell

Timbales bell

FIGURE 4.25 *"Anacaona," both bell patterns against the* clave, *as heard on CD track 18.*

reproduces the rhythmic parts transcribed in Figure 4.25, beginning with the *clave* and then adding the bongo and *timbales* bell patterns.

> **ACTIVITY 4.16** *Practice the individual* cáscara *and bell parts recorded on CD tracks 17 and 18 and notated in Figures 4.24 and 4.25. Try starting on the "two side" and the "three side" of the* clave *in order to orient yourself both ways. Then, with friends combine the various parts against one another. Later, listen again to "Anacaona" (CD track 16) and see if you can hear the notated bell parts performed as they appear in the transcriptions.*
>
> *Try learning the chorus harmonies to the piece as well, as notated in Figures 4.26 and 4.27. Lyrics to Figure 4.26 are translated in the earlier partial listening guide. The second chorus in Figure 4.27 translates as "Anacaona, the* areíto/song *of Anacaona."*

The keyboard style in salsa music is ultimately derived from patterns played on the *tres* in rural *son* music, as mentioned earlier. Lilí Martínez (1915–1990), pianist in Arsenio Rodríguez's *conjunto* for many years, is recognized as one of several important innovators who first adapted the *tres* style to the keyboard, imitating the *tres'* doubled strings (by playing in octaves) and its syncopated melodies.

In modern salsa, keyboard technique takes various forms. Free rhythmic *comping*, the playing of entire chords as in jazz performance, is common in verse sections. This may or may not be accompanied by improvised melodies in the right hand. Chordal comping may also occur to a preestablished rhythm, performed jointly with the bass player and/or horns. The effect is used to create variety, for instance, in a bridge section,

FIGURE 4.26 *Chorus 1 harmonies, "Anacaona."*

FIGURE 4.27 *Chorus 2 harmonies, "Anacaona."*

and often the percussion will continue playing, even solo, against this sort of sparse harmonic accompaniment. Finally, in later sections of the piece and in the *montuno*, the keyboard plays a specific repeating riff in a *"claved"* rhythm. This pattern (yes, it is confusing!) can also itself be referred to as a piano *"montuno."* The latter style is ultimately what corresponds most closely to earlier performance on the Cuban *tres*.

Figure 4.28 demonstrates roughly what the keyboardist plays in the *montuno* section of "Anacaona," for instance, at 1:25 and 4.22. Note that it consists of a repeated eight-measure figure, a loop. In actual performance, keyboardists often play these melodies in octaves and vary them considerably. The rhythms performed by the keyboardist lock in particular ways with the *clave* and with other instruments; the even-numbered, "straighter" measures that include a note on the downbeat correspond to the "two side" of the *clave*. They are intended to be played against bell patterns and other percussion parts that also correspond to the "two side." CD track 19 reproduces the piano line transcribed in Figure 4.28 together with the *clave*.

Though salsa has remained popular since the 1970s, its audience among Latin Americans and Latino immigrants has declined somewhat in recent decades. There are various reasons for this. Beginning in the 1980s, salsa began to lose ground to *merengue*, which experienced a boom in popularity and continues to attract large numbers of enthusiasts. As Latin American immigrants and their children have begun to

FIGURE 4.28   *"Anacaona," piano* montuno, *as recorded on CD track 19.*

learn English and become more accustomed to North American culture, their listening preferences have changed. Many now prefer rock, rap, *reggaeton*, or other musical styles rather than salsa. Another important factor for the decline derives from changes in the sound of commercially released salsa itself. The genre became big business in the 1980s, and large corporations began to record and distribute it, buying out Fania and other smaller labels in the process. Major labels have tended to be less interested in urban working-class concerns and instead do their best to create a product that can be sold to the widest possible audience. Their releases usually avoid politicized lyrics in order not to offend anyone. Many also sound quite slick in comparison to the salsa of past decades. Producers may mix the original sound with influences from rock, pop, or romantic ballads in Spanish. Fans of classic-era salsa have disparagingly referred to much repertoire from the 1980s and early 1990s as *"salsa romántica"* or *"salsa monga"* (literally, "limp salsa"). Not every artist conforms to this trend, but it holds true as a general rule.

> **ACTIVITY 4.19** *Compare the sound of salsa recordings or Internet clips from the 1970s by Eddie Palmieri or Willie Colón ("salsa dura" artists) with those of the 1980s and 1990s by Willie González, Frankie Ruiz, Luis Enrique, and others ("salsa romántica" artists). Now compare both of these groups with recordings since 2000 by singers La India, Gilberto Santa Rosa, and Victor Manuelle.*

As an epilogue of sorts to this discussion of salsa, I should note that within Cuba itself *son* music has developed differently since 1959. In the late 1960s and 1970s, dance bands did not receive strong government support. State cultural agencies instead promoted classical music performance and education, as well as the dissemination of socially engaged protest music known as *nueva trova* (see Chapter 6). Beginning in the late 1980s, however, dance bands proliferated once more, playing a style of music known as *timba*. *Timba* is highly eclectic, a blend of traditional *son* and New York salsa music with elements of funk and local Afro-Cuban folklore. *Timba* bands often replace the bongo drum with a U.S.-style drum set. A synthesizer keyboard is often used in addition to an acoustic piano that plays riffs at particular moments to add variety to the sound. Drums, *timbales*, and congas combine with the bass and the two keyboards to create a very dense texture. Bass lines are unpredictable, incorporating fast runs, sustained notes, glissandi, chromatic passages, and slaps. Horns frequently play their lines in unison as this is believed to create a driving sound, and their melodies demonstrate the influence of jazz. African American groups such as Earth, Wind, and Fire and P-Funk influenced *timba* composers heavily as the style emerged in the late 1980s. Recently, many new fusions of *timba* with *reggaeton* and rap have emerged as well in the repertoire of Bamboleo, Manolito Simonet, and others.

ACTIVITY 4.18 *Find representative recordings or video clips of* timba *music to listen to and to compare with New York salsa. Make a list of musical similarities and differences. Groups that would serve as a good introduction to* timba *include Azúcar Negra, Bamboleo, NG La Banda, and Klímax.*

You may have noticed that, as in the case of the music described in most other chapters, few women are represented overall in dance repertoire from the Hispanic Caribbean; this merits consideration. Much of the marginalization of women may derive from broader restrictions they face in Latin American society. Dance music is usually performed late in the evening in nightclubs, contexts for drinking or even drug use that families may not want their daughters to frequent. Many parts of the Spanish-speaking Americas continue to subscribe to a form of machismo that encourages women to stay at home or to venture out to nightclubs only in groups rather than alone. And the late hours required of dance-band musicians are difficult to reconcile with the heavy emphasis on raising children and on family life in the Hispanic Caribbean. Despite such obstacles, women have created an increased presence artistically in recent years. To early figures such as Celia Cruz have been added all-female *son* bands in Cuba such as Son Damas and Anacaona, Puerto Rican *merengue* artist Giselle, Puerto Rican salsa singer La India (Linda Viera Caballero), or *timba* vocalists Haila Mompié and Vania Borges. In many instances, however, women continue to be confined to the role of singer rather than composer, arranger, or instrumentalist.

All of the creole dance music discussed in this chapter has come to represent people and places nationally and internationally. *Merengue* is one of the most immediately identifiable forms of Dominican culture today, for instance; the same could be said of *plena* and *son* in their respective countries. All of these folkloric musics seemed doomed to marginality for many years. Derived from working-class Afro-Caribbean heritage, they were rejected by middle-class professionals as distasteful. As in the case of the Argentine tango and early jazz, they first gained popularity in brothels, seedy bars, and other venues on the margins of respectable society. Only with time did Caribbean populations come to accept such culture for what it was and is: a powerful symbol of creolized sensibility, a complex representation through sound of the New World experience.

The emergence of salsa music and commercial *merengue* took this sort of mass identification to entirely new levels. In the context of immigration to the United States, Latin performers managed to fuse elements of folkloric practice from various islands into a single style. They created music designed not only for audiences from one island but also for those from various backgrounds. The phenomenal popularity of commercial salsa and *merengue* among Latinos and Latin Americans alike since the 1970s is quite striking and suggests that it speaks to many groups. It has also become fashionable among Anglo-Americans, Europeans, Africans (especially those in French-speaking countries), Japanese, and others. The prominence of Afro-Caribbean musical traditions globally and their impact on public forms of socialization has been so marked that it has been described by Enrique Patterson (1996, 61) as a form of "inverse colonization," a cultural incursion into the mainstream on the part of those on the margins. As in the case of the United States, music from poorer and blacker communities in the Hispanic Caribbean has become a tremendous force to be reckoned with.

CHAPTER 5

Transnational Caribbean Musics

∞

The Caribbean has functioned since the earliest colonial days as a nexus of intersecting trade routes, and its cultural forms have always incorporated influences from diverse sources. In such a region, it is impossible to understand cultural development without considering the regional and international circulation of culture. Chapters 2 and 3 made reference to the trans-Atlantic flow of people and music during centuries of colonization of the Caribbean, but this represents only one aspect of a broader phenomenon. Caribbean culture has also influenced Europe in significant ways. Caribbean islands influence one another as well as exchanging music with other Latin American countries and the entire hemisphere.

Transnational cultural dialogues in the Caribbean continue to accelerate with the advent of new global communication and transportation systems, as well as the constant movement of residents back and forth between their home islands and other locations. The latter is a significant trend: Over 10% of Dominicans and Cubans now live outside of the Caribbean region, primarily in the United States. Amazingly, over half of Puerto Ricans now live in the United States. Multinational corporations market a variety of music to Latin American immigrants at home and abroad, who may listen to it as is or creatively blend it with traditional genres of their own. The popularity of funk, rap, reggae, and related music in the Hispanic Caribbean and among Latinos generally attests to this trend. With the spread of the Internet, music downloads, and channels such as MTV, a global public sphere is emerging that cannot be controlled by any particular country or region. We live in an era of cultural and geographic displacement on an unprecedented scale in which musical products and practices refuse to "stay put."

This chapter explores a few representative examples of music that has emerged as the result of transnational influences, both within the Caribbean and by Caribbean artists living abroad. It begins with a brief overview of genres from past centuries such as the *contradanza* in order to underscore the extended history of such processes, then analyzes others from more recent times in greater detail. These include the

Latin American *bolero* and its eventual transformation into Dominican *bachata*, as well as *reggaeton*.

THE COLONIAL *CONTRADANZA*

In the eighteenth and nineteenth centuries, a form of dance music influenced both by European models and local recreations of them began to develop in the Hispanic Caribbean. Creolized versions of the contradance (*contradanza* in Spanish) and variants such as the quadrille and the square dance, among others, flourished and came to be a sort of musical common denominator on many islands. By 1800, versions of the contradance had become popular in virtually all of the New World.

Contradance first became popular in continental Europe, especially in France and the Netherlands, in the mid-seventeenth century. It emerged as part of music events performed by multiple couples who formed themselves into circles, squares, or lines. All of the choreographies derive from English "country dance" traditions, thus the name. Interestingly, contradance was one of the first European social activities to cut across class lines and gain popularity among rich and poor; this seems to have reflected the gradual democratization of society. While much less complex than its elite predecessor the minuet, contradances did involve a series of four or five distinct steps whose sequence would be determined by a caller, much as in the case of square dancing in the United States. Various groups played this music, from very simple, rustic ensembles to polished high-society orchestras. The most common ballroom groups in the Caribbean that played it included clarinets, violins, trumpets, bass, and percussion (Fig. 5.1). This instrumentation underscores the strong influence of military bands at the time on popular culture.

Changes to the European contradance in the Hispanic Caribbean involved the addition of new elements of syncopation and percussion, as well as changes to the choreography. Melodic syncopation manifests itself in the incorporation of figures such as the *cinquillo, tresillo,* and *habanera* rhythms into the melody or accompaniment (see Chapter 1). These rhythms eventually influenced music making in other countries; they are found in U.S. ragtime pieces, for instance, as well as in Argentine tango. Creolized percussive elements in the Caribbean *contradanza* often took the form of repeated rhythms, similar to the *clave* patterns discussed in Chapter 3. In some cases the rhythms seem to have been identical to West African bell patterns, although most were played on the *timbales*, a creolized instrument patterned after the European timpani. Adaptations of this nature demonstrate how African-influenced culture can permeate local sensibilities yet not be recognized as such.

FIGURE 5.1 *A state-supported dance band in Cuba (El Piquete Típico) that specializes in* contradanzas, danzas, danzones, *and related nineteenth-century repertoire. Note the tympani-like drums (a predecessor of the modern* timbales*), the violins, the wind instruments, and the* güiro. *(Photo by the author, 2008).*

Nineteenth-century *contradanzas* incorporated a simple two-part form, AABB, usually consisting of short eight-measure sections and simple harmonies. Pieces could be written in either duple or triple meter. In performance, entire songs might repeat multiple times to facilitate dancing or elide seamlessly with additional songs. Melodies tended to be simple and in major keys. The A section usually adopted a moderate rhythm in contrast to the B section, which more frequently included creolized, polyrhythmic additions. The two-part form of nineteenth-century Caribbean dance music resembles that of more modern styles, such as the *merengue* and *son,* and may well have influenced their development.

Afro-Caribbean listeners appear to have taken to the *contradanza* at least as quickly as Euro-Caribbeans. In part, this reflected the fact that the performance of European music constituted an important form of employment for them. It also may be that the *contradanza* and its variants seemed familiar, given that many traditional West African dances involve line or circle choreography. European descendants for their part increasingly embraced the creole polyrhythms in such music as their own, choosing not to recognize their African origins.

In the 1840s, the *contradanza* began to cede popularity to a related style known simply as *"danza."* Apparently influenced by the vogue of the waltz, it sounded much the same but emphasized figure dancing in smaller groups and on occasion incorporated even more Afro-Caribbean polyrhythm in the accompaniment. Officials in Puerto Rico attempted to ban the dance as early as 1849 on the grounds of indecency, believing it involved too much physical contact between partners. There and in the Dominican Republic, the mid-nineteenth century *danza* was referred to at times as a *"merengue."* While distinct from the modern *merengue*, it appears that the name first gained widespread usage at that time.

Puerto Rican composer Juan Morel Campos (1857–1896) deserves special mention as a prominent composer of *danzas* and one who was adept at creating stylized versions of them for solo piano, intended for presentation in the salon or concert context. A mulatto composer from Ponce, Morel Campos is known within Puerto Rico as "father of the *danza.*" He was one of the first formally trained musicians to write music perceived as in a uniquely "Puerto Rican" style, and thus his pieces soon became associated with nationalist sentiment as island residents began to rebel against Spanish rule in the 1850s and 1860s (see Chapter 6). Morel Campos' stylized *danzas* are clearly sectional, with repeated sections of eight, sixteen, or thirty-two measures that often modulate to a different key. Similar composer figures in Cuba include Manuel Saumell (1818–1870) and Ignacio Cervantes (1847–1905), known primarily for their stylized *contradanzas*.

In the final decades of the nineteenth century, yet another *contradanza* variant, known as the *danzón*, developed in Cuba and soon spread to the Dominican Republic and Puerto Rico. Its first recognized composers were well-to-do black musicians from the city of Matanzas. While virtually identical in sound to the *contradanza* and *danza*, the *danzón* utilized a somewhat more complex structure known as *rondo*, typically ABACA or ABACAD, with the B, C, and D musical segments each corresponding to a specific dance step. The final D section, if included, tended to be the most lively; dancers used the A section, the *paseo* or promenade, to walk out onto the dance floor or to rest and converse. *Danzones*, along with *danzas*, represented one of the first popular genres from the Hispanic Caribbean to be danced by independent couples rather than in groups or squares, a development that seemed morally suspect to critics. *Danzones* also incorporated a unique repeated rhythmic pattern, most often played on the *timbales*, which consisted of a *cinquillo* followed by four quarter notes (Fig. 5.2). Percussionists developed a style of executing this figure

FIGURE 5.2 *Danzón clave.*

derived from West African traditions. It involved dampening and releasing the head of the *timbales* with one hand as they struck it with a stick. In the transcription in Figure 5.2, slash heads indicate dampened strokes, while rounded note heads indicate open tones. Keep in mind that this represents only one way of performing the pattern, which is frequently varied in actual performance. The incorporation of the *danzón* rhythm on the timpani or *timbales* also became the subject of criticism among those who wished to keep Cuban culture free of "Africanisms." Yet by the late 1880s the genre had gained widespread popularity.

> **ACTIVITY 5.1** *See if your library has a copy of the Smithsonian Folkways CD* The Cuban Danzón: Its Ancestors and Descendants *(FE 4066). This excellent collection provides recorded examples of dance music throughout the nineteenth century, including the genres discussed here. Note the use of the* danzón *clave and its many variations. Analyze the form of several compositions, seeing if you can tell which adopt the* rondo *structure. Also, listen for the marked switch from wind bands to the* charanga *flute and violin format at the turn of the twentieth century.*

Both *danzas* and *danzones* maintained a prominent place in Cuban, Dominican, and Puerto Rican popular culture at the turn of the twentieth century, vying for prominence with the Spanish two-step and early jazz dances such as the cake walk and turkey trot. Clearly, the cultural histories of all three islands are intimately entwined and reflect the influence of European and North American musical forms.

Though the *contradanza* and its descendants are less common in the Hispanic Caribbean now, they continue to influence present-day traditions. Many Puerto Ricans still consider the *danza* to be a cherished musical idiom and compose in that style. Classical musicians of the Hispanic Caribbean have incorporated influences from the *contradanza*, *danza*, and *danzón* in their symphonic and chamber works. A slower, sung version of the *contradanza* known as the *"contradanza habanera"* or simply *"habanera,"* continues to be popular in Spain and has influenced numerous European classical composers; one example is the *habanera* included in George Bizet's opera *Carmen*. Modern Dominican *merengue* (e.g., CD track 10) derives some of its structure, such as its initial *paseo* or promenade, from the *danza*. Genres such as the *danzón* appear to have influenced the development of ragtime jazz and Dixieland music in significant ways. *Danzón* orchestras of the 1930s and beyond gradually adopted musical influences from the *son*, and this led to the development of the *chachachá* and groups known as *"charangas."* The latter performed *son*-based repertoire as well as *danzones* but retained instruments from nineteenth-century bands such as the flute and violin. César Rondón (2008) provides some information on these groups in his book on salsa history, recently translated into English.

Finally, many Cuban *son* or salsa dancers, as of the 1960s, perform in groups led by a caller in a style known as *"rueda de casino,"* or "casino circle." This choreography hearkens back to older quadrilles and square dancing figures, fusing them with movements derived from African-influenced folkloric traditions and ballroom dancing (see Fig. 5.3). The

FIGURE 5.3 Rueda de casino *dancers in Austin, Texas, performing a choreographed move as a group that involves lifting women up on the interlocked arms of their partners. Most of the styles of music and dance we discuss in this book have spread far beyond the Caribbean and have gained popularity among new audiences.* (Photo by the author).

dancers execute synchronized moves as indicated by the caller, passing their partners around the ring at various moments. The legacy and adaptations of the *contradanza* and its variants demonstrate that music and dance in the Caribbean have been part of a trans-Atlantic dialogue for centuries, as well as dialogues with the music of neighboring islands. The remainder of the chapter will focus on case studies from more recent times to demonstrate how these processes have been perpetuated.

ACTIVITY 5.2 *Search the Internet for information about* rueda de casino *dancing and for video clips, to see what it looks like. Try to find an instructor in your area; take a few lessons yourself and try executing basic dance moves associated with the* rueda de casino *such as* guapea *(strut),* dame *(give me your partner), or* exhbíbela *(show her off).*

BOLERO AND BACHATA

The Latin American *bolero* in its many permutations serves as another excellent example of a transnational musical form in the Hispanic Caribbean and one that bridges the history of the nineteenth and twentieth centuries. *Boleros* are best defined as romantic songs that developed out of influences from European parlor music, as well as from musical influences specific to the Spanish-speaking Americas. The term *"bolero"* comes from Spain, where it is used to refer to a particular genre of largely urban popular music played in 3/4 time to the accompaniment of string instruments and castanets. A specifically Latin American *bolero* seems to have first developed in eastern Cuba in the late nineteenth century. Performers there—relatively affluent urban blacks or mulattos who performed music recreationally—used the term in a different way. They applied it to songs in 4/4 time, usually performed as a vocal duet and accompanied by two guitars and *claves* that tapped out the basic *danzón* beat (Fig. 5.2). These new *boleros* were slow, sentimental, and harmonically complex. They were not intended for dancing but, rather, for listening in small neighborhood venues or private homes. One guitar played bass notes and provided a basic chordal accompaniment, while a second plucked out improvised melodies in counterpoint with the voices. A number of early *boleros* contained overtly patriotic lyrics as they emerged during the years of Cuba's independence struggle against Spain (1868–1898). The lyrics tended to be very refined, even metaphorical, reflecting nineteenth-century middle-class taste.

Research remains to be done on the early history of Latin American *boleros*, especially since most of the early songs were never recorded or transcribed and have apparently been lost. One prominent figure in the development of this genre was José ("Pepe") Sánchez (1856–1918), an Afro-Cuban employee in a textile firm and resident of the city of Santiago. Sánchez avidly followed opera and supported local arts initiatives. In addition to hobnobbing with major military figures of the revolutionary effort against Spanish rule —Antonio and José Maceo, Quintín Banderas, Guillermón Moncada—he organized regular musical gatherings in his home, which became one of the first sites for *bolero* performance. He also led choral groups that included younger musicians (Sindo Garay, Manuel Corona, Rosendo Ruiz Suárez, etc.) who would popularize the *bolero* across Cuba in the 1910s and 1920s.

ACTIVITY 5.3 *Locate the city of Santiago on a map of Cuba. Investigate the Wars of Independence against Spain in the late nineteenth century that affected all of the Hispanic Caribbean so that you have a better feel for their duration and scope as well as the issues driving colonial subjects to revolt. Finally, research the histories of figures such as Cuban Antonio Maceo, Dominican Máximo Gómez, and Puerto Rican Lola Rodríguez de Tió.*

CD track 20, "La tarde" ("The Afternoon"), is a recreation of an early *bolero* from 1907 with music composed by Sindo Garay, one of Sánchez's protégés. "La tarde" illustrates many of the features of the early *bolero* and exemplifies additional transnational influences, given that the first half of the text was penned by Mexican Amado Nervo and the second half by Puerto Rican Lola Rodríguez de Tió. Note the prominent switch from a major to a minor key that occurs at about 0:51 as the song passes from the first section to the second, common both in older *bolero* repertoire and in the sung *habanera*. This version of "La tarde" features a *tres* playing improvised lead melodies against a guitar, a less common instrumental combination than two guitars but not unheard of. Most *bolero* texts are gender-neutral, as is this example; one doesn't know whether a man or a woman is singing necessarily, or to whom, by looking at the lyrics alone.

Partial Listening Guide for CD Track 20

"La tarde"

View the complete guide at www.oup.com/us.moore

0:00–0:13

A brief instrumental introduction featuring *tres* on lead melody, guitar accompaniment, and the *claves* playing the *danzón*-style *cinquillo* rhythm.

0:14–0:53

The first segment of lyrics, sung by Pablo Milanés on lead vocal and Luis Peña on the lower countermelody. Both instruments continue to play, but the *tres* switches to an arpeggiated style more suited to accompaniment. At 0:51 the minor mode of the harmony switches to major.

La luz que en tus ojos arde	The light that burns in your eyes
Si los abres amanece	If you open them the day dawns
Cuando los cierras parece	When you close them it seems
Que va muriendo la tarde	That the afternoon is dying away

As in the case of Pepe Sánchez, Sindo Garay is said to have been a prolific composer who wrote hundreds of pieces, but very few of them have survived to the present. Garay is an interesting figure who claimed indigenous heritage in addition to African and European. As opposed to Sánchez, he came from a very poor, illiterate family and spent much of his life as a virtual vagabond, wandering throughout Cuba and abroad (Haiti, Dominican Republic) in search of gainful employment. He worked in many capacities aside from that of a musician, including circus acrobat and clown! In his biography, Garay mentions never liking "black music" much (apparently referring to folkloric drumming), preferring strongly European-influenced genres like the *bolero*. He is one of the first early *bolero* artists to spend considerable amounts of time in Havana and to popularize the style there. Latin American *boleros* from the outset have largely been an urban phenomenon and, because of their ties to parlor music, are associated most often with cosmopolitanism and middle-class sophistication, Garay's own biography notwithstanding.

> **ACTIVITY 5.4** *Try learning to sing the first half of the "La tarde" vocals as notated in Figure 5.4, to the accompaniment of guitar or piano and the* danzón clave.

Beginning in the 1930s, Mexico became an important center of *bolero* performance, even more influential than Cuba. The genre, introduced into Mexico via Veracruz and the Yucatán Peninsula at the turn of the twentieth century by traveling entertainment troupes and through sheet music sales, soon became a featured component in the repertoire of musicians such as Manuel Ponce (1882–1948), Guty Cárdenas (1905–1932), María Grever (1884–1951), and Agustín Lara (1897–1970). These pioneers fused the Cuban style of performance with influences from their own *canción* or romantic song tradition, influences from light opera, and other elements of international popular song that were beginning to circulate on radio stations, on 78 rpm records, and in motion pictures. In this effort they took inspiration from seminal *boleristas* who had begun fusing the *bolero* with jazz such as Cubans Luis Casas Romero (1882–1950),

FIGURE 5.4 *Vocal transcription of the first half of "La tarde" (CD track 20).*

Nilo Menéndez (1902–1987), and Gonzalo Roig (1890–1970), as well as Mexican Emilio Pacheco (1891–1964). Menéndez proved especially influential in composing *boleros* for the piano rather than the guitar.

Agustín Lara rose from humble origins as a self-trained pianist performing in Mexico City's red light district and in informal bohemian *peñas* or artistic gatherings to become perhaps the most famous composer of *boleros* from the early twentieth century. A prolific composer, Lara owed his meteoric rise in fame in the 1920s and 1930s to the recording and film industries as newly established star performers began to feature his work. Indeed, his marriage to the prominent actress María Félix reflects such relationships. Lara's musical style involved writing *boleros* in a slightly slower tempo and without the *danzón clave* figure, scoring works for piano and extended ensemble (bass, violins, sometimes other orchestral instruments) rather than for guitar and *tres*, composing for a single voice, and incorporating harmonic influences from jazz. These changes helped to convert the *bolero* into a style that could be easily assimilated by the international music market and to instigate what is often referred to as the "golden era" of the *bolero*, roughly 1935–1950. Much of Mexico's influence in the early years derived from its film industry, much more advanced at that time than anything that existed in the Caribbean.

The media introduced Mexican versions of the *bolero* to audiences throughout Latin America, where performers adopted it and shaped its sound according to their preferences. *Boleros* became extremely popular in the mid-twentieth century, rivaling all other commercial genres. Composers in the Hispanic Caribbean (e.g., Puerto Ricans Pedro Flores, Rafael Hernández, and Mirta Silva; Dominicans Bienvenido Brens and Luis Kalaff) and in virtually every Latin American country listened to the works of *boleristas* from other countries as well as their own versions. It became common to dance the *bolero* at this time, rather than merely listen to it, usually with a simple slow step similar to that of the fox trot. During the same period a standard set of relatively simple rhythms on the *maracas, clave,* bongos and congas derived loosely from the Cuban *son* came to define the international accompaniment of the *bolero* (Fig. 5.5). The *clave* pulse employed in this accompaniment was (and is) the same as that of the *son,* typically beginning on the "three-side." Bongos can perform either the line transcribed in Figure 5.5 or the more standard *martillo* rhythm (see Fig. 4.10).

Another major stylistic innovation of the mid-century was the development of the trio format, in which three (usually male) musicians interpreted *boleros* in tight, multipart harmonies to the accompaniment of guitar, a smaller string instrument designed to play lead melodies known as the *requinto,* and *maracas* or other percussion. The most

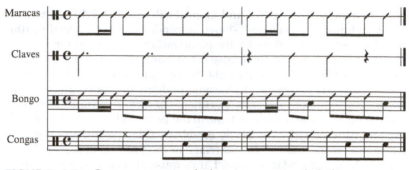

FIGURE 5.5 *Common percussion rhythms accompanying the* bolero.

influential trio of the period was Los Panchos, an ensemble formed in New York in 1944 by Mexicans Alfredo Gil and Chucho Navarro and Puerto Rican Hernando Avilés. The group had undoubtedly been influenced by the Trío Matamoros from Cuba (established in 1925) but took the vocal arrangements associated with the trio format to new levels of sophistication. Their beautiful recordings for Columbia Records inspired countless imitations and continue to generate sales to this day. Singer Alfredo Gil is also credited as the inventor of the *requinto*. Los Panchos repertoire became decidedly cosmopolitan as their influence spread; the group adopted local songs from Venezuela, Peru, and countless other nations and "boleroized" them as a means of appealing to more diverse audiences.

ACTIVITY 5.5 *Search your local libraries and/or the music collections of friends and family for* boleros *by authors from various countries and decades in order to compare them both to each other and to CD track 20. Listen for the percussion patterns notated in Figure 5.5. Compare the trio sound with that of individual vocalists, and see if you can recognize the sound of the Mexican* requinto, *comparing it to the* tres, *also on CD track 20. Search for photos of the* requinto *and for biographical information on major* bolero *figures such as those mentioned here.*

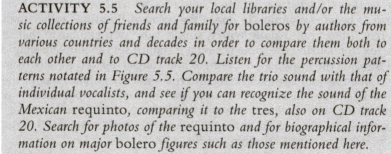

Since the 1950s, the *bolero* has continued to develop and change, even as earlier formats retain a certain loyal following. In the 1940 and 1950s, *bolero* music accompanied by large "big-band" orchestras became popular. Many groups imitated the instrumentation and elaborate score arrangements of jazz bands from the United States such as the Glenn Miller Orchestra; this includes the group featured on *I Love Lucy* and directed by Ricky Ricardo (Desi Arnaz). In Cuba of the 1950s, a distinct style of *bolero* also emerged known as *"filin"* (or "feeling"), characterized by a single vocalist and guitar, the use of more complex jazz harmonies, almost constant vocal improvisation, and emphasis on a rhythmic tension between a loose *rubato* feel on the part of the vocalist and relatively straight time marked by the accompanist. César Portillo de la Luz, José Antonio Méndez, Ángel Díaz, and others first championed this style.

Perhaps the most influential *bolero* innovation as of the 1960s was the emergence of the *balada*, a fusion of elements of the earlier "classic" *bolero* of the 1950s with elements of international pop music. *Baladas* often incorporated the drum set, synthesizer, electric guitar, and background string arrangements to accompany the vocals. Mexican Armando Manzanero and Brazilian Roberto Carlos established themselves as early exponents of this variant. The *balada* is considered "watered-down" Latin American music by some critics, who characterize it as nondescript and uninteresting, too heavily influenced from abroad. Yet it has proven very successful commercially, especially among working-class listeners. As of the 1990s an even more overtly "rockified" *bolero* became all the rage, as exemplified in the recordings of Mexican Luis Miguel and others. Individuals such as Miguel have often simply rerecorded older pieces from the mid-twentieth century, altering the original sound so as to appeal to the youth market.

In the Dominican Republic, *bolero* repertoire from Mexico, the Hispanic Caribbean, and elsewhere contributed centrally to the development of the music now referred to as *bachata* (CD track 21). The history of this unique variant, best documented by Deborah Pacini Hernández (1989, 1995), helps underscore the ways in which international traditions may become "localized" over time in terms of musical sound and broader social meaning. *"Bachata"* as a term has existed for some time, though in earlier periods it usually referred broadly to rowdy working-class parties and the music associated with them. The genre emerged in the wake of mass immigration to cities such as Santo Domingo on the part of rural migrants searching for better educational and employment opportunities. Early artists such as Luis Segura and Leonardo Paniagua performed in the 1970s on acoustic guitars with small ensembles accompanying them that featured the bongo, *maracas*, or *güira*. *Bachata* recordings initially gained popularity in the Dominican Republic through sales of cheaply produced cassettes; locals often listened to them as they socialized outside of neighborhood corner stores and drank, smoked, danced, and played dominos during free moments. At this time, *bachata* could be defined only as the music of a class of people—the urban poor—and referred to all styles that appealed to them including international *boleros* and acoustic *merengues*.

Since the mid-1980s, however, the term has come to represent a distinct sound. This *bachata* is best described as a relatively slow form of dance music. It represents the synthesis of Cuban, Mexican, local Dominican, and other influences but derives primarily from the international *bolero*. *Bachata* ensembles perform at a slightly faster tempo compared to older *bolero* repertoire and adopt a more percussive sound. On occasion, pieces incorporate influences from the *merengue* as well, shifting to a double-time feel. *Bachata* bands feature electric guitars and bass as well as additional percussion instruments including drum set and drum machine. Artist Blas Durán (Fig. 5.6) is credited with helping to define the commercial *bachata* sound. He adopted a distinct flanged timbre by hooking his guitar to an electronic effects box and began to

FIGURE 5.6   *Blas Durán.*   *(Photo courtesy of Blas Durán).*

accompany himself by arpeggiating his chords in a unique and almost constant fashion while playing. One of the first pieces to employ that technique was his 1987 hit "Mujeres hembras" ("Women's Women"). The sharp staccato arpeggio on the electric guitar has become a defining characteristic of the modern *bachata*.

The unique *bachata* dance step that has emerged involves taking three steps to each side in alternation followed by a distinctive hop-like motion. The dance is performed by couples, most frequently in a tight embrace and moving their hips markedly (the latter may also derive from the *merengue*).

Bachata is a male-dominated and working-class musical form, and this perspective is evident in song lyrics. Indeed, many pieces from the 1970s and 1980s could easily be described as sexist. As in the case of much Mexican rural music, *bachatas* for years employed colloquial forms of expression, the "language of the street," rather than the refined lyrics associated with early *boleros*. *Bachata* lyrics may express despair, suffering, indignation, and longing; glorify excessive drinking; boast about sexual conquests; or protest mistreatment by women. Bawdiness and sexual double entendre are common features. On occasion, lyrics also make reference to the harsh realities of life in urban ghettos. Because of all this, *bachatas* during the genre's formative period were also known as *canciones de amargue*, "songs of bitterness." The repertoire appears to have emerged as a coping mechanism of sorts for rural migrants in desperate economic conditions. As one might imagine, early *bachatas* struck middle-class and elite listeners as crude, vulgar, and by extension a symbol of cultural "backwardness." Most established radio stations refused to include them in their programming for some time. Of course, since the music has gained a broader public, its lyrical content has conformed more to that of other international popular music.

ACTIVITY 5.6 *Search available libraries and record collections, as well as YouTube, for examples of* bachata *music. If possible, listen to early* bachatas *by Luis Segura or Leonardo Paniagua and compare them to songs from the 1980s by Blas Durán, to the early Cuban bolero on CD track 20, and to CD track 21 (our commercial* bachata *example). Make a list of similarities and differences among the various pieces that will help underscore how the genre developed over time. Check to see if the lyrics of particular composers are available on the Internet so that they can be examined for content. Finally, search for video examples of* bachata *dancing, and try a few steps yourself.*

CD track 21, "Que vuelva" (I Want Her to Return), written by Alberto "Tico" Mercado and performed by Alex Bueno, comes from an anthology of *bachata* hits from 2001. The piece exemplifies the modern, commercial sound most typical of recordings heard today. Alex Bueno is a second-generation *bachatero* (*bachata* player) who first began performing as an adolescent about 1980. For a time he sang with a band known as Alex Bueno and the Liberation Orchestra but has since gone solo.

Note the fairly simple harmonies, primarily in a major key, and the rhythmically straightforward bass pattern (typical of *boleros*) consisting of a half note followed by two quarter notes or some variant of that pattern. A flanged electric guitar takes the melody from the outset in the instrumental introduction. Percussion consists of what seems to be a synthesized drum set track that marks an eighth-note pulse, with occasional fills by percussive, *güira*-like flourishes (also part of the synthesized drum's high-hat sound), and a bongo drum. Note the prominent arppegiation or outlining of chords on the guitar, first heard at about 0:12–0:18. A listening guide and the lyrics to the first half of "Que vuelva" are provided in the box. The complete lyrics are available on the Global Music Web site.

Partial Listening Guide for CD Track 21

"Que vuelva"

View the complete guide at www.oup.com/us.moore.

0:00–0:24

Instrumental introduction performed on the electric guitar and electric bass, with synthesized and acoustic percussion.

0:25–0:56

First verse, divided into two equal sections of nearly identical music. Two male voices enter at the outset, singing in parallel thirds. At particular moments the second harmonizing voice drops out, then returns.

Anda, ve a decirle que yo estoy sufriendo	Go on, tell her that I'm suffering
Dile que no puedo con las penas	Say that I can't take the pain any more

Tú que te das cuenta que la quiero	You who realize that I love her
Ve a decirle que mi alma se quema	Go say to her that my heart is burning
Tú que eres su amiga sabes de mi sueños	You, her friend, know of my dreams
Cuéntale que el mundo se me acaba	Tell her that my world is ending
Vamos, date cuenta que me muero	Come on, you know it's killing me
Que sin ella no soy nada	That without her I am nothing

As mentioned, *bachata*'s popularity had increased to such an extent by the early 1980s that major record labels and other music media began to include it in programming and promotion within the Dominican Republic and beyond. It was at this time, with the inclusion of the genre on mainstream radio and in DJ dance contexts, that the style of the music became more fixed. New labels emerged specifically to promote *bachata* releases including Discos José Luis, Unidad, Negra, and Marisol; even multinationals such as Sony have now signed prominent perform- ers. Some characterize the current sound, represented by CD track 21, as "pop-*bachata*," given the strong promotion of certain artists to the international Spanish-speaking community, the slick studio production of recent CDs, and the greater emphasis on youth and the visual image of performers. Partial credit for the legitimization and rise in popularity of *bachata* is due to superstar Juan Luis Guerra and his 1990 release *Bachata Rosa*. While Guerra's carefully crafted studio compositions didn't sound exactly like other *bachatas* from the same period—he tended to blend the 1980s style with elements from traditional *boleros* and with international pop and *balada*—his work nevertheless contributed to the embrace of the working-class form by the elite of Dominican society.

It is worth mention that musicians continue to experiment with fusions of *bachata* and *merengue*. Blas Durán did so on numerous occa-sions in the 1980s; composers associated with this *"bachata-rengue"* style in more recent decades include Antony Santos, Raulín Rodríguez, Joe Veras, and Luis Vargas. *Merengue* stars such as Wilfrido Vargas have also created *"merengue*-fied" versions of previously released *bachata* hits, suggesting that the influence of the music continues to grow. Performers of *reggaeton*, discussed in the following section, have also borrowed samples and rhythmic elements from *bachata* and from *merengues*, further hybridizing all three genres and making *bachata* even more popular among younger listeners.

REGGAETON

Reggaeton (also spelled *reggaetón* or *reguetón*) is the final example of transnational dance music considered in this chapter, one that developed as a result of the movement of cultural influences throughout the Caribbean and circum-Caribbean. *Reggaeton* is most closely associated with Puerto Ricans, who constitute a majority of stars in the present; but it is performed widely in the Hispanic Caribbean and beyond. The genre as a distinct commercial entity emerged quite recently in the early 1990s. It is fundamentally creolized, with roots in dancehall music of Jamaica and the British Caribbean and rhythmic ties to Trinidadian *soca* as well as to Colombian *champeta*. *Reggaeton* incorporates a diversity of elements from black North American music, as well as influences from folkloric genres of the Hispanic Caribbean. Characterized by rapped lead vocals, a danceable beat, and background choruses or instrumental figures reminiscent of U.S. soul, *reggaeton* might be thought of as a fusion of Spanish-language dancehall and Spanish-language rap, with a specific rhythm called the Dem Bow (nearly identical to the *habanera* rhythm) underlying most tracks. Lyrics in recent commercial songs tend to focus on partying and romantic relationships, but others also reference issues of pan–Latin American and pan-Latino pride, racial consciousness, or other social concerns.

The roots of *reggaeton* can be traced back to interactions between the Caribbean and Central America and specifically to Jamaican immigrants living in Panama. Many Jamaicans came to Panama as workers on the canal construction project at the turn of the twentieth century, bringing their music with them. Large numbers settled there, creating a community that retained ties to their island home even as they adopted influences from Hispanic culture. In the 1960s and 1970s, Jamaican-descended DJs and musicians in Panama began to perform new versions of popular reggae hits, changing the lyrics to Spanish and in some cases adding additional musical elements from Spanish-language dance music (especially Latin percussion tracks) to the mix.

In the late 1980s, Edgardo A. Franco—known as "El General" because he often wears military uniforms on stage—became one of the first Jamaican Panamanian performers to achieve international success with his unique synthesis of what became known as reggae-*español*. Born in the late 1960s to a half-Trinidadian, half-Jamaican mother and a half-Panamanian, half-Colombian father, Franco began his musical career at an early age. After receiving a scholarship to attend school in New York City, he returned to Panama and began to write a series of popular songs in a Jamaican dancehall style, such as "Muévelo" ("Shake It") and "Te Ves Buena" ("You're Looking Good"). Interest in his songs in Latin America and the United States played an important role in paving the way for later *reggaeton* artists.

In the United States, interest in reggae-*español* (which might more aptly be called "dancehall-*español*") first became evident in cities with large numbers of Latin immigrants such as Los Angeles, Miami, and New York. Spanish-speaking club-goers of many nationalities came to appreciate the sound, promoted in some cases by immigrant Panamanian DJs themselves. Compilation albums of the music began to receive regular rotation, both on nightclub playlists and on Spanish-language radio. Spanish-only stations in the United States have increased tenfold in number over the past two decades incidentally, currently numbering about 900. Interest among listeners in the reggae-*español* repertoire seems to have derived both from its unique sound and perhaps to an even greater extent from the dance moves associated with it, often of a provocative and sexually explicit nature. Probably the best known of these, *el perreo* (roughly, "doggy-style"), involves a man standing behind his female partner, both with legs slightly bent; the two lock pelvises and grind against each other in various ways. Similar moves are executed by couples facing one another as well, sometimes with the female dancer stretched out on the ground or laying back on her knees. Choreography of this sort has a history in the British Caribbean among dancehall enthusiasts dating back to the 1980s, but it represented something new and rather controversial in Latin clubs of the 1990s. The overt sexuality of many moves and of some song lyrics became the focus of considerable criticism in the press.

ACTIVITY 5.7 *Search on the Internet or in the library for recorded collections of Jamaican reggae and dancehall, then compare them to reggae–*español* music and specifically the early hits of Edgardo Franco. Make lists of the musical characteristics that distinguish the musical styles from one another and those that they share.*

Independently of the development of reggae-*español*, a similar process involving the development of Spanish-language rap music had begun in

Puerto Rico and in New York City. Puerto Ricans enjoy special status as U.S. citizens and travel between Puerto Rico and the United States constantly. Many of them live in neighborhoods such as East Harlem or northwest Chicago that directly border African American communities, so it is no surprise that they should have involved themselves in hip-hop culture from its earliest years. By the mid-1980s, Puerto Rican rappers already constituted a visible presence. At the time they tended to take existing instrumental tracks from popular African American rap tunes and create new Spanish (or "Spanglish" or even English) lyrics for them. By the end of the decade, however, many developed unique styles of musical accompaniment for their rhymes as well.

One of the first Puerto Rican rappers to become influential as part of this movement was Luis Armando Lozada Cruz (b. 1971), known by his stage name "Vico C." Vico C earned a reputation among his peers for thoughtful and socially engaged commentary. His first hit came in 1989 with the song "La recta final" (roughly, "The End of Times"). This piece and its video, which make reference to a variety of topical subjects such as international military aggression, drug trafficking, poverty, and political corruption, became phenomenally popular within Puerto Rico and inspired numerous imitators. Other hits followed, including "Saboréalo" ("Enjoy the Taste") and "María." Vico's compositions into the 1990s, and those of his contemporaries, were engaging but in musical terms still sounded essentially like North American rap.

As mentioned, modern *reggaeton* is most clearly defined by the constant use of a repeated *habanera* figure as the rhythmic basis of the composition, a slight modification of that shown in Figure 1.3. Often, the groove is created out of interaction between a synthesized bass drum playing a steady pulse on 1 and 3 of the 4/4 measure and a *tresillo* played against it by a contrasting percussive sound, for instance, that of a sampled high hat, snare drum, or bell (Fig. 5.7).

Most critics trace the first usage of this pattern in electronic dance music to Jamaican dancehall artist Shabba Ranks and his popular song

FIGURE 5.7   *Basic* reggaeton *beat.*

"Dem Bow" from the 1991 CD *Just Reality*. It appears that "Dem Bow" circulated in numerous Caribbean and Latin American countries and eventually influenced the releases of Panamanians such as Edgardo Franco, Puerto Ricans including Luis Armando Lozada Cruz, and others. By the mid-1990s, Puerto Rican DJ Blass had produced entire albums based on the Dem Bow groove. Commercial *reggaeton* developed from this process of musical cross-fertilization: the adoption of British Caribbean dance beats by Puerto Rican rappers and the growing influence of rap itself on Spanish-language dancehall. The resulting music can take many forms depending on the artist in question. It foregrounds the *reggaeton* beat but may include introductions or interludes of an entirely different rhythm or character. In order to keep the music interesting, artists usually change the timbre of electronic samples, playing the *tresillo* rhythm at various times throughout the piece, in addition to working with contrasting harmonies, background melodic figures, and so on.

The visibility of *reggaeton* among Spanish-speaking audiences achieved a major boost around 2000 owing to the efforts of a production duo known as Luny Tunes. The two men involved, Francisco Saldaña (b. 1979) and Víctor Cabrera (b. 1981), are Dominicans raised in Massachusetts who later immigrated to Puerto Rico. In 2003 they released a well-received compilation album (*MasFlow*) featuring *reggaeton* backbeats with vocals by many up-and-coming stars of the new style. These included Puerto Ricans Don Omar (William Omar Landrón), Tego Calderón (Tegui Calderón Rosario), Baby Ranks (David Luciano Acosta), and superstar Daddy Yankee (Ramón Ayala). A follow-up album from 2005 also sold well and charted on Billboard. The Luny Tunes duo has produced some of the genre's biggest international hits to date, including Don Omar's "Dale Don Dale" ("Go On, Don, Go On," 2003) and Daddy Yankee's "Gasolina" (2004). In the studio they have been known to sample widely from genres such as *merengue, bachata, bolero, cumbia,* and *salsa* and to combine elements from them into the overall *reggaeton* groove. They also mix North American–style rapped segments into their compositions, a common practice.

CD track 22, "Oye mi canto" ("Listen To My Song"), dates from 2005 and features N.O.R.E. (Victor Santiago, b. 1976), a half–African American, half–Puerto Rican singer born in New York City, along with *reggaeton* singers Daddy Yankee, the duo Nina Sky (Nicole and Natalie Albino, Puerto Rican Americans), Gemstar (Rolphy Ramírez, Dominican American), Big Mato (Leonardo Vasquez, Dominican American), and others. "Oye mi canto" is important in the history of the genre because it represents one of the first to attract audiences beyond Spanish-speaking fans. Santiago proved an excellent crossover artist since he could sing in two languages and thus market himself to rap enthusiasts in the

United States as well as to Latinos and Spanish-speaking immigrants. His music has been frequently played on BET (Black Entertainment Television) and MTV and helped create a more diverse audience for *reggaeton* among the North American public.

An excerpt of the at times startling lyrics to "Oye mi canto" appear in the next box. Most are in English, with particular Spanish words and phrases translated in brackets. An introductory statement (0:00–0:22) includes a list of the various performers and groups taking part in the release. The creation of a sense of pan-Latino youth identity is clearly a central theme in *reggaeton*, as noted both in the spoken introduction and in the chorus, which identifies collectively with immigrants from many countries. The text moves seamlessly between English and Spanish, appealing most strongly to those familiar with both languages. Also evident are non-standard Spanish words used primarily by immigrants, such as *"ringa"* for "ring" and *"bloque"* for "city block."

One can't help but note as well the use of profanity and crude references to sex and to various parts of the female body. This is typical of much *reggaeton* and U.S. rap today and has contributed to its controversial reception, as mentioned. The primary perspective represented here is that of young men and could be viewed justifiably as demeaning to women. Nevertheless, such themes have become so commonplace in rap and *reggaeton* that apparently misogynistic lyrics often fail to provoke a response among listeners. *Reggaeton* artists, as in the case of *bachata* singers, are overwhelmingly male; the relatively small number of successful female artists or groups (Ivy Queen, Glory, Nina Sky) have not succeeded in influencing mainstream lyrical messages.

ACTIVITY 5.8 *Initiate a discussion with your friends or classmates about what constitutes appropriate material for inclusion in song lyrics. How much profanity is too much? What sorts of discussions of sex, violence, or related speech should be accepted in popular music and played on mainstream radio or on MTV? Should any restrictions be imposed, and if so, what sorts of criteria should be established to define them?*

In musical terms, note the frequent studio manipulation of sound to produce echoes, reverb, and so on. The background harmony alternates between only two chords, B♭ minor and G♭ major, providing a steady vamp over which singers can improvise. Chords are outlined constantly by means of a single electronically generated melodic line that sounds vaguely like a harpsichord. The melody often presents arpeggios in a syncopated fashion reminiscent of folkloric *tres* or *cuatro* performance, as described in Chapter 4. Much more prominent is the electronic *reggaeton* beat itself, absent in the introduction and more subdued under Daddy Yankee's and Big Mato's lead vocal but otherwise dominating the song. The *reggaeton* groove alternates every other measure between a standard *habanera* figure and one that begins with two eighth notes instead of a single quarter note. Both this pattern and the synthesizer line give the impression of being *"claved"* because of their two-measure structure. The Nina Sky duo adopts a strongly melismatic and African American–influenced vocal style, inflected with "blue notes," flattened fifths, and thirds.

Partial Listening Guide for CD Track 22

"Oye mi canto"

View the entire listening guide at www.oup.com/us.moore.

0:00

If you're proud to be Latino right now stand the f*** up. Double cut, double cut, let's go. SBK. Alive, we comin' up, comin' up. Nina Sky. N.O.R.E., Da-ddy Yan-kee, Gem Star, Gem Star, Big Mato, Big Mato, c'mon, c'mon.

0:23

[CHORUS sung by the Nina Sky duo over *reggaeton* beat]
Whoa, whoa, whoa, whoa (what you say?)
Boricua [Puerto Rican], *morena* [dark woman], *dominicano, colombiano*
Boricua, morena, cubano, mexicano
Oye mi canto [Listen to my song]

0:43

[N.O.R.E.] You see this is what they want, they want *reggaeton* (what, what?)
They want *reggaeton, esto e' lo que quieren* [this is what they want]
Toma reggaeton [take *reggaeton*] (¿qué, qué?), *toma reggaeton*
You see, I'm N.O.R.E., keep my story, my story
I always kick it (¿qué? [what?]) when I bone shorty [slang for girl]
I slap *culo* [ass] and listen (¿qué?)

ACTIVITY 5.9 *Search the Internet for music videos of "Oye mi canto" and other representative* reggaeton *pieces. Analyze the images that artists choose to include. How are the performers dressed, what body postures and gestures do they adopt, and what sorts of messages do these images send? How are women depicted as opposed to men? Is "Latin-ness" or nationality referenced in any way? More broadly, what nonmusical images appear in the videos, and how do they relate (if at all) to the song lyrics?*

Many other *reggaeton* stars have achieved international popularity and commercial success. Afro-Puerto Rican Tego Calderón (b. 1972) is an especially interesting figure who has also contributed significantly to the popularization of the genre. His compositions are characterized by insightful social content, racially conscious or even Afro-centric lyrics, and the incorporation of *bomba sicá* and other folkloric rhythms into studio mixes. This makes sense given the artist's upbringing in Loíza Aldea, a predominantly Afro-Puerto Rican neighborhood outside of San Juan that is known for its preservation of local drumming styles. Calderón has taken part in extramusical social activities including Latino voter registration drives, AIDS awareness concerts, and public criticism of exploitative business practices on the part of multinational corporations that have sought his sponsorship. He represents a counterpart of sorts to the more hedonistic and profit-driven *reggaeton* music that dominates the market.

Among Latino and Latin American youth audiences, the popularity of *reggaeton* continues to expand; it has become popular in Mexico, Panama, Venezuela, Colombia, and Peru. Successful *reggaeton* performers have emerged in all these countries, as well as in Canada, Honduras, Nicaragua, Spain, even England. Artists continue to experiment with the form, fusing it with other world musics. Recent hybrid subgenres of *reggaeton* include *"salsaton," "rocketon," "merenton,"* even *"bhangraton"* (a blend of *reggaeton* with commercial *bhangra*, itself a hybrid dance music with influences from India and Pakistan). Within Cuba, *reggaeton* with a local twist has also attracted a wide audience. Performer Papo Record (Andrés Rivalta Hechevarría) made a name for himself by developing hits that incorporated sacred Yoruba phrases into the lyrics of songs and in other ways referencing Santería practice. He recently defected while on tour and now resides in the United Kingdom. Other prominent Cuban groups—Baby Lores & Insurrecto, Clan 537, Eddy K, Gente de Zona—experiment creatively with local folklore and in fusing *reggaeton* with elements of *timba* dance music discussed in Chapter 4.

Many transnational forms have emerged in the Hispanic Caribbean other than the examples mentioned here. One of the most prominent is Latin jazz, a dynamic body of music discussed in Chapter 7. Another is *boogaloo* (or *bugalú*), a fusion of the Cuban *son* and *chachachá* with elements of R&B that emerged in the early 1960s, primarily among Puerto Ricans and so-called Nuyoricans (Puerto Rican immigrants living in the New York area). Yet another is Latin rock, a genre with countless devotees throughout the Hispanic Caribbean and Latin America.

The histories of North American and Caribbean popular music have been in dialogue for centuries, as evident in the analysis of the colonial-era dance genres that began this chapter. The Caribbean's *tresillo* and *son clave* patterns can be found in rock 'n' roll songs by Bo Diddley from the 1950s as well as in the *contradanza*; the ubiquitous *habanera* beat appears not only in *reggaeton* but also in the bass line of compositions by Scott Joplin, even in Brazilian piano music from the turn of the twentieth century and the dance rhythms of North African Berbers. It is probably more useful to think of all these musical forms as unified in many respects, linked through international commerce, technology, and shared history.

Writers on the topic of transnationalism suggest that while in the past cultural diversity may have been located in distinct folkloric styles, in the present it is more often based on interrelations. Immigrant performers, or those in the developing world, interact constantly with influences from a gamut of sources, both local and global. They achieve critical success not necessarily through isolationism or the rejection of First-World commercial sounds but more often through critical dialogue and the revision or editing of existing forms to suit their own tastes. In the case of the Hispanic Caribbean musical "revisions" or creolizations have a venerable history dating back to the earliest years of colonization. The spread of the *contradanza*, the *bolero*, the *bachata*, and subsequent musical phenomena indicates that regional or national senses of self on the islands derive to a significant extent from forms of expression that have their origins elsewhere.

These realizations lead back to questions about the best way to study Caribbean music and how to define it more generally—topics broached in Chapter 1. The study of world music frequently requires fieldwork in out-of-the-way places, one-on-one interviews and music lessons with performers, and close ethnographic attention to community experiences. This sort of approach has proven invaluable over the years in documenting the expression of groups who have been marginalized from textbooks and official histories of music. Yet ethnographic analysis often privileges local views and processes over those based on broader systems of cultural interaction. The future study of world music will require increasing attention to analytical approaches that reconcile paradigms based on fieldwork and ethnography with the complex transnational realities of the present.

CHAPTER 6

Political Song

∞

This chapter examines the ways in which the Caribbean's turbulent political history has inspired music making of various kinds. It begins with reflections on factors that led to the rise of leftist politics throughout Latin America in the post–World War II period and to a pan-regional musical form known as *nueva canción* or "new song." The chapter then focuses on specific examples of *nueva canción* from the Hispanic Caribbean. The first is music associated with Puerto Rican independence movements, beginning in the nineteenth century and most visible as of the 1970s in the compositions of Roy Brown, Andrés Jiménez, and others. The second example is that of music performed in the Dominican Republic following the assassination of dictator Rafael Trujillo. Subsequent attempts to redefine the country culturally and politically in more democratic terms led to experimentation by folklorists and music ensembles, among them Expresión Joven and Convite. The final example is that of protest song from Cuba in the form of *nueva trova* and socially conscious rap. Prominent musicians of recent years have continued the socially committed messages of the early revolution but have couched them in terms appealing to younger listeners and to the Afro-Cuban community.

THE RISE OF *NUEVA CANCIÓN*

The 1940s and 1950s witnessed heightened levels of political activity in much of the developing world, owing in large part to uprisings against colonial occupation. With the aid of advanced military technology (rifles, cannons, gunships), Western nations such as Spain, Portugal, France, and England managed to occupy and control vast areas of the globe for centuries. European leaders and intellectuals felt little need to justify the subjugation of other people or the taking of their lands and resources. Colonizers believed their culture and society (not to mention the "white race") to be inherently superior to others. They believed they were helping other groups become "civilized," to progress in various ways that would benefit them.

These attitudes only shifted decisively after World War II, when peoples of Asia, Africa, the Middle East, Latin America, and elsewhere demanded independence. Such tendencies coincided with the struggles of minorities and underrepresented groups for full rights within other nations. In the Caribbean, the 1950s and 1960s gave rise to independence movements in Jamaica and Trinidad, *negritude* and *noirisme* (black arts movements) in Haiti and Martinique, calls for independence from the United States in Puerto Rico, and challenges to U.S.-backed military dictatorships in the Dominican Republic and Cuba. It was in this overarching context that new forms of expression such as *nueva canción* emerged. The music is linked to the development of protest song elsewhere, for instance, that of U.S. folk singers Bob Dylan and Joan Baez, Joan Manuel Serrat in Spain, and Bob Marley in Jamaica.

Nueva canción is best defined as a genre of socially engaged song that became popular in the Spanish-speaking Americas during the 1960s and 1970s. Most of its early performers and listeners were teenagers and young adults, primarily middle-class and college-educated. They sought an alternative to music dominating the media that they perceived as overly commercial. *Nueva canción* performers attempted to create a new kind of music, one of high artistic quality; in some cases they adopted local forms of folklore or instruments that earlier generations considered of little interest. The lyrics of early compositions touched on many subjects, drawing attention to social injustice or discussing more conventional themes such as love or romance in fresh, unconventional ways. In order to promote their songs, initially rejected by the cultural establishment, performers created alternative spaces for themselves known as *peñas* (clubs) or *tertulias* (informal artistic gatherings).

Nueva canción in the Caribbean owes a conceptual debt to the efforts of musicians in Chile and Argentina, who were among the first to champion the style. Argentine Atahualpa Yupanqui (Héctor Roberto Chavero, 1908–1992) was an influential figure who studied the arts of indigenous peoples. Chilean Violeta Parra (1917–1967) and Uruguayan Daniel Viglietti (b. 1939) emerged shortly thereafter as prominent activists in much the same vein, inspiring countless others to continue their efforts. Support for early *nueva canción* among listeners throughout Latin America developed partly in response to the onslaught of popular music from the United States and Europe heard in the post–World War II period. The power of multinational music corporations to inundate developing countries with recordings by artists such as Elvis Presley or Chuck Berry and their frequent disregard for local expression created a backlash of sorts.

STRUGGLES FOR INDEPENDENCE IN
THE HISPANIC CARIBBEAN

Most countries in Latin America achieved their independence early in the nineteenth century. The political and economic impositions of Spanish authorities generated considerable discontent on the part of many colonists; this, in combination with Napoleon's invasions of Spain and Portugal (1807–1808) and the temporary collapse of the Spanish monarchy, facilitated successful transitions to self-rule. Haiti and the Dominican Republic achieved independence from Europe at this time. Cuba and Puerto Rico represent an exception to the overall trend, however; both remained colonies of Spain until 1898. In the case of Cuba, reluctance to break ties to Spain resulted from the large numbers of slaves imported between 1800 and 1840 and a perceived need on the part of the white elite to have the backing of the Spanish military to control them should a rebellion occur. In Puerto Rico, loyalty to Spain resulted partly from a large Spanish military presence on the island and from the relatively small and socially fragmented state of the colony during much of the nineteenth century that made collective action difficult.

Puerto Rico's political debates since the mid-nineteenth century and much of its protest music have centered around the issue of sovereignty. As in the case of Cuba, the latter half of the nineteenth century gave rise to a series of attempts by Puerto Rican landholders either to wrest control of the island from Spain or at least to achieve a greater degree of autonomy. The issue came to a head most famously in a brief and unsuccessful rebellion in September 1868 known as the *Grito de Lares* or "Cry of Lares," named after the town where it took place. Some of the first examples of Puerto Rican independence song date from this period, for example, the island's revolutionary anthem "La borinqueña." Lola Rodríguez de Tió penned the lyrics in Cuba, where she and her husband moved after being banished by Puerto Rican colonial authorities. As is evident, the author took inspiration from the onset of the Cuban Wars of Independence that also began in 1868, exhorting Puerto Ricans to rise up against the Spanish. The first three verses read as follows.

¡Despierta, borinqueño	Arise, Puerto Rican
Que han dado la señal!	The call to arms has sounded!
¡Despierta de ese sueño	Awake from your sleep
Que es hora de luchar!	It is time to fight!

A ese llamar patriótico	Doesn't this patriotic call
¿No arde tu corazón?	Set your heart on fire?
¡Ven! Nos será simpático	Come! We will take pleasure
El ruido del cañón.	In the roar of the cannon
Mira, ya el cubano libre será	Come, Cubans will soon be free
Le dará el machete su libertad	The machete will give them their liberty

Puerto Rican leaders continued to lobby the Spanish for greater autonomy in ensuing decades, with some success. But shortly after new agreements had been formalized, the island became embroiled in what has become known in the United States as the "Spanish–American War." This conflict actually began in 1895 as the last in a series of wars of independence initiated by Cuba. Cuban fighters appeared to be on the brink of defeating Spanish forces by 1898. Just at that moment the U.S. government entered the conflict, justifying its intervention because of the mysterious bombing of one of its naval vessels while in Havana's harbor.

The massive strength of the U.S. army and navy relative to that of Spain or Cuba soon put an end to the war. In the aftermath, the U.S. military occupied Cuba for four years; it eventually granted the island nominal independence only after forcing the election of a hand-picked and pro-U.S. president, establishing multiple military bases on the island and making the new Cuban government agree to let it intervene militarily in Cuban affairs any time it cared to. One of the military bases created through this process was the now famous outpost at Guantánamo Bay. At the same time, the U.S. government annexed the island of Puerto Rico outright, claiming it as a war prize without any thought to offering its residents independence. It took possession of Guam and the Philippines at the same time.

PUERTO RICAN PROTEST SONG

Though some factions within Puerto Rico welcomed their new relationship with the United States, points of strain soon developed. Much of this had to do with the desire of U.S. authorities to "anglicize" Puerto Rico, essentially to strip it of its Hispanic heritage. Early governors made English the only language of instruction in public schools and forbade the use of Spanish in many other contexts. They tended not to recognize or encourage the perpetuation of Spanish-derived holidays and generally demonstrated a lack of regard for, even condescension toward, local ways of life. Colonial authorities banned displays of the Puerto Rican flag for fifty years, a fact which helps explain the passion many Puerto Ricans currently express for waving their flag in collective gatherings. Tellingly, the revolutionary lyrics of "La borinqueña" proved too controversial to adopt openly under U.S. rule. Various new lyrics took their place in the early twentieth century as composers created "nonconfrontational" versions of the hymn that could be taught in public schools and used in official events. Lyrics penned by Manuel Fernández Juncos in 1903 became the official text of the song as of 1977. Fernández Juncos' version begins in this way (Malavet Vega 1993, 276).

La tierra de Borinquén	The land of Borinquen
Donde he nacido yo	Where I have been born
Es un jardín florido	Is a florid garden
De mágico fulgor	Of magical brilliance
Un cielo siempre nítido	A sky always clean
Le sirve de dosel	Serves as its canopy
Y dan arrullos plácidos	And placid lullabies are given
las olas a sus pies	By the waves at her feet

For some years, Puerto Ricans did not protest U.S. control of their island vociferously. They believed their colonial status to be temporary and enjoyed certain advantages such as funding for education and public works, as well as U.S. citizenship (granted in 1917). But as colonial control continued into the 1930s, many began to lose patience. These feelings were exacerbated by the onset of the Great Depression, which curtailed U.S. imports and resulted in massive unemployment among Puerto Rican workers. Those who immigrated to the United States often suffered discrimination and found themselves unable to integrate easily into English-speaking society.

The 1930s thus represents the first rise of strong anti-American sentiment in Puerto Rico, as manifest in the compositions of individuals such as Rafael Hernández (1892–1965). Perhaps the most famous of all Puerto Rican musicians today, Hernández was an amazingly versatile and prolific composer who traveled frequently and absorbed influences from many sources. This Afro-Puerto Rican began his professional career in San Juan, where he played in various municipal bands. During World War I he joined a segregated infantry troupe and played jazz under the direction of African American bandleader James Reece Europe. The 1920s and early 1930s found him living in New York, where he founded the Borinquen Trio and Victoria Quartet. In 1932 he moved to Mexico, directing radio and dance orchestras before returning to Puerto Rico in 1947. Hernández composed over 2,000 songs, many of which continue to be performed and recorded (fig. 6.1).

In the 1930s, Hernández turned from composing songs of romance to themes of nationalism. One of his best-known works is "Lamento borincano" ("Puerto Rican Lament," 1930). This piece, written as a slow *bolero* in a minor key, tells the tale of a humble *jíbaro* who makes a long journey into town to sell his produce, only to return empty-handed because the market has closed owing to the depression. It has been recorded by hundreds of performers including contemporary salsa star Marc

FIGURE 6.1   *Rafael Hernández in 1935.*   (Photo courtesy of José Ruiz Elcoro).

Anthony. Other patriotic numbers from the same decade include "Linda Quisqueya" ("Beautiful Dominican Republic," 1928) and "El buen borincano" ("The Good Puerto Rican," 1939), which extol the independence of the Dominican Republic and express a desire for Puerto Rico to achieve the same status. Hernández's most controversial song from the 1930s is undoubtedly "Preciosa" ("Beautiful," 1935), in which he refers obliquely to the United States as a "tyrant." The song has been recorded many times, often by artists who replace the word *"tirano"* ("tyrant") with *"destino"* ("destiny") in order to alter the meaning, depending on their political leanings.

Preciosa te llaman los bardos	The bards who sing your history
Que cantan tu historia	Call you beautiful
No importa el tirano	No matter that the tyrant
Te trate con negra maldad	Treats you with pure evil
Preciosa serás sin bandera	You remain precious without a flag
Sin lauros, ni gloria	Without laurels, nor glory
Preciosa, preciosa, te llaman	Precious, precious they call you
Los hijos de la libertad	The sons of liberty

Though a great deal of Puerto Rican protest music has been inspired by reactions to North American control, there are of course many other kinds of political music on the island. One of the most common genres associated with protest, frequently between striking workers and businesses, is the *plena*, discussed in Chapter 4. Because *plena* in its initial folkloric form involved only singing and performance on hand-held percussion instruments, it proved an excellent medium for street demonstrations. As early as the 1930s, labor unions and others used *plenas* as a means of voicing their dissent, and the tradition continues today. Much as in the case of the Mexican *corrido* or the Cuban *rumba*, *plena* music has functioned as a form of oral history, spreading information about important working-class events. It played an even more important role earlier in the century when the illiteracy rate was far higher. The twenty-minute video documentary *Plena Is Work, Plena Is Song* (New York: Cinema Guild, 1989) provides an excellent introduction to the links between *plena* political activism.

Three political parties have dominated Puerto Rico in the twentieth century, each corresponding to distinct attitudes about U.S. control. The

Puerto Rican Independence Party (PIP) advocates for complete sovereignty. One early leader of this faction was Pedro Albizu Campus (1891–1965), a mulatto activist who suffered imprisonment on several occasions for challenging U.S. authority. Albizu Campos has achieved nearly mythic status among *independentistas* and is mentioned in many political songs, including one of our examples (CD track 23). The Popular Democratic Party (PPD) supports the ambiguous "commonwealth" status Puerto Rico currently enjoys, neither a part of the United States nor separate from it. This is the party that has held the greatest sway among the electorate in recent years. The New Progressive Party (PNP) advocates statehood for the island and, thus, full integration into the United States.

The most notorious period associated with the independence struggle internationally extended from the 1950s through the 1970s. Ironically, this was also when the island achieved major concessions, especially the right to elect governors locally rather than having them imposed from the United States and the achievement of commonwealth status. Even so, open discussion of Puerto Rican independence remained a crime in the 1950s, apparently the result of McCarthy-era fear of communism and the spread of left-wing political agendas. Though they represented a minority, activists such as Lolita Lebrón (Dolores Lebrón Sotomayor, b. 1919), Pedro Albizu Campos, and others continued to protest. In March 1954 Lebrón and three male co-conspirators entered the U.S. House of Representatives and began firing guns in order to raise awareness about their cause. Lebrón claims to have fired only at the ceiling, but at least one of her cohorts wounded five congressmen. She served twenty-five years in prison and was only released in 1979 following a pardon by Jimmy Carter. Her life has been immortalized in song by Puerto Rican musician Danny Rivera and Cuban Carlos Puebla.

> **ACTIVITY 6.1** *Conduct research on the lives of Lolita Lebrón and Pedro Albizu Campos and on the Puerto Rican independence movement of the 1950s. Also, search for copies of the Arhoolie Records CD collection Lamento Borincano (2001) with insightful liner notes (in Spanish) written by Cristóbal Díaz Ayala. The release includes early recordings of the independence movement, in addition to well-known Rafael Hernández repertoire.*

Many Puerto Rican *nueva canción* performers emerged in the 1970s and 1980s, inspired by their counterparts in South America, Cuba, and elsewhere. Virtually all believed fervently in Puerto Rican independence and addressed the issue through song, in addition to discussing other issues of the day such as the Vietnam War. Prominent musicians included Roy Brown Ramírez (b. 1945) and Antonio Cabán Vale ("El Topo" or "The Mole," b. 1942). Brown grew up in Orlando, Florida, the son of an American naval officer and a Puerto Rican mother. He enrolled in the University of Puerto Rico in the late 1960s; his first LPs date from the following decade, including *Yo protesto* ("I Protest", re-released in 2005) and *Basta ya, revolución* ("Enough Already, Revolution," 1970). Brown is a prolific artist, with at least eighteen releases to his name. He is a friend of Cuban Silvio Rodríguez, discussed later, and has performed and recorded with him on various occasions.

The profile of Antonio Cabán Vale is in many respects similar. He also attended the University of Puerto Rico in the 1960s and after graduation became a schoolteacher. Cabán Vale is perhaps best known for forming a group called Taoné. In all, he has recorded over twenty albums and performed throughout the Caribbean, Latin America, and the United States. Cabán Vale's best-known compositions date from the 1970s, including "Verde luz" ("Green Light"), a song written as a slow *danza* whose lyrics call for independence. It is considered an unofficial national anthem. To a greater extent than Brown, Cabán Vale is known for the use of local Puerto Rican instruments and musical genres in his compositions.

During its heyday, Puerto Rican *nueva canción* artists performed in many contexts. The Silvia Rexach Theater in Santurce, named after a prominent local composer, represents one important venue for such music; El Topo, Lucecita Benítez (b. 1942), and Danny Rivera (b. 1945) all staged various presentations there. Grupo Taoné began performing in the Claridad Festival, an annual fund-raiser for a socialist newspaper of the same name that began publication in the 1970s. Another event featuring *nueva canción* singers was the Tierrazo Festival, which has taken place annually as of 1977 in the Roberto Clemente Coliseum. Other, more modest and bohemian venues in the Old City included the Cafe Teatro la Tea, El Ocho Puertas, and Corral de la Cruz, the latter an experimental theater. The University of Puerto Rico and the Institute of Culture also regularly sponsored artists associated with *nueva canción*.

Our example of Puerto Rican *nueva canción* (CD track 23) was written by yet another artist, Andrés ("El Jíbaro") Jiménez (b. 1947, Fig. 6.2). Jiménez comes from a large *jíbaro* family in Orocovis, Puerto Rico, in the mountainous heart of the island. He moved to New York as a teenager, was drafted by the U.S. army and served for a time in Vietnam, then returned home. During his university studies, Jiménez performed in Taoné, singing together with both Brown and Cabán Vale. Samples of their music can be heard for free on the Smithsonian Folkways Web site (http://www.folkways.si.edu/albumdetails.aspx?itemid=2254); they contributed to compilation albums such as *¡Viva Puerto Rico libre!* ("Long Live Free Puerto Rico") in collaboration with Cubans Pablo Milanés and Amaury Pérez. Liner notes for the release are also available for free in pdf format.

Over the years, Jiménez has developed a style of *nueva canción* that is more closely linked to Puerto Rican folkloric traditions than that of most of his contemporaries. His releases often sound nearly identical to the traditional *seis* and *música jíbara* discussed in Chapter 2, though the lyrics carry more of a political edge. In recent years, Jiménez has also

FIGURE 6.2 *Andrés ("El Jíbaro") Jiménez on the cover of his* En la última trinchera *album from 1997.* *(Photo courtesy of Andrés Jiménez).*

experimented more widely with Puerto Rican and Hispanic Caribbean music (*plena*, salsa, *rumba*, religious *décimas*, etc.); in 2000, he recorded an album in collaboration with *salsero* Ismael Miranda entitled *Son de Vieques* ("*Song from Vieques*"). His 2007 release *Mi Parranda* ("*My Party*"), consisting primarily of *aguinaldos* and Christmas repertoire, has proven his most commercially successful to date.

> **ACTIVITY 6.2**   *Find the island of Vieques on a map, and search information on the recent controversy that has surrounded it, pitting many Puerto Ricans against the U.S. government.*

CD track 23, "Libertad y soberanía" ("Liberty and Sovereignty"), comes from Jiménez's 1997 album *En la última trinchera* ("*In the Final Trench*," Fig. 6.2). The *trinchera* serves as a metaphor for the battle lines of the electoral process. Puerto Ricans have taken nonbinding votes since the 1950s to determine whether the population desired independence from the United States. In 1998, the most recent vote took place; it seemed especially important since the U.S. Congress for the first time appeared willing to support Puerto Ricans in their decision for independence, should they choose that option. The vote dealt a blow to the PIP when it became clear that those in favor of independence constituted only a small minority. In fact, virtually all recent referenda have indicated that Puerto Ricans prefer commonwealth status or even statehood rather than independence. Yet the matter remains unresolved: New legislation on the status of Puerto Rico was drafted in Washington, D.C., for consideration in 2007 (House Resolution 900 and Senate bill 1936, searchable on the Library of Congress website under the first session of the 110th Congress: http://thomas.loc.gov/home/c110query.html).

"Libertad y soberanía" (CD track 23) is written as a "salsified" *plena*, one that includes instruments such as trombones and piano usually associated with salsa music. The full instrumentation includes *panderetas*, congas, timbales, *güiro*, piano, electric bass, accordion, *cuatro*, trombones, and vocals. You may recognize the *plena* rhythm from the discussion in Chapter 4 and from CD tracks 14 and 15. The two-sided pattern here begins on the syncopated or "jumped" side, what we might describe as the "three side" if relating it to an implicit *clave*. The *timbales* play a backbeat rhythm on the bells, striking on "two-and" and "four-and" of the 4/4 measure (i.e., one and *two-and* three and *four-and*). The form of the composition is relatively simple, alternating between a verse section sung by Jiménez, a chorus, and an instrumental passage. It may surprise you to hear accordion in this piece; accordions no longer appear frequently in the *plena*, but in earlier decades they were common.

Partial Listening Guide for CD Track 23

"Libertad y soberanía"

View the full guide at www.oup.com/us.moore.

0:00–0:17

Instrumental introduction, with the accordion on the lead melody for the first ten seconds, followed by the trombones. The *cuatro* plays a countermelody in the background in response to the accordion and trombone phrases. *Panderetas*, the *timbales* bell, and *güiro* can be heard clearly. The bass plays a straight half-note rhythm on 1 and 3 of the 4/4 measure, as is common in dance-band *plenas*.

0:18–0:36

First entry of Jiménez on lead vocal. He sings the refrain by himself, setting up the choral entrance at 0:37. The texture becomes thinner as the piano and trombones drop out and the bass shifts to playing shorter quarter notes on 3 and 4 of the 4/4 measure for a time (0:18–0:26). Chordal accompaniment is provided only by the accordion, with an occasional note or two added on the *cuatro*.

Se escucha este canto en la tierra mía [2×]	This song is heard in my land [2×]
Quiero que en mi patria	I want my country to have
Haya libertad y soberanía [2×]	Liberty and sovereignty [2×]

0:37–0:53

The chorus enters, singing the same text. Trombones provide support with syncopated background figures, together with the piano. The bass by this point returns to a straight rhythm on 1 and 3, typical of dance-band *plena*, making the sound fuller.

ACTIVITY 6.3 *Conduct research on the issue of Puerto Rico's political status in order to understand better the justifications for various positions in the debate and the ways Puerto Rican attitudes have shifted on this issue over the years.*

NUEVA CANCIÓN IN THE DOMINICAN REPUBLIC

As mentioned in Chapter 2, the Dominican Republic developed from the Spanish colony that Christopher Columbus established on Hispaniola in the 1490s. French forces occupied the western half of the island in the late seventeenth century and established their own colony, now known as Haiti (an indigenous term meaning "mountainous"). The histories of the Dominican Republic and Haiti are closely bound together. Haiti gained its independence from France in 1804 as the result of a massive slave uprising, becoming the first free nation in all of Latin America and the Caribbean. In 1822, Haitian troops attacked and took over the entire island, so when the Dominican Republic gained its own independence in 1844, it did so from Haiti rather than from Spain. In the early 1860s, military leader Pedro Santana attempted to revert the Dominican Republic to colonial status, thinking that, with the backing of Spain, his country would never again be subject to attack by Haitians. Complete independence proved too attractive to most residents, however. In 1870, the United States nearly annexed the Dominican Republic in a move supported by the Dominican leadership and Ulysses S. Grant, but the U.S. Senate rejected the proposal by a single vote.

Through the early twentieth century, the Dominican Republic continued to be led by military figures who used their office to enrich themselves. Several were assassinated by political opponents, leading to turmoil and unrest. In 1916, President Woodrow Wilson made the decision to occupy the country in order to protect U.S. business investments there and to help establish democratic rule. The occupation lasted for eight years. It had some positive effects including the quelling of internal violence. But most Dominicans chafed under North American occupation; those years are associated with a sharp rise in nationalist sentiment and eventually the adoption of local folkloric genres such as the *merengue* as the epitome of Dominican expression to the exclusion of foreign music.

General Rafael Trujillo dominated Dominican politics for decades, beginning with his rise to power in 1930. He took control of the country through a series of illicit electoral maneuverings and by the time he died controlled approximately half of the country's financial assets. Aside from suppressing freedom of expression and killing or jailing Dominican political opponents, Trujillo committed horrendous acts against Haitians. These included the massacre of tens of thousands of poor squatters near the border who had crossed into the Dominican Republic illicitly. Similarly ruthless tactics employed by the dictator against high-profile political adversaries eventually led to increasing opposition against him and to his assassination in May of 1961.

In the aftermath of Trujillo's death, Dominicans faced the challenge of refashioning the nation so as to be more democratic. Essayist and politician Juan Bosch won presidential elections in February of 1963 in one of the first democratic transitions of power in the Dominican Republic's history. Bosch championed a new constitution that guaranteed rights such as freedom of expression and freedom of the press. Despite popular support, he soon faced powerful enemies. Bosch's distribution of land to the rural poor drew the ire of large agriculturalists. Leaders of the Catholic Church criticized him as too secular, and the army balked under the command of a president with no military experience.

Seven months after he had taken office, a military coup deposed Bosch. In protest, sectors of the military and the population rose up in an attempt to reinstate him, resulting in street fighting and chaos. This led Lyndon Johnson to send 42,000 U.S. marines to occupy the country once again in 1965, setting the stage for elections in which former Trujillo associate Joaquín Balaguer would take office in 1966, backed by the United States. Dominican *nueva canción* emerged in this turbulent context. It represented a reaction on the part of urban youth to armed insurrection against a dictator and his assassination, democratic elections overturned by a military coup, armed foreign intervention, and the installation of an unpopular Trujillo crony, all within the space of a few years.

Rafael Trujillo and his brother Petán maintained tight control over the mass media and inhibited the movement of musicians to and from the island. The international promotion of music interested them little, and as a result the mid-century Dominican music industry never realized its full potential. The fall of Trujillo created new opportunities for musicians and aspiring entrepreneurs, however. Record labels and radio stations appeared across the island that afforded artists additional opportunities to perform. Commercial *merengue* orchestras flourished and toured as never before, and *bachata* artists began signing contracts with national and international labels as well. Foreign music entered the country at an accelerated pace, especially commercial music from the United States and Europe, *balada* recordings, and New York salsa.

Considerable debate ensued about the best ways to redefine the nation culturally in a post-Trujillo era. Many artists engaged in what performer Luis Días has described as *"la lucha sonora"* (Pacini Hernández 1991), a sonic struggle to envision a more equitable and democratic future. This struggle manifested itself in varied and somewhat contradictory ways. Young, middle-class urbanites generally wished to integrate more fully into the international community, to perform and consume the latest songs and videos from abroad; and they created new markets for such repertoire. Rural listeners tended to prefer *merengue típico, salves,* or *bachata* that had for the most part been marginalized prior to the 1960s. A smaller group of *nueva canción* activists for their part began to search for a music that would effectively represent the activist spirit of the times and spur the population to engagement with political reform. This group has often been referred to as the "Generation of the 1970s."

Dominican *nueva canción* performers of the 1970s included singer-songwriters Luis Días (b. 1952), Sonia Silvestre (b. 1952), and Víctor Víctor (Víctor José Víctor Rojas, b. 1948). Some also associate Juan Luis Guerra (b. 1957) with the group, though he is slightly younger than the others and his artistic career took a different path, as we shall see. *Nueva canción* musicians of the period performed largely acoustic, guitar-based music. Many songs were influenced by the *bolero* or by South American folk dance repertoire performed by Violeta Parra and others. Members of groups such as Los Macopejes ("The Tadpoles") and Expresión Joven ("Young Expression") commonly recited speeches or poetry over minimalist musical accompaniment as well. They wrote songs criticizing the presence of multinational corporations in the Dominican Republic (the U.S.-based Alcoa and Gulf and Western, Canada-based Falconbridge Mining), viewed as complicit in supporting oppressive leaders such as Trujillo and Balaguer. Other piecess exhorted listeners to revolutionary action or eulogized the lives of martyrs in the armed struggle to reinstate Bosch. Artists played most often on the campus of the Universidad Autónoma de Santo Domingo (UASD, Autonomous University of Santo Domingo). A sampling of Expresión Joven songs from the album *Dominican Republic: ¡La hora está llegando!* can be accessed on the Smithsonian Folkways Web site (http://www.folkways.si.edu/albumdetails.aspx?itemid=2245).

The group Convite may have made the most lasting contribution to early Dominican *nueva canción* by doing their best to learn about their nation's folklore and to incorporate aspects of it into socially conscious music. The term *"convite"* is used in both the Dominican Republic and Haiti. It refers to a communal work effort of some kind—for instance, house construction or harvesting—in which participants help each other without payment but are promised support from others in the future as necessary with their own labors. The principal founding members of the ensemble were musician Luis Días, sociologist Dagoberto Tejeda, and folklorist Iván Domínguez. Convite did not constitute a performing ensemble as such but, rather, consisted of individuals with a common desire to study, valorize, and disseminate Dominican heritage. They expressed special interest in African-derived musical genres that had largely been ignored prior to that time.

Convite remained active through 1981. They took trips to rural areas of the Dominican Republic to record and study traditional music and established annual folklore festivals such as the Festival de Sainagua. At the height of the group's popularity, members made television appearances and gave performances at venues such as the Casa de Teatro, a prominent cultural institution in Santo Domingo. They collaborated with commercial musicians of the day such as *merengueros* Johnny Ventura and Wilfrido Vargas, who arranged some of their folkloric material for dance bands. Convite organized conferences on folk music as well as international festivals of *nueva canción* that featured Silvio Rodríguez and Noel Nicola of Cuba, Mercedes Sosa of Argentina, Antonio Cabán Vale and Danny Rivera of Puerto Rico, and others. The most renowned of the festivals, Siete Días Con el Pueblo ("Seven Days with the People") is said to have attracted over 200,000 listeners. It took place in 1974 in two different stadiums: the Centro Olímpico of Santo Domingo and the Estadio Cibao in Santiago de los Caballeros, with support from the Central General de Trabajadores, a national trade union. In the aftermath, the government of Juan Balaguer denied further entry into the country of all international artists who had participated in an attempt to suppress oppositional political song (Dagoberto Tejeda, personal communication).

In more recent years, Luis Días, Tony Vicioso, and others have continued Convite's efforts by fusing traditional Afro-Dominican folkloric rhythms with rock and jazz. Unfortunately, very little of this experimentation is available for purchase, but an interesting example of Luis Días' work, a piece entitled "Palo mayor," can be seen on YouTube. It contrasts images of the Dominican working classes in urban settings with vocals and percussion derived from rural *palo* traditions, a prominent Kongo-derived drumming style (see Fig. 3.8). Eventually, electric guitar enters the musical mix in the video as well, alongside the sound of electric saws and motorcycle engines. Most scenes make reference to poverty or to typical aspects of everyday life: the shining of shoes on a street corner, the cutting of green coconuts, the homeless asleep on the sidewalk, women carrying baskets on their heads, children at play. The video provides a window of sorts into Convite's artistic efforts.

Nueva canción groups such Expresión Joven employed overt and rather heavy-handed Marxist terminology in their lyrics, making reference to "the workers," "the struggle," and "the peasant." They approached music making with great earnestness but not always with humor; their intent seemed to be to teach (or preach) rather than to entertain. Both Expresión Joven and Convite rejected *merengue* and *bachata* as too commercial for their efforts, representing more what they were trying to distance themselves from rather than a vehicle with which to communicate to the masses. Their compositions thus differed greatly both from Dominican folklore and from contemporary commercial releases, and as a result they struggled to create and sustain an audience base.

Juan Luis Guerra represents the most successful of the Dominican musicians who came of age in the era of political song, having won ten Grammys to date. Born and raised in an affluent middle-class family in Santo Domingo, Guerra was a teenager in the mid-1970s and admits to having preferred rock music to the sorts of protest song promoted by Expresión Joven or Los Macopejes. After studying at the Dominican National Conservatory and at Berklee College of Music in Boston, he formed a vocal quartet in the 1980s patterned after the jazz fusion group Manhattan Transfer. Guerra too expressed skepticism about composing in mainstream styles such as *merengue* and had to be repeatedly urged to do so by his promoters. Thankfully, he eventually did, making an initial splash with his 1985 album *Mudanza y acarrero* (*Moving and Transport*) and with later projects such as *Ojalá que llueva café* (*May It Rain Coffee*, 1987).

FIGURE 6.3 *Juan Luis Guerra (right), performing early in his career in the 1980s with members of 440. The other vocalist pictured is Mariela Mercado. (Photo by Víctor Camilo).*

Guerra masterfully blends elements of jazz, Brazilian dance music, South African vocal genres, and other elements into his *merengues*. At the same time, his sophisticated arrangements are often matched by lyrics that engage with important issues such as immigration or the difficulties of rural life. "Visa para un sueño" ("Visa for a Dream") represents a good example of this sort of composition. Deborah Pacini-Hernández (1995, 204) believes that Guerra "spiritually renovated" the *merengue* in the late 1980s, bringing its focus back to local concerns of the Dominican population. Later experiments include *Bachata Rosa* from 1990, in which the composer created *bachata* music in a similarly unique and cosmopolitan style, and *Areíto* (1992), a release with two tracks written in the indigenous Arawak language, as well as one ("El costo de la vida," "The Cost of Life") with anti-capitalist undertones.

Nueva canción singers Sonia Silvestre, Luis Días, Víctor Víctor, and others continue to perform but have done so largely as individual artists and not as part of a movement. It is interesting to speculate further as to why Dominican *nueva canción* has not flourished to the same extent as elsewhere. One reason may be that the Dominican Republic does not have the pressing concern of colonialism to contend with as does Puerto Rico and is not as directly involved in international political struggle as Cuba. Tourism, one of the Dominican Republic's primary sources of income, may serve as an impediment to the popularization of *nueva canción* as it creates potential friction with the developed nations on which the economy relies. Its university-educated population base—the primary audience for *nueva canción*—is smaller than in Cuba or Puerto Rico. And finally, there is the issue of style: Dominican *nueva canción* has yet to find a resonant voice, a musical aesthetic to match its message that attracts mass audiences. One exception to this trend may be the recent experiences with Afro-Dominican fusion music mentioned briefly in Chapter 7.

CUBAN *NUEVA TROVA*

Nueva trova is the label Cubans use to describe to their own version of *nueva canción*. The term *"trova"* has been employed on the island for almost a century. It derives from *"trovador"* or "troubador" and refers to older romantic, guitar-based repertoire including the *bolero* and *canción*, most of which dates from the 1910s and 1920s. The term *"trovador"* is also used in Puerto Rico to refer to performers of *música jíbara*. *Nueva trova*, by contrast, is the music of Cuban youth who were raised in the aftermath of the Cuban Revolution (1959) and the subsequent sociopolitical changes that took place in the 1960s and 1970s. In a stylistic sense, *nueva trova* repertoire is quite diverse, though guitar-based music is usually the medium of choice. Some of the best-known pieces are influenced by rock and folk rock, though others, especially those written after 1980, experiment broadly with influences from Cuban dance music, folkloric drumming, jazz, and rap.

As in the case of Puerto Rico and the Dominican Republic, Cuba has a troubled history with the United States. At least some of the impetus for the 1959 revolution derived from many Cubans' perception that North Americans played too much of a role in domestic politics. As mentioned, American troops intervened in the Cuban War of Independence (1895–1898) and occupied Cuba for four years. In deliberations with Spain at the end of the conflict, U.S. representatives refused to allow Cubans to take part, making all negotiations unilaterally. During the early twentieth century, U.S. officials refused to allow Cubans to choose their own political leaders freely, insisting on candidates viewed as friendly to North American interests. North Americans initiated massive investment in the war-ravaged island beginning in 1902 that soon placed control of most large industries and utilities in their hands. The importance of the U.S. ambassador increased to such an extent in the early twentieth century that virtually no important decision could be made in the Cuban legislature without authorization through his office. As in the case of other Caribbean islands, conflicts between Cuba and the United States gave rise to a considerable body of protest song in the early twentieth century as manifest in *décimas*, *sones*, and the popular theater.

Military leader Fulgencio Batista (1901–1973) was the most important figure in Cuban politics immediately prior to the Cuban Revolution. He first entered the national spotlight in 1934 after helping stage a U.S.-sponsored coup against a democratically elected president deemed too independent and left-leaning to please Washington. Batista ran successfully for Cuban president himself in the 1940s in relatively free elections and—despite embezzling state funds and collaborating with the mafia—functioned as a reasonably competent head of state. However, in 1952 he staged a coup for a second time against then-president Carlos Prío Socarrás with the aid of the military. This outraged much of the population and led to civil war. Countless individuals took part in the insurgency against Batista, most famously Fidel Castro Ruz (b. 1926), his brother Raúl (b. 1931), and Ernesto ("Che") Guevara (1928–1967). The struggle continued for years but culminated in the departure of Batista for Miami on January 1, 1959.

ACTIVITY 6.4 *Conduct independent research on the history of the Cuban Revolution in order to understand more about its origins, the friction it generated in the 1960s with the United States, and its effect on Cuba in political and social terms.*

Investigate topics such as the U.S. trade embargo, the Bay of Pigs attack, and the Cuban missile crisis, as well as the biographies of revolutionary leaders.

The success of the revolution against Batista and the eventual decision of the new leadership to embrace Soviet-style socialism resulted in fundamental changes within Cuba, not the least of which were cultural. Cuba of the 1940s and 1950s had been a center of tourism, record production, and wild nightlife. Revenue for the countless nightclubs and cabarets (more than in Manhattan at that time, by all accounts) came largely from gambling revenues. The revolutionary government instigated changes such as the nationalization of all private enterprise, the outlawing of gambling and prostitution, and the abolition of copyright and royalty agreements that fundamentally changed the country's musical environment. In their attempts to create a more just and progressive society, revolutionary leaders offered free health care, free education, and a guaranteed right to work to all citizens. But the tensions that developed with the United States and with Cuban exiles also led to the imposition of limitations on travel for Cuban nationals, on access to the media, and on freedom of expression. This is the context in which Cuban artists of the 1960s and 1970s were raised, one of strong political rhetoric as well as a fundamental questioning of societal norms as they had existed earlier.

Political song during the revolution soon gained prominence. Traditional performers of *son* and *música guajira* such as Carlos Puebla (1917–1989) wrote songs extolling initiatives such as housing and agrarian reform and later his famous "Hasta siempre" ("Until Forever," 1967) in memory of Che Guevara. In contrast to most of the individuals we have discussed, his work supported rather than criticized government initiatives of the day. *Nueva trova* artists rose to prominence slightly later, beginning in the late 1960s, representing a younger generation. In general, they too supported the revolution, though they could be more critical. Among the most prominent figures in the movement's early years were Silvio Rodríguez (b. 1946, Fig. 6.4) and Pablo Milanés (b. 1943, Fig. 6.5). Milanés, an Afro-Cuban, grew up in eastern Cuba and demonstrated an interest in incorporating aspects of traditional genres (*son*, *bolero*, *rumba*) into his music. His well-known compositions of the 1970s include "Son de Cuba y Puerto Rico" ("Song of Cuba and Puerto Rico"), based on the poetry of Lola Rodríguez de Tió, and "De que callada manera" ("In What Quiet Way"), with lyrics by Cuba's national poet, Nicolás Guillén. Both pieces incorporate unique picking patterns on the guitar inspired in part by the syncopated melodies performed on the Cuban *tres*.

Probably the most famous *nueva trova* artist of all time is singer-songwriter Silvio Rodríguez (Fig. 6.4), a renowned poet and prolific composer whose songs span a vast array of styles. Early in his career Rodríguez took inspiration from folk and rock artists such as Bob Dylan and The Beatles. In this sense he was more of an internationalist than Milanés, reflecting the preferences of most urban Cuban youth at the time. His music is harmonically complex but also noteworthy for its asymmetrical phrases, abrupt key changes, and vocals in a high melodic range. The lyrics of Rodríguez's songs are especially daring, incorporating surreal imagery and powerful but extended metaphors so that the literal meaning of the text is far from transparent. He was the first *nueva trova* artist recognized as such, appearing on Cuban television in 1968. Among his many noteworthy compositions from the 1960s and 1970s are "Oleo de mujer con sombrero" ("Oil Painting of a Woman in Hat"), "En estos días" ("In These Days"), and "Esto no es una elegía" ("This Is not an Elegy"). The CD *Al final de este viaje ("At the End of This Voyage")* contains many beautiful songs accompanied only by acoustic guitar that provide insights into Rodríguez's performance style.

FIGURE 6.4 *Early* nueva trova *artist Silvio Rodríguez in a photo taken about 1980.* (Photo courtesy of the Cuban Ministry of Culture).

ACTIVITY 6.5 *Search for more information about the lives and compositions of Silvio Rodríguez and Pablo Milanés. Compare their styles of composition; make a list of similarities and differences.*

The 1980s was the heyday of Cuban *nueva trova*; it witnessed both the emergence of new artists and the diversification of the genre stylistically. Groups performed frequently at the University of Havana, at the Americas House (Casa de las Américas) cultural center, in parks, in theaters, and in the mass media. Milanés and Rodríguez by this time had achieved superstar status and continued to record and perform internationally, experimenting with extended ensembles and studio arranging. Some singers, such as Pedro Luis Ferrer (b. 1952) and Gerardo Alfonso (b. 1958), continued to compose for acoustic guitar in a style reminiscent of the 1970s, with notable differences. Ferrer, for instance, came from a rural family and demonstrated his affinity for *música guajira* through an emphasis on *décima* poetry. Alfonso incorporated influences from U.S. jazz and Brazilian music in his songs, often employing extended, complex harmonies. The duo Gema y Pável (Gema Corredera, b. 1964, and Pável Urkiza, b. 1963) developed an eclectic, international sound similar in many respects to that of Alfonso. Rather than foregrounding sociopolitical critique, their compositions instead challenged established practice by redefining Cuban culture in more inclusive, hybridized terms. They combine elements of Afro-Cuban religions and rhythms from the *son* with cello, electric guitar, and musical citations of international pop repertoire. Gema y Pável eventually left Cuba, pursuing their careers while residing in Spain, as have a number of their contemporaries. The reasons for their departure were primarily economic as they find it easier to tour and record based in capitalist countries and tend to earn more money. They continue to have a devoted following within Cuba nevertheless.

Individuals such as Frank Delgado (b. 1960), Santiago Feliú (b. 1962), Polito Ibáñez (b. 1965), and Carlos Varela (b. 1963, Fig. 6.5), by contrast, have adopted electrified rock music as their protest medium. This may be the style of *nueva trova* that best characterizes Cuban political song of the late 1980s and early 1990s. Varela's compositions and ensemble proved especially popular, drawing inspiration from the likes of U2 and Sting. His pieces vary from sweet lyrical ballads employing a lone keyboard or guitar to minimalist R&B grooves and half-spoken vocals reminiscent of Dire Straights to raunchy hard-driving rock with prominent distortion. Clearly a gifted musician, Varela nevertheless has

FIGURE 6.5 *Carlos Varela (right), performing alongside first-generation* nueva trova *artist Pablo Milanés (left).* *(Photo by Héctor Delgado).*

gained widest recognition for his lyrics. They address domestic social concerns with a directness that is startling. Examples include "Cuchillo en la acera" ("Razor on the Sidewalk"), graphically describing the rise in violent street assaults typical of mid-1990s Havana and the period of economic desperation following the collapse of the Soviet Union. Rock artists struggled for years in Cuba against a cultural establishment wary of a musical form associated so closely with the United States and Britain, but in the last two decades they have established themselves as a legitimate presence. Since the late 1980s the government's position toward rock has become more tolerant, and rockers perform frequently in theaters such as the Karl Marx, in festivals of protest song organized in various cities, and in centers dedicated to promoting *nueva trova* repertoire such as the Centro Pablo de la Torriente Brau in Havana.

CUBAN *RAP CONSCIENTE*

One of the most recent trends related to the history of politically engaged music within Cuba has been the emergence of a vibrant rap scene. As in the case of rockers, rap musicians struggled for recognition in a context not always welcoming of North American music or of expressions of racial pride. The Cuban Communist Party concerns itself with the welfare of poorer citizens, among which blacks are prominently represented. But it has never allowed the black community an independent political voice such as a radio or television show, newspaper, or magazine. Cuban rap eventually became an important medium for the expression of black concerns, especially during the height of its popularity, roughly 1995–2003. Along with *timba* dance music, it represented a grassroots Afro-Cuban corollary to *nueva trova*, which had always been associated primarily with white and middle-class Cubans.

From the outset, Cuban rap never embraced the themes of violence typical of much commercial rap in the United States. One reason may be that government regulation of worker salaries has moderated the disparities that exist between rich and poor in much of the capitalist world. Marginal and demographically blacker neighborhoods exist in some areas of Cuba but are not nearly as large as the ghettos of major U.S. cities. Cuban authorities do not permit most citizens to own guns unless they are in the military, and thus, lyrics about automatic weapons and the like make little sense. Perhaps most importantly, Cuban performers who began listening to U.S. rap via Miami radio broadcasts did not all speak English or know how to interpret black street slang. They were attracted to the sound and urgency of rap music, as well as its associations with the black community there, but wrote song lyrics to conform to their own experiences and needs.

One of the earliest rap groups to gain a following in the early 1990s was a band known as Amenaza ("Threat"), which later changed its name to Orishas. Founding members Yotuel (Yotuel Omar Romero Manzanares, b. 1976) and Ruzzo (Hiram Riverí Medina, b. 1972) initially performed as a duo in Havana. During a scholastic exchange in France, they joined forces with Roldán (Roldán González Rivero, b. 1971) as well as others, eventually releasing their first CD in 2000, *A lo cubano* ("In the Cuban Way"), which became an international hit. Many cuts used looped samples of older Cuban dance music as backtracks over which to speak and incorporated segments of Afro-Cuban religious music into the overall mix. In this way songs manifested uniquely "Cuban" elements while still conforming to the broader rap aesthetic.

Orishas remains one of the few Cuban rap groups to have recorded with a major label and whose releases are easily available internationally. The Cuban government does not have extensive recording facilities and can never accommodate as many performers as wish to make records; virtually no private recording industry exists. Scores, perhaps hundreds, of groups across the island remain unknown outside of their local communities for this reason. One of the most significant anthology releases of Cuban rap is *Cuban Hip Hop All-Stars*, vol. 1 (Papaya Records, 2001), which contains compositions by various groups (Hermanos de Causa, Explosión Suprema, Cuarta Imagen) who helped to define the socially engaged Cuban rap genre (known as *rap consciente*) in its early years. DVD documentaries of the Cuban rap movement have also been produced of late, such as *La Fabri-K: The Cuban Hip-Hop Factory* (Gato Films, 2005).

Cuban rappers managed to establish themselves as a viable artistic presence much faster than rockers, even though the latter had been performing since the 1970s. Rap artists developed a winning strategy: They postured themselves as the champions of revolutionary themes such as social equality. At the same time that their songs addressed sensitive, nearly taboo issues such as racism, they made reference to martyrs of the revolution, sported Che Guevara T-shirts, and claimed that they were carrying on the work of the revolution in the street. Interestingly, black North Americans in Cuba including former Black Panthers helped advise a number of early rappers in terms of both their lyrical messages and stage personae. Beginning in 1995, rappers established a major annual festival outside of Havana that was sanctioned by the government. By 1999, minister of culture Abel Prieto declared rap an "authentic expression" of the Cuban experience. Shortly thereafter he established an independent agency (la Agencia Cubana de Rap) to further the careers of the most prominent groups.

Lyrical themes of many sorts are apparent in *rap consciente*. As mentioned, references to Afro-Cuban religions are central, for instance, in the Orishas song "Canto para Elewa y Changó" ("Song for Elegguá and Changó"). Religious subjects became much more common in virtually all styles of music following Cuba's Fourth Party Congress in 1991 and the decision by the Central Committee that belief in God would no longer be considered "unrevolutionary."

Probably the most prominent theme in Cuban *rap consciente* is racial tension; one way this is addressed is to dialogue with Cuban music or poetry of the past in such a way as to bring themes related to race to the fore in new ways. Examples include the Hermanos de Causa ("Brothers of the Cause") release "Tengo" ("I Have"). It takes the name of a famous poem by Nicolás Guillén discussing the social gains of the revolution but evaluates the situation critically from the perspective of black youth. Another example is the all-female group Instinto's ("Instinct") remake of the 1930s song "Quirino con su tres" ("Quirino with His *Tres*"). The original text, also by Guillén, pokes gentle fun at a black adolescent who parties all day while his mother works to support him. Instinto emphasizes the inherently feminist message of this song, converting it into an ode to Afro-Cuban motherhood and to the song's original interpreter, Santería devotee Merceditas Valdés (1922–1996).

CD track 24 features an example of Cuban rap, "La llaman puta" ("They Call Her Whore"), written in 2002 by Magia López (b. 1970) and Alexey Rodríguez (b. 1972) of the duo Obsesión (Fig. 6.6). It alludes to prostitution, a phenomenon that has witnessed a resurgence in Cuba with the onset of the economic crisis of the 1990s and the growth of the

FIGURE 6.6 *Magia López* (l) *and Alexey Rodríguez* (r) *of Obsesión.* *(Photos by Héctor Delgado).*

tourism industry that caters to visitors from Mexico, Europe, Canada, and elsewhere. Many Cuban families now live in rather desperate conditions, without enough money to provide adequately for their families in terms of food, clothing, or domestic goods. One way young women have reacted to this situation is to seek out relationships with foreign visitors who may pay them for sex, buy them gifts, or marry them and take them away to live abroad. The Cuban media tend to vilify such women, describing them as amoral; but Magia contests that view and explores the motivations that would logically bring women to sell their bodies.

Based in Regla, López and her husband Rodríguez began performing as Obsesión in 1996. They have various goals, two of which are the promotion of black pride and getting more Cuban youth involved in the arts. Obsesión works together with another rap duo, Doble Filo ("Double Edge," Yrak Saenz and Édgar González), in a collective known as La Fabri-K (pronounced *"la fábrica,"* meaning "the factory"). The founding of the two groups, their collaborations, and their trip to New York involving interactions with various North American artists (Afrika Bambaataa, Kanye West, etc.) are the subject of the DVD *La Fabri-K* mentioned earlier. Since 2007, López has served as director of la Agencia de Rap Cubano.

Partial Listening Guide for CD Track 24

"La llaman puta"

View the full guide at www.oup.com/us.moore.

0:00–0:53

An instrumental introduction begins the piece that features a freely improvising acoustic bass, a *chéquere* playing constant eighth notes, and a sparse bell pattern. *Chéqueres* are an instrument closely associated with Ochún, the Afro-Cuban goddess of beauty and physical love. Magia's voice begins at 0:16. At 0:21, under the line *"Loca, carne que invita,"* *batá* drums enter as well, adding emphasis to the track's associations with Santería and Afro-Cuban heritage.

La llaman puta	They call her whore
Para todos no es más	For everyone she's no more
Que una mujerzuela	Than a bimbo
Disfrutando el hecho de ser bonita	Enjoying the fact that she's pretty
Loca, carne que invita	Crazy, meat that invites
Que incita, provoca	That incites, provokes
Menudo oficio que le toca	The lowly job is her lot
Esa chica ambulante	That slut girl of the streets
Ese *look* evidente	That obvious look
Que hace proposiciones indecentes	That makes indecent propositions
Es un cuerpo de cuerdas	Her body is made of strings
Que se agita	That resonate
Traduciendo fuego interior	Translating an interior fire
Que no siente	That she doesn't feel
Dientes se clavan en sus senos	Teeth bite on her breasts
Llegó el momento de gritar	The moment to yell has come
Y ensayar locura	And to show emotion
Apura sus caderas	She hurries her hips
Porque afuera espera otro cliente	Because outside another client waits

Puede ser un borracho	He could be a drunk
Puede ser un demente	He could be demented
Un tipo elegante	An elegant guy
O un asesino que vino escondido	An assassin who comes disguised
En un cuerpo masculino	In a masculine body
Cuántas no van por ese camino	How many have died that way
Y entonces la llaman puta	And so they call her whore

When the peak of the *rap consciente* movement ended in about 2003, many artists continued to perform politicized rap. Increasingly, however, the public that once flocked to rap festivals have spent their time dancing to *reggaeton*. Rappers and others committed to social issues, a minority, frequently deride *reggaeton* groups for composing in what they describe as a trite and mindless style. Singers in top *reggaeton* bands such as Eddy-K, Cubanos en la Red, and Cubanitos 20-02 earlier enjoyed careers as rappers; their decision to "switch sides" and "sell out" to larger audiences has generated considerable controversy. Key Cuban *rap consciente* artists and DJs have also left the country in recent years, taking some wind out of the sails of the movement. Virtually all performers now feel pressure to create music that will sell CDs and attract the attention of international record labels, regardless of their politics. This is indicative of overall economic changes within Cuba in the new millenium and the country's gradual reintegration into international circuits of trade at the same time that political discourse remains decidedly socialist.

The histories of Puerto Rico, Cuba, and the Dominican Republic have many parallels, so it is not surprising that protest music on all three islands demonstrates commonalities as well. All three struggled in the nineteenth century to establish their independence. Various pressures related to the slave trade, the relatively small size of the settlements, and/or their vulnerability to invasion by neighbor states made the severing of ties with the Spanish government difficult. Similarly, all three have struggled more recently to define their relationship to the United States. The twentieth century witnessed the rise of the United States as a global superpower; its government has dominated the Americas and intervened militarily on countless occasions, heightening regional tensions and often fostering anti-U.S. sentiment. Finally, all three islands have had to define their relationship to the powerful international music industry and to musical trends of the moment that have promoted English-language genres to the exclusion of local music, political or otherwise.

Of course, significant differences exist in the histories of protest song from the Hispanic Caribbean as well. In Puerto Rico, *nueva canción* has maintained a small but devoted audience for many decades. In large part this is due to the status of the island as a U.S. protectorate and desire on the part of some for complete autonomy. Puerto Rican *nueva canción* tends to be strongly rooted in local folkloric traditions, which is attractive to many local listeners. But its focus on a single issue and its marginality to mainstream labels has resulted in limited audiences elsewhere. In the Dominican Republic, the extreme political volatility of the 1960s led to the emergence of a significant body of *nueva canción* patterned largely after the songs of South American and Cuban protest singers. The movement eventually flagged, however, largely because of the lack of a distinctly Dominican sound with broad appeal—the efforts of Convite members and others notwithstanding. Dominican consumers of the 1970s also had their interests divided between *nueva canción* and a barrage of new commercial genres entering the country and generated from within for the first time. To the extent that socially engaged Dominican repertoire has become widely popular, it has drawn heavily from popular music traditions.

In Cuba, political song flourished to a greater extent than in Puerto Rico or the Dominican Republic, owing largely to the revolution in 1959 and the emergence of a state cultural policy that encouraged engagement with social concerns as part of music making. *Nueva trova* singer-songwriters achieved widespread popularity beginning in the 1970s and 1980s with guitar-based repertoire. More recently, *rap consciente* has come to represent the voice of politically engaged youth, especially from the black community. Yet political song in Cuba also faces challenges, including the increasing popularity of commercial dance music (*timba*, *reggaetón*) and an international context in which artists remain isolated, unable to record, and largely unknown outside their own country.

This chapter may have overemphasized distinctions between *nueva canción* and other forms of what is often considered "apolitical music." Certainly, all songs have the potential to make charged statements. The promotion of staged Afro-Dominican folklore by members of Convite caused considerable controversy in the Santo Domingo of the 1970s, for example, despite the fact that the lyrics of the songs contained no political references; many listeners did not care to admit to the prominence of African cultural heritage in the country. Commercial genres also touch directly upon political themes in many instances. Rafael Hernández's anti-imperialist "Preciosa" was written as a *bolero* and sold widely; the Tite Curet Alonso salsa composition "Anacaona," discussed in Chapter 4, and Juan Luis Guerra's *merengues* constitute another example of the same phenomenon: commercial music (in this case for dance bands) alluding to serious issues. Political song from the Hispanic Caribbean comes in many forms; *nueva canción* represents only one way that the political experiences of local residents manifest themselves in a rich legacy of music, all of which deserves greater attention.

CHAPTER 7

Dialogues with Blackness

∞

Among the central concerns of this book has been the impact of the Atlantic slave trade in the Hispanic Caribbean and the hybridization or creolization of cultural elements from diverse sources there over time. As you now realize, creolization has taken place in different ways, to different extents, and for different purposes. Chapters 1 and 4 discussed the fact that creolized culture has become emblematic of the Caribbean and is embraced as a powerful symbol of local experience. And yet that process of acceptance has not been simple or rapid; on the contrary, it has often been fraught with contradictions. Despite its symbolic position and although it is an essential element of Caribbean music, African-derived heritage is still not well understood or appreciated by many residents. Overall, black music has yet to achieve its rightful place in educational curricula and music conservatories. Cuba, the Dominican Republic, and Puerto Rico share with many post-slave societies (including the United States) certain biases against the music of Afro-descendant populations, though many positive changes have taken place in recent decades.

This chapter describes in broad strokes the process by which African-influenced culture has been accepted as national expression by inhabitants of the Hispanic Caribbean to the extent that it has, drawing connections between attitudes toward music and distinct racial formations and underscoring how much attitudes have changed over the past 150 years. It concentrates on three distinct moments that illustrate that process. The first is the turn of the twentieth century, one in which negative middle-class and elite attitudes toward Afro-Caribbean culture gave rise to blackface entertainment that depicted African descendants in stereotypical and negative ways. The second comes in the early to mid-twentieth century, when classically trained composers first attempted to integrate Afro-Caribbean content into their works. Finally, the chapter focuses on Latin jazz of the 1940s and beyond, in which Afro-Caribbean musicians themselves have been more equal partners in the process of developing and defining the region's artistic expression, typically in ways that consciously establish ties with other Afro-diasporic traditions.

EARLY REPRESENTATIONS OF BLACKNESS

The struggles of Afro-Caribbean people in postcolonial societies for equal citizenship have been paralleled in the cultural realm by the emergence of styles of music and dance that manifest distinct attitudes toward African-derived heritage—some positive, others negative. We should not be surprised at this since music inevitably emerges in specific contexts and represents the diverse views of performers and listeners. Music is thus structured by the society in which it is heard. But society is also musically structured since artistic performance represents an important way in which attitudes and beliefs are manifested, disseminated, and perpetuated. One could rightly expect that attitudes about African culture would have a central and contested place in debates surrounding national expression in the Hispanic Caribbean.

The individual histories of Cuba, the Dominican Republic, and Puerto Rico are distinct, as we have seen; and discourse about African-derived culture varies on each island. In the Dominican Republic, the early period of the country's history was characterized by an antagonistic relationship with Haiti, a nation of predominantly former slaves whose culture demonstrates strong African influences. As a result of Haitian occupation of the Dominican Republic, multiple border disputes, and other conflicts, dominant Dominican society has tended to demonize Haiti and, by extension, African culture of any kind. For years, many Dominicans distanced themselves from African heritage; thus, open recognition of Afro-Dominican elements of national expression has been slow to emerge. In Puerto Rico, limited formal recognition of black heritage began in the 1930s and has continued to the present. But because the island is demographically the whitest of the three, identification with African culture is less central. Cuba is the country where debates over the "proper place" of African heritage have the longest history, owing to the presence of both European and African immigrants in large numbers and to the long duration of the slave trade. For these reasons, Cuba's cultural policies and musical entertainment at the turn of the twentieth century serve as my initial focus of analysis as a means of addressing issues applicable to the Hispanic Caribbean more broadly.

Much has been written about the inhuman practice of treating Africans as property in the New World—buying and selling them, breeding them, working them to death, and replacing them with others. Somewhat less has been written about the ideological justifications for such actions. Remember that up until the 1940s most academics and historians in the West ascribed to notions of European superiority, as described in Chapter 1. In order to justify the enslavement of other human beings, European colonists needed to convince themselves that Africans and, by extension, other non-European groups were inherently inferior. A tremendous amount of pseudoscientific literature from the nineteenth and early twentieth centuries attempted to prove this through studies that compared the size of African skull cavities, for instance, to those of Europeans, concluding that the former were smaller or misshapen. Africans were characterized as morally weak, poor thinkers, lazy, overly emotional by nature, inclined to criminality, and unfit for citizenship. Historian Aline Helg quotes a prominent author who described blacks in 1906 as "a race vegetating in childhood," adding that they had only brought to the Caribbean "their musical sense, their exhibitionism and lasciviousness, and their lack of foresight" (1990, 48). Clearly, notions about African-influenced music and culture contributed to a particular racial formation involving the stratification of society and the subjugation of the black population, just as they did in the United States. These ideas persisted well beyond the abolition of slavery.

Slave music in the early and mid-nineteenth century served as further evidence of this assumed inferiority and became an object of derision for many Spanish colonial authors. One primary focus of interest was the annual Kings' Day celebration on January 6 in which Africans processed through the streets playing music in traditional costumes (see Fig. 3.1); numerous descriptions of the event by contemporary observers have been collected by Fernando Ortiz and subsequently translated to English and published by Judith Bettelheim (2001). In the mid-nineteenth century, commentators often expressed repulsion for the spectacle but also a perverse fascination; it seems to have helped to justify their sense of superiority. Following abolition, however, as blacks began to move en masse into urban areas in search of an education and work opportunities, attitudes about Afro-Cuban culture began to change. African-derived cultural forms that had existed on the islands for centuries in relative obscurity (largely on plantations or in the countryside) now suddenly could be heard in squalid tenement housing in the poorer areas of major urban areas. Middle-class and elite Cubans began to perceive Afro-Cuban culture as more threatening at this time, and municipal authorities passed numerous new laws to restrict its performance in various ways.

The early twentieth century witnessed a continuation of this tendency, a crackdown and intense regulation of Afro-Cuban music, dance, and religion. At the same time that the newly created federal government attempted to demographically whiten the nation through the subsidizing of Spanish immigration, they instituted campaigns against

Santería ceremony, which involved imprisoning religious leaders and confiscating or destroying drums and other religious objects. By writing sensationalist reports in local newspapers, they frequently (and falsely) accused Santería devotees of kidnapping children to sacrifice in bloody rituals (Chávez Alvarez 1991). The press coverage resulted in national legislation banning African-derived religions in 1922. Authorities instigated campaigns to eradicate African-derived *Abakuá* brotherhoods derived from traditions in Cameroon as well. Parallel processes in the political realm led to the massacre of blacks attempting to form their own political party during roughly the same period (Helg 1995). Rogelio Martínez Furé (1991, 27) suggests that the destruction of Afro-Caribbean percussion instruments represents an analogue of sorts to other sorts of repression experienced by the population of color.

In the realm of popular entertainment, the mid-nineteenth century witnessed the rise of a form of comic theatrical entertainment in Cuba performed by white artists who blackened their faces with burnt cork and imitated black music, dance, and speech. Those who have read about blackface minstrelsy in the United States will notice obvious parallels, and in fact U.S. minstrels did tour in Cuba during the Civil War and influenced traditions there. Characters from the North American stage such as Jim Crow, a happy-go-lucky country bumpkin, had their counterpart in the *negro bozal*, a recently arrived African slave who spoke only broken English. Likewise, the Zip Coon of North American minstrelsy closely resembles the Cuban *negro catedrático*, an urban want-to-be sophisticate who overdresses and tries to speak grandly while mispronouncing large words. By means of the latter character, theatergoers learned that being well educated, reading serious books, or writing verse was "white" behavior and any blacks doing so should be viewed as pretenders, "ludicrous interlopers in a white world" (Lane 2001, 76).

Three primary stage characters came to dominate blackface theater shows by the early twentieth century: the *negrito* or comic black man (in various incarnations), the *mulata* or sensual mixed-race woman, and the *gallego* or Spaniard from the northern province of Galicia. These characters interacted with each other in various ways; plots often revolved around attempts by the *negrito* and *gallego* to compete against each other in seducing the *mulata*. All characters became the butt of numerous jokes. The *mulata* most typically appeared as a male-defined stereotype, the epitome of sexuality but also of danger, a potential source of temptation, familial discord, and social conflict. As in the case of the *negrito*, the *mulata* loved singing and dancing, and (like the *negrito*) her character spent considerable amounts of time doing both. *Mulatas* were most often portrayed by white women in blackface or occasionally by

FIGURE 7.1 *Two* negrito *stage characters.* Left: *Possibly Paquito Rodríguez, playing a conga drum.* Right: *Sergio Acebal, a renowned whistler, composed and recorded CD track 25.* *(Archives, Centro Odilio Urfé).*

light-skinned black women themselves. The *gallego* for his part tended to be depicted as a shopkeeper with a heavy Spanish accent, rather unmusical and with poor dancing skills. Often, he had more education and wealth than the other characters and more often acted within the confines of the law. But his accent and his obsession with *mulatas* made him laughable all the same.

In the early twentieth century, a number of artists recorded comic sketches taken from the blackface theater on 78 rpm records. This repertoire has never been comprehensively studied, and none of the songs has been rereleased as part of an anthology. The few I have been able to listen to nevertheless provide important insights into the now nearly forgotten world of blackface humor in the Hispanic Caribbean and into racial discourse of the period. The example on our CD, track 25, dates from 1928. As opposed to some comic recordings that consist of dia-logues between characters, this example is a monologue from the perspective of a single *negrito*; the performer is Sergio Acebal (1889–1965), a prominent Cuban entertainer from the 1910s into the 1940s (see Fig. 7.1b). Music accompanying the end of the sketch does not include overt references to Afro-Cuban culture beyond the lyrics, as was fairly common; it reflects instead the influence of Tin Pan Alley and other popular music styles of the day.

As you listen to CD track 25, you might be able to detect the presence of dialectical Spanish (slang) and the occasional conscious use of incorrect grammar as in *"como me has ponido"* ("look what a state you've got me in") at 0:55. The correct phrase would be *"como me has puesto,"* with an irregular conjugation; poor grammar references the *bozal* and *catedrático* traditions. In the boxed translation and in the full on-line transcription, you should look for the implicit associations between blackness and a host of negative qualities in the piece, as well as between black male behavior, emotion, belief in "African superstition," infidelity, and violence.

Partial Listening Guide to CD Track 25

"La negra monguita" ("The Foolish Black Woman")

View the full guide at www.oup.com/us.moore.

Desconflautado, desesperado y abollado.	Disjointed, despairing, and stunned.
Me ha dejado ese negro desgrasiado,	She has left this unfortunate black man
Que la gallina me ha volado. Esto no será verso, pero es *"verdá."* Soy el negro más fatal que ha tenido negra.	My chick has run off. That's not very lyrical, but it's true. I am the unluckiest black guy who's ever had a black woman.
Todo es negro para mí. Mi madre negra, mi padre negro, y mi estrella más negra que la situación que atravesamos.	Everything is black for me. My mother a black, my father, and my star blacker than the situation I face.
Y para más fatalidad ahora estoy sufriendo por causa de una negra en quien había puesto todo mi querer.	And to make matters worse I'm suffering for a black woman to whom I had offered all my love.
Que ¿qué más me pasa? Casi nada...que se me corrió	What else has happened? Not much...she ran off with my

con mi amigo Serafín, que también es negro, dejándome la colombina vacía y vacío el corazón. Ay, cómo estoy sufriendo. Desde que se fue estoy desganado, no le entro a la chaúcha, nada. Ay, monguita, como me ha *"ponido."*	friend Serafín, who is also black, leaving my cot empty, and my heart too. Oh, how I am suffering. Ever since she left I don't want to do anything, I can't even eat, nothing. Ay, foolish girl, look what you done to me.

Blackface comedy continued into the mid-twentieth century on radio and early television and attracted performers and listeners from other countries including Puerto Rico. Yeidy Rivero (2005) has written on this topic, describing the influence of Cuban comedians and radio scripts on that island and the use of blackface among some Puerto Rican performers, most notably Ramón Rivero (1909–1956). Rivero's two *negrito* characters for which he is most famous are Diplomacia ("Diplo" for short) and Calderón. Diplomacia became well known to Puerto Rican listeners as the result of a popular radio show called *El Tremendo Hotel* (*The Crazy Hotel*); Calderón appeared later on early Puerto Rican television. Rivero seems to have combined elements of the *negro catedrático* and U.S. Zip Coon persona in his sketches, as well as voicing aspects of his own political agenda, which on occasion included veiled critiques of U.S. imperialism. Rivero's blackface characters might be considered "antiheros" of sorts—illiterate, dishonest, and lazy yet street-smart, conniving but occasionally endowed with class or political consciousness. Rivero can be seen performing on YouTube, and background info is available at http://www.diplo.org/tv/us/tv_us.htm.

Cuban blackface comedians Leopoldo Fernández and Tino Acosta emigrated to Puerto Rico following the Cuban Revolution of 1959 and performed there for some time. The presence of blackface comics is especially noteworthy given that Afro-Puerto Rican actors and actresses themselves could find virtually no work in the theater or on television in Puerto Rico in the 1960s (Rivero 2005, 63). With a few notable exceptions, the same is generally true in Cuba and in the Dominican Republic. The few roles available to black actors tended to be those of domestic servants or of slaves in historical dramas. That sort of overt discrimination began to disappear in the 1970s, in part as the result of influence from the civil rights and Black Power movements in the United States. Rafael Cortijo and his dance band, discussed in Chapter 4, are significant for having been some of the first Afro-Puerto Ricans to premiere on Puerto Rican television and for having helped create alternative and more positive representations of blackness in the media. Ironically, Yeidi Rivero (2005) notes that during some of Cortijo's earliest television broadcasts he was introduced by comedians in blackface.

In contrast to Cuba and Puerto Rico, no blackface tradition ever existed in the Dominican Republic. Some believe it never caught on because until recently the population as a whole refused to concede the existence of Afro-Dominicans! For reasons related to conflicts with Haiti, the country has tended to emphasize its Spanish and indigenous roots strongly rather than its African heritage. The consensus that African ancestry is unimportant, even nonexistent, has been perpetuated on national ID cards, which continue to categorize the population as "*indio claro*" (light-skinned Indian) or "*indio oscuro*" (dark-skinned Indian) rather than *mulato* or *negro* (black), as noted by Deborah Pacini Hernández (1995). In a country whose population is overwhelmingly of black or of mixed descent, blackface as a medium of expression may also lack a point of reference and be less meaningful. Or the issue may be too uncomfortable to serve as a basis for mainstream comedy.

CREOLE HERITAGE AND CLASSICAL MUSIC

Latin American classical composition has a long history dating back to the earliest years of Spanish colonization. Many early pieces, as one might expect, derive from church music written to accompany the Catholic mass and related activities; these works differ little from the sorts of repertoire performed in Spain during the same period. For centuries, the wide social divisions between colonizer and colonized, between European immigrants and blacks, indigenous groups, and those of mixed race had their corollary in distinct musical traditions. It took centuries for any sort of rapprochement to begin between European classical composition and local creole genres. Well into the twentieth century, classically trained musicians continued to search for a unique voice, a way to reconcile erudite European forms with local realities and practices. This process took especially long because of biases against working-class expression inherited from earlier generations.

The nineteenth-century political struggles that led to independence from Spain in the Hispanic Caribbean helped intensify the search for unique forms of cultural expression that could be embraced by all social classes. Argeliers León (1991) and Thomas Turino (2003) have argued that musical nationalism in the Spanish Americas consisted of at least two distinct phases. In the first, nationalist cultural forms represented exclusively the products of elites, who did not necessarily share a common language or ethnicity with the majority of residents in the regions where they lived. This phase, labeled "white nationalism" by León, is characterized by the creation of music that borrowed very little from local sources and instead closely emulated European models. Nineteenth-century national anthems based on march rhythms provide a good example of such music. The desire to homogenize and Europeanize the cultural differences of various groups meant that the nation came to be defined exclusively on elite terms. A second phase, beginning in the 1920s and described by León as "black nationalism," had somewhat more populist and inclusive tendencies; and it is this next moment I examine.

ACTIVITY 7.1   *Search for biographical information on colonial composers in the Hispanic Caribbean such as Esteban Salas, and check local libraries to see if they have recordings of works by such individuals that you can listen to analytically.*

Chapter 5 includes a brief discussion of early nationalist composers in Cuba and Puerto Rico who created stylized versions of dance repertoire such as the *danza* and *contradanza* for solo piano. They included Cubans Manuel Saumell (1818–1870) and Ignacio Cervantes (1847–1905) and Puerto Ricans Manuel Gregorio Tavárez (1843–1883) and Juan Morel Campos (1857–1896). Often, the pieces these individuals wrote incorporated rhythms such as the *tresillo, cinquillo,* and *habanera*; despite being performed on European keyboard instruments, their works did demonstrate subdued local influences, which today we would describe as Afro-Caribbean. But if such influences were evident, they tended not to receive recognition as African-derived. It is important to note as well that black Cubans, Dominicans, and Puerto Ricans and those of mixed race contributed significantly to the Hispanic Caribbean's "white nationalist" phase. Juan Morel Campos himself was a *mulato,* and various *mulato* performers such as José White (1836–1918) and Claudio Brindis de Salas (1852–1911) established international reputations for themselves during this period by performing music in the European classical tradition.

Juan Bautista Alfonseca (1810–1875) is considered the father of musical nationalism in the Dominican Republic. A clarinetist initially, he worked in the cathedral of Santo Domingo for a time and later became known for short, rhythmic compositions inspired by popular dance music. In addition to waltzes, quadrilles, and other European genres, he began composing works inspired by *danzas, merengues*, and other local forms. One of his best-known works is a song cycle entitled *Cantos de guerra* (*Songs of War*) from 1852. Bautista Alfonseca was the first to establish an urban repertoire of music that had a distinctly national character and create stylized versions of the *merengue* for the salon and concert hall. In the 1840s, as the country struggled for independence from Haiti, Bautista Alfonseca wrote a national anthem based on another local rhythm, a creolized folkloric dance in 6/8 time called the *"mangulina."* Perhaps because of its close associations with working-class expression, this composition never gained widespread acceptance among the urban elite.

Nationalism of the Twentieth Century. The most significant trend in classical music of the Americas in the twentieth century was the rapid growth of nationalist sentiment of a somewhat more populist sort. Instead of perpetuating elite European forms such as opera or incorporating folkloric melodies or themes into works that sounded decidedly European, composers in the twentieth century began to study traditional music more seriously in their search for new ways to express a Latin American reality. As a result, they paid more attention to the contributions of indigenous and Afro-descendant peoples. The movement developed in part out of a response to U.S. imperialism as well as through the influence of musical trends in Europe and (ironically) the United States. But it reflected also a gradual democratization of Latin American society and ways of conceiving the nation that more directly incorporated non-European influences. Composers who played a role in this effort throughout the hemisphere include Carlos Chávez in Mexico, Heitor Villa-Lobos in Brazil, Alberto Ginastera in Argentina, and Teodoro Valcárcel in Peru. Similar trends are evident at roughly the same time among classical artists in the United States and in the realm of popular culture, as evident in the emergence of the Harlem Renaissance in the United States and the vogue of "exotic" genres such as the tango and jazz internationally.

Various factors complicated the efforts of these nationalist composers. The first was the fact that Latin American and Caribbean nations continued to suffer from deep divisions of class and race in the early twentieth century. In the Hispanic Caribbean, for instance, practices of discrimination and segregation too often divided the middle classes and elites from the bulk of the population. A majority of rural inhabitants remained illiterate on all three islands through the mid-century, worked for the most part in agriculture, and had few opportunities for social advancement. Notions of cultural evolutionism (see Chapter 1) remained largely unchallenged through the 1940s as well. Composers struggled to reconcile their interest in local, working-class musical forms with a perception that they were simplistic, monotonous, and largely undeserving of study. Many sought to tap into a vitality and excitement that they perceived in African-influenced music, even though they did not consider it "artistic" per se. Modernist composers of the first half of the twentieth century represented the progressive thinkers of their time and did much to pave the way for the greater acceptance of African-influenced culture as legitimate in subsequent decades. But ultimately their views on the superiority of Western music reflected contemporary biases.

Finally, composers of the period also frequently adopted experimental techniques in their music associated with modernism, a pan-artistic trend that emerged in Europe and whose early musical advocates included Arnold Schoenberg, Igor Stravinsky, and Edgard Varèse. In their desire to expand the horizons of classical music making, modernists not only incorporated unconventional sources of inspiration, such as folkloric drumming and indigenous flute melodies, but also left many basic conventions of European music making behind. Some invented new scales or instruments, some avoided the use of functional harmony or any harmony, some began to experiment with electronically generated sounds or recorded sounds. As one might imagine, many people did not immediately warm to the compositions of classical modernists. Though hailed by the international artistic community as visionaries, they often had trouble generating audiences.

Probably the most important composer of this Afro-Caribbean nationalist trend from Cuba and the first to write pieces in a style from the Hispanic Caribbean was Amadeo Roldán (1900–1939, see Fig. 7.2). A violinist of note as well as a composer, Roldán grew up for the most part in Paris, the son of a Cuban mother and a Spanish father. He studied music in Madrid before moving back to Cuba in 1919 and, thus, arrived with an outsider's curiosity for local traditions. In 1923 he began attending Afro-Cuban religious ceremonies—something unheard of in middle-class society, especially as the federal government had recently criminalized involvement in such events—and transcribing melodies and rhythms. The first major symphonic work to result from Roldán's interest in Afro-Cuban culture was his *Obertura sobre temas cubanos* (*Overture on Cuban Themes*) from 1925. In addition to incorporating folk melodies, it included passages for solo percussion (drums, *güiros*, *claves*, and cowbells) that generated considerable controversy as Afro-Caribbean percussion had never been used in the concert hall before.

FIGURE 7.2 *Amadeo Roldán.* *(Photo courtesy of José Ruiz Elcoro).*

Other well-known pieces by Roldán include music for the ballet *La rebambaramba* (*The Big Commotion*, 1928), inspired by the African drumming and dance of nineteenth-century Kings' Day celebrations (see Fig. 3.1), and *Rítmicas*, a series of six chamber pieces. Sections of *La rebambaramba* feature a recurrent two-measure ostinato figure played by the string and wind section that is *"claved,"* as discussed in Chapter 3, thus referencing a host of local folkloric styles. Roldán's orchestral scoring is influenced by Stravinksy's *Rite of Spring*, with strong, unpredictable rhythmic accents throughout and extended harmonies. *Maracas* and other Caribbean hand percussion are employed by the orchestra. Roldán is said to have used actual folkloric drummers in at least some performances of the piece, whom he would allow to play for a time "in their own fashion" (Benítez-Rojo 1996, 77).

Ritmicas, by contrast, is a composition written for a small chamber group. Movements 1 through 4 are scored for flute, oboe, clarinet, bassoon, trumpet, and piano. The final two, however, utilize exclusively percussion instruments, something that had never been attempted by anyone in the European classical tradition. A glance at the first page of the score is instructive (Fig. 7.3) as it lists the various percussion instruments employed by the ensemble: multiple *claves* of different pitches, *maracas*, bells, a *quijada* or jawbone of a donkey (a traditional Afro-Latin instrument that is struck with the fist so that the teeth rattle), bongo drums, *timbales*, tympani drums, *bombo* or bass drum, and a *marímbula* (see Fig. 1.8). The piece incorporates small percussive motives from Afro-Cuban folklore (most notably the *tresillo*, repeated in Fig. 7.3 by multiple instruments) but superimposes them upon one another

FIGURE 7.3   *First page from the score of Amadeo Roldán's* Ritmicas, *movement 5.*
(Copyright 1967 by Southern Music Publishing Co., Inc. Used by permission).

and manipulates them in nontraditional ways. Movements 5 and 6 of *Rítmicas* have become standard repertoire for modern-day percussion ensembles, and various presentations of the piece can be seen on YouTube.

Music written by Roldán, his contemporary Alejandro García Caturla (1906–1940), and a few others immediately became a lightning rod for public criticism. Some viewed them as brilliant, while others accused them of "debasing" the Western classical tradition by fusing it with "primitive" and distasteful forms of expression or of being too experimental. The orchestral community actually split in two over these issues; conservative factions within the Havana Symphony refused to perform any works by Cuban modernists, and Roldán was eventually forced to create a second symphony (the Philharmonic) in order to premiere contemporary works. For conservatives, Afro-Cuban drumming clearly had not yet become "Cuban." Unfortunately, both Roldán and García Caturla died young, the former from cancer in 1939 and the latter a year later at the hands of a gunman.

The black nationalist phase initiated by classical modernists influenced other forms of music making, for instance, operatic and popular repertoire; and it is this music that began to circulate in Puerto Rico by the 1930s. One early figure involved in it was Ruth Fernández (b. 1919, Fig. 7.4), an Afro-Puerto Rican singer who initially entered the media spotlight singing popular songs known as *afros*, which featured poetry referencing Afro-Caribbean subject matter. The first song she popularized, with poetry by Fortunato Vizacarrondo and music by Domingo Colón, appeared in 1939 and was entitled "¿Y tu abuela onde etá?" ("And Your Grandmother Where Is She?"). Vizacarrondo's poem is written in a quasi-*bozal* style with incorrect spellings, referencing black working-class slang. Asking about someone's grandmother in this context suggests that many apparently white Puerto Ricans may have relatives who are black or of mixed heritage and would prefer not to admit that fact.

The popularity of Fernández's early recordings led Cuban composer Gonzalo Roig to invite her to perform in a nationalist opera he had composed, *Cecilia Valdés*. In this famous work, whose plot involves a love triangle between a black man, a *mulata*, and a white man in the nineteenth century, Fernández played the role of Dolores Santa Cruz, a slave. Her *aria* or feature song, "Po, po, po," also involved singing in *bozal*-style speech and required that she adopt a rough, nonclassical vocal timbre. Decades later, the singer recreated this presentation at the behest of the Puerto Rican National Foundation for Popular Culture; it was filmed and is available on YouTube. Parallels exist between *Cecilia Valdés* and stage productions such as *Showboat* or *Porgy and Bess* in the United

FIGURE 7.4 *Puerto Rican singer Ruth Fernández, making a recording of a song from the zarzuela Cecilia Valdés. Havana, 1948.* (Photo courtesy of José Ruiz Elcoro).

States. Fernández subsequently recorded an entire LP of songs with Afro-Caribbean subject matter entitled *Ñáñigo* in 1955. As the first commercially successful black female singer in Puerto Rico, this artist broke through many color barriers, though from the perspective of the present her early stage roles seem dated and heavily typecast.

The first classical composer in Puerto Rico to write in a style similar to that of Amadeo Roldán was Héctor Campos-Parsi (1922–1998). Considered one of the primary exponents of twentieth-century musical nationalism on that island, Campos-Parsi studied in both the United States at the New England Conservatory, in private lessons with Aaron Copland and Olivier Messiaen, and Europe, with Nadia Boulanger. By the 1950s he returned to Puerto Rico and accepted a position as professor of music at the University of Puerto Rico. Donald Thompson (2002) describes Campos-Parsi's stylistic development as following two parallel tendencies: on the one hand, that of incorporating rhythmic elements from the *plena* and other folkloric forms into concert repertoire and, on the other, experimentation with electronically generated sounds and aleatoric music. The latter approach is characterized by the composer's decision to let certain elements of a composition be determined either by musicians themselves or by chance in the act of performance. *Divertimiento del sur* (*Entertainments of the South*) from 1955 provides a good introduction to both of these tendencies in Campos-Parsi's work.

Other Puerto Ricans who have experimented along similar lines include Jack Delano (1914–1997) and, more recently, Ernesto Cordero (b. 1946). Delano, the child of Ukrainian immigrants, spent most of his youth in the United States studying viola and composition in Philadelphia. By the mid-1940s he had settled in Puerto Rico and established himself as a documentary filmmaker and musician with the debut of a score for the film *Desde las nubes* (*From the Clouds*, 1946). Delano adopted a more tonal musical vocabulary than Campos-Parsi but also experimented with dissonance and twentieth-century modernist techniques, blending them with elements of folklore. The work *Burundanga* (1988) for voice and orchestra is said to be one of his most successful in terms of blending these materials. A classical guitarist by training, Cordero studied in Puerto Rico, Spain, and Italy. His musical style is relatively accessible as well; many of his pieces are written for voice and guitar, incorporating sung *décimas* as a prominent traditional element. His *Cantata del valle de México* (1981) for soprano, flute, cello, and guitar represents an interesting aggregate of elements such as Catholic chant and rhythmic aspects of Puerto Rican *seis* together with modernist techniques (Quintero Rivera 1999, 356).

The dictatorship of Rafael Trujillo in the Dominican Republic between 1930 and 1960 stifled the intellectual and artistic experimentation required for avant-garde composition. Trujillo's own musical tastes tended to be populist, involving support for gentrified versions of working-class dance music. Experimental pieces did not appeal to him; he preferred works more reminiscent of nineteenth-century nationalists that incorporated folk melodies and rhythms into tonal orchestral compositions. Trujillo's patronage of the arts, by establishing a national symphony in 1941 as well as a national conservatory and various music schools in the capital shortly thereafter, greatly influenced the production of this style of music.

Dominican musical nationalists of the mid-twentieth century include Juan Francisco García (1892–1974), Julio Alberto Hernández (1900–1999), and Rafael Ignacio (1897–1984). García established himself as an advocate of utilizing folkloric material with a composition in 1918, *Ecos del Cibao* (*Echoes from the Cibao Region*), that featured the melody of a well-known *merengue*, "El juangomero"; this appears to have been one of the first truly "symphonic *merengues*" ever composed. García's *String Quartet #1* from 1922 employs similar material and represents one of the first nationalist pieces in that idiom written by a Dominican. In 1925 García traveled to Cuba, met poet Nicolás Guillén who had heavily promoted the use of Afro-Caribbean subject matter, and wrote at least one composition inspired by his work. Probably García's best-known piece is the *Sinfonía quisqueyana* (*Quisqueya Symphony*, "Quisqueya" being an indigenous name for the island of Hispaniola) from 1935. Most of it is written in a European style but includes a *"scherzo criollo*," or creole scherzo, section incorporating folkloric rhythms and melodies. The term "scherzo" comes from the Italian word for joke and implies a playful orchestral movement, often rhythmic and lively.

Rafael Ignacio is one of the few composers from the mid-twentieth century whose works directly referenced specifically Afro-Dominican traditions. A bass player by training, Ignacio was born in Santiago and began his career playing in military bands. He helped organize performers in Santo Domingo to perform symphonic repertoire in 1932 and served as the first conductor of the National Symphony. Bernarda Jorge notes (1982, 101) that his *Suite Folklórica* from 1942 is an especially significant piece in terms of its incorporation of influences from percussion. In the first movement of the work, "Al son de los atabales" ("To the Sound of the Drums"), various instruments are said to imitate the rhythms of folkloric *palo* drumming (see Fig. 3.8). Sadly, no recordings are currently available for purchase in recorded form by either García or Ignacio.

Though African cultural influences are as strong in the Dominican Republic as anywhere else in the Hispanic Caribbean, or stronger, the country until recently has not recognized them. Trujillo himself, despite being a mixed-race individual with a Haitian grandmother, persecuted

Afro-Dominican religions actively and flatly denied the influence of African heritage on the nation. It has only been since Trujillo's death that researchers, writers, composers, and musicians have been at liberty to more fully and openly explore these dimensions of their culture.

ACTIVITY 7.2 *Summarize the ways in which the Caribbean classical composers mentioned in this section reference local cultures. Use this as a means to review the various sorts of classical music that have emerged in the region and the ways in which it conforms to or deviates from European models. See if you can find recordings of any of the music mentioned to listen to yourself.*

LATIN JAZZ

The preceding two sections have described what might be considered "top-down" musical processes involving representations of creolized culture on the part of middle-class or elite society. The individuals creating such representations often were not black or of mixed race themselves and/or grew up exposed primarily to European-derived traditions. In important ways, their music represents an outsider's perception of Afro-Caribbean culture. The final section of this chapter focuses on the development of Latin jazz, a form of music in which performers of all backgrounds have had more room to express themselves, fusing elements from folkloric, popular, or classical sources and often emphasizing African heritage in unique ways. Latin jazz has proven a more democratic musical space in this sense; it has given rise to fusions of African- and European-derived music in terms of more equal parity, as well as with other creolized musics from the African diaspora throughout the hemisphere. Latin jazz is one of the most fecund and influential areas of experimentation among all present-day jazz performers.

As discussed in Chapter 1, influences from the Hispanic Caribbean have been in circulation within the United States from the earliest periods of its history. New Orleans, known as the birthplace of jazz, is a port city facing the Caribbean that had sustained commercial contact with all of the islands mentioned here since the eighteenth century. The plantation economies of the American South and the Caribbean are very similar, as are the demographics of both regions. Musicians from Mexico and the Hispanic Caribbean lived in early twentieth-century New Orleans and directly contributed to the development of what is now called "jazz." The nineteenth and twentieth centuries witnessed a constant process of exchange between the Hispanic Caribbean and the United States, beginning with the dance traditions discussed in Chapter 5 such as the *danzón* and *habanera*. This process continued with the popularity of genres such as the *son*, *chachachá*, mambo, and salsa in the United States and with interest in ragtime music and various other forms of jazz in the Caribbean. Not only are the histories of jazz and Latin jazz fundamentally linked, but it is more useful to think of them as one and the same phenomenon, parts of a single story.

Before continuing, it would be useful to define the terms "jazz" and "Latin jazz." Both have existed in very different styles through the years, which complicates the matter; any comprehensive definition tends to be so vague as to be virtually useless. North American authors stress that jazz developed out of the interaction of African American musical aesthetics with European music and that it foregrounds improvisation, individual expression, and spontaneous interactions between performers. This doesn't help differentiate the two styles as the same could be said of most Caribbean creolized music. As a general rule, the complexity of jazz lies in its harmonies and arrangements, while the complexity of much Afro-Latin music lies in its rhythms, its ostinato patterns, and the ways in which it stacks particular melodic or rhythmic ideas on top of one another. Traditional Latin music tends to be less complex harmonically than jazz and to consist of shorter formal structures. It is closer to its West African roots in this sense. Styles of soloing are often quite different between mainstream jazz and Latin jazz artists as well and are worth comparing. Since Latin jazz artists cannot rely on frequent harmonic changes to generate interest during their solos, they develop more innovative uses of rhythm, repeated melodic shapes known as "sequences," and other techniques.

ACTIVITY 7.3   *Come up with your own definitions of "jazz" and "Latin jazz" using library resources. As part of this process, search for recorded examples of North American jazz from the 1930s and 1940s. Compare these to recordings of traditional Caribbean genres on our CD, such as tracks 3, 10, and 15. Make a list of similarities and differences. Listen also to Larry Harlow's piano solo on CD track 16 and consider how it compares to standard jazz piano solos.*

Despite similarities, significant differences exist between jazz repertoire and traditional Caribbean music that have made them difficult to
reconcile with one another. The scales used in both can vary; for instance,
the tendency to emphasize so-called blue notes in North American jazz
has no counterpart in the Hispanic Caribbean. Likewise, the notion of
"clave" (see Chapter 3), of a repeated rhythmic cell as a structural basis
for a composition central to much music from the Caribbean, does not
appear in most jazz. The basic time sense of the two musics is also distinct: The "swung note" feel of mid-twentieth-century jazz is at odds
with the very straight feel of Caribbean dance music and its frequent
emphasis on weak beats or off-beats rather than strong beats. Thus, it
took some time for performers in each style to learn to appreciate each
other's music and to create workable fusions of the two. Perhaps the
most common solution has involved the blending of jazz harmonies and
big-band jazz instrumentation with rhythmic ostinato patterns derived
from Caribbean folklore. Another approach has been to take segments
of Caribbean music and insert them into works that otherwise sound
more like North American jazz. This could include a piano *montuno*
interlude (see Chapter 4), a rhythmic shift, or the incorporation of a well-
known Latin melodic fragment.

Ruth Glasser (1995) has documented much of the early history of Latin
jazz, beginning with the drafting of Puerto Ricans into the U.S. Army in
1917 and their exposure to North American music through performance
in military bands. Bandleader James Reece Europe, for instance, formed
an orchestra to entertain troops abroad that included over a dozen
Puerto Ricans, most famously Rafael Hernández (see Chapter 6). Puerto
Rican and Cuban immigrants have been intimately involved with jazz
performance in New York as well, beginning in the 1920s. They often
had more formal musical training than African Americans of the time
and, thus, found work easily in many Broadway pit orchestras and in
segregated black venues of Harlem.

The trend toward collaborations between African Americans and
Hispanic Caribbean immigrants intensified in the 1930s as greater
numbers of performers arrived in search of employment during the
Depression, especially Puerto Ricans. Juan Tizol (1900–1984) was a
prominent trombonist and arranger in Duke Ellington's band who
wrote early Latin-influenced hits such as "Conga Brava." A host of dance
orchestras proliferated in the 1930s led by Caribbean immigrants including Augusto Cohen, Xavier Cugat, Enrique Madriguera, Noro Morales,
Alberto Socarrás, and others. The repertoire of these early groups
consisted primarily of formally arranged jazz pieces, with little room
for improvisation, as well as jazzy versions of popular song from the
United States; the so-called Latin pieces they played tended to represent

Caribbean or South American musical elements rather superficially. In some cases this reflected a lack of knowledge about Afro-Caribbean folklore on the part of composers. In other cases it represented a conscious decision to give the mainstream U.S. public "watered-down" versions of Latin music in the belief that they would not appreciate more traditional repertoire.

The mid-1940s is the period in which the first pieces recognized as Latin jazz per se were written involving true collaborations between Caribbean and North American artists. Cuban Mario Bauzá (1911–1993) is often credited with writing the first Latin jazz piece, though the issue is debatable; regardless, he is a key figure in the development of mid-century Latin jazz. A child prodigy, Bauzá played classical clarinet and oboe in the Havana Philharmonic orchestra as a young man. After moving to New York in the early 1930s, he taught himself to play trumpet and performed in the jazz bands of Noble Sissle, Chick Webb, and Cab Calloway, becoming intimately familiar with jazz arranging. "Tanga," a Bauzá piece written in 1943, might be considered a milestone in the history of Latin jazz to the extent that it prominently foregrounds percussion rhythms associated with the Cuban *son* while reed and brass instruments play extended notes against one another that imply complex jazz harmonies. This sort of composition had little precedent.

Perhaps the most famous Latin jazz composition of the period, however, and one which even more effectively fused elements of jazz and Latin influences, is "Manteca" ("Pork Fat"), a song cowritten by jazzer Dizzy Gillespie (1917–1993) and Cuban percussionist Chano Pozo (1915–1948) in 1947. In this work one can hear the very distinct sound of the first section of the piece written by Pozo and the bridge or second section written by Gillespie. Pozo's contribution is based on a single chord; it creates musical interest by layering one looped musical idea upon another in traditional West African style, first on the conga, then bass, then baritone saxophone, then entire sax and trumpet sections. Gillespie's contrasting section is quite different, employing a complex sequence of chords, a "walking bass" pattern typical of mid-century jazz, and a swing feel on the drum set. This and other Latin jazz experiments of the 1940s can be heard on the CD *The Original Mambo Kings* (Verve/Polygram, 1993).

The 1950s, a sort of "golden age" of jazz and Latin dance music, was dominated in the United States by the presence of large orchestras with prominent percussion that often performed for dancers in New York's Palladium Ballroom at 53rd St. and Broadway. This venue is important in several respects, not the least of which was the fact that it created one of the first consistently integrated entertainment spaces in the country where Latinos, African Americans, and Anglo-Americans could socialize together. *Timbales* players were a central focus of the emerging big-band Latin jazz sound; the 1950s is the first period in which conga drums, the bongo, and *timbales* all began to be used together in the same ensembles. Prominent bandleaders of the era included Puerto Ricans Tito Puente (1923–2000, Fig. 7.5) and Tito Rodríguez (1923–1973). Of the two, Puente had an especially long and influential career. After serving in World War II, he went to the Juilliard School of Music on the GI Bill, specializing in vibraphones and percussion. As opposed to mainstream jazz of the period, which had shifted to bebop and cool jazz styles, Latin jazz retained its connections to dancers. Indeed, Puente himself believed that being danceable was a fundamental component of Latin jazz repertoire. Orchestras such as his often arranged jazz standards or popular songs of the day for their ensembles, adding the appropriate Latin percussion (usually derived from the Cuban *son*) and often playing pieces instrumentally rather than with vocals. Also influential

FIGURE 7.5 *Tito Puente performing early in his career, in 1957. Gilbert López sits at the piano, Santito Colón on the* timbales, *and Nilo Sierra on bass. Colón was the featured vocalist on Puente's top-selling* Dance Mania *LP, which helped to establish his career.* (*Josephine Powell archives*).

during this period were Havana's jazz bands, such as the house band for the Tropicana nightclub.

Paul Austerlitz (2005) has provided important insights into the history of Dominican musicians and their involvement with jazz through the years, part of the Hispanic Caribbean story that is not always told. According to Austerlitz, jazz has been read in distinct ways by Dominican performers: as an attractive and a relatively familiar musical style related to their own Afro-diasporic traditions and in a more ambivalent or negative way as a form of imposed culture brought to their country as the result of occupation. The backlash against the U.S. military presence beginning in the 1910s led to an increasing acceptance of the *merengue* as national music, as mentioned in Chapters 4 and 6. Yet at the same time many performers found themselves drawn to jazz harmonies and orchestrational techniques, exactly as had been the case with Cubans and Puerto Ricans. The traditional *merengue* itself allowed for a great deal of improvisation and embellishment on the part of instrumentalists and percussionists, so the basic parameters of jazz soloing did not prove difficult for Dominicans to assimilate.

By the 1950s, *merengue* orchestras had been influenced strongly by the instrumentation of mid-century jazz bands, and it was common for an instrument such as the trumpet to take an extended improvised solo during dance pieces, often to the accompaniment of traditional arpeggiated countermelodies on the saxophone. Prominent figures who have experimented with fusions of the *merengue* and other Dominican folkloric forms with jazz include saxophonists Tavito Vásquez (1929–1995) and Mario Rivera (1939–2007, Fig. 7.6). Austerlitz considers Vásquez to be the single most important innovator of a uniquely Dominican form of jazz. In the 1950s he helped standardize the improvised solo as part of the orchestral *merengue* sound. Subsequently, he experimented with smaller groups, stripped-down combos consisting only of piano, bass, *tambora*, *güira*, and saxophone. These ensembles used *merengue* percussion as a basis for bebop-like improvisations; the *tambora* and *güira* players would play in a relatively traditional manner, but piano and saxophone would soar over the top with extended harmonies, employing lightning-fast runs and phrases. Vásquez was a featured soloist on Juan Luis Guerra's first *merengue* LP, *Soplando*, in 1984.

Mario Rivera is remembered as a talented multi-instrumentalist who played piano, trumpet, percussion, and flute in addition to his primary instrument, the saxophone. During his early years, he performed folkloric *merengue*, but in 1961 he moved to New York and began to collaborate with numerous jazz groups. These included the orchestras of Tito

FIGURE 7.6   *Mario Rivera.*   *(Photo courtesy of the Rivera family).*

Rodríguez (1963–1966), Tito Puente (1966–1972), Machito and his Afro-Cubans, Eddie Palmieri, Giovanni Hidalgo, and other greats. Rivera toured in Europe with Dizzy Gillespie for a time and played *tambora* and sax on the Grammy-winning release *Live at Royal Festival Hall*

(1989). He formed two groups of his own through the years, the Salsa Refugees and the Mario Rivera Sextet, but sadly recorded only a single album, *El Comandante: The Merengue Jazz* (1996) with North American artist George Coleman. Many of the compositions on *El Comandante*, such as "Afternoon in Paris," "Dominicanize" jazz standards with folkloric percussion in a manner reminiscent of Tavito Vásquez. Rivera had firsthand exposure to expression such as *palo* drumming (see Fig. 3.8). He appears to have been the first to experiment with the fusion of *palo* percussion with jazz, though he did not have the opportunity to record music in that style before his death.

One can point to many tendencies in Latin jazz that have emerged since the 1960s. One has been toward diversification of style. In the 1940s and 1950s, most Latin jazz in the United States was based on percussion patterns associated with traditional Cuban dance music; in recent decades, countless new forms of experimentation have taken place, including the compositions by the Dominican artists mentioned here. Virtually every Latin American country—Brazil, Haiti, Panama, Puerto Rico, Venezuela, etc.—now has well-known performers who compose using elements of unique local folkloric music. Especially prominent figures of recent decades from the Hispanic Caribbean would include Cubans Jesús "Chucho" Valdés, Paquito D'Rivera, and Gonzalo Rubalcaba; Dominicans (in addition to those already mentioned) such as virtuoso pianist Michel Camilo; and Puerto Ricans Bobby Sanabria, David Sánchez, and Miguel Zenón. The technical difficulty and virtuosity of Latin jazz have increased as more players now begin their careers with extensive formal training from music schools and conservatories. Another shift has involved movement away from a focus on dance repertoire. Many continue to play danceable Latin jazz, but others create contemplative music for listening in the club or concert hall. This latter approach is often accompanied by influence from the world of contemporary classical music with its search for new sounds and its emphasis on experimentation.

In recent Latin jazz one also hears much more sophisticated engagement with African diasporic traditions than had been the case previously. In part this is because Afro-Caribbean artists themselves have had an increasingly central role in performing Latin jazz themselves and bring to the stage a depth of knowledge about particular styles that their predecessors lacked. In the 1950s and 1960s, for instance, many experts in folkloric traditions such as *batá* drumming (see Fig. 3.2) or the rhythms and songs of Santería began to collaborate with North American jazz artists. Drummers initiating this trend include Mongo Santamaría, Armando Peraza, and Carlos ("Patato") Valdés. More recently, individuals such as Cubans Elio Villafranca and Yosvany Terry have conducted research on obscure Dahomeyan-derived traditions and have used them as the basis of jazz compositions. The deeper engagement with Afro-Caribbean forms has also resulted from a gradual destigmatization of such music, a realization on the part of listeners as to its complexity and cultural significance. Just as North American jazz itself played an important role in the 1920s and 1930s in portraying African Americans and their heritage in a positive light for the first time, Latin jazz has become a means of educating audiences about forms of Afro-Caribbean expression that remain poorly understood.

Finally, the ongoing hybridization of jazz and Latin jazz with multiple musical styles is a prominent trend. In the same composition one might hear Latin instruments and/or folkloric influences from several countries played simultaneously. Collaborations between Latin jazz artists and those from other parts of the world are increasingly common, as in the case of pianist Bebo Valdés' collaborations with flamenco singer Cigala (Diego Jiménez Salazar), in which the two perform Brazilian bossa nova hits together. Ongoing fusions between jazz and rock or other forms of popular music are also common. Angelina Tallaj (in press) has documented the emergence of Dominican *música de fusión* in the 1980s as one example, a genre that mixes historically marginalized Afro-Dominican drumming styles with rock and jazz as a means of expressing racial pride. Building on the efforts of Convite (see Chapter 6), artists attempt to alter perceptions about Afro-Dominican heritage by making it a central feature of their performances. Prominent bands/artists include Domini-Can directed by José Duluc, Luis Días' Transporte Urbano, Edis Sánchez's Drumayor, the ensemble Licuado directed by Crispín Fernández, and performers Toni Vicioso and Xiomara Fortuna. Of these, the music of Duluc, Días, and Sánchez tends to be primarily rock-oriented, while Fernández, Vicioso, and Fortuna incorporate more jazz influences.

The final listening example on our CD (track 26) reflects many of the recent trends mentioned here and is performed by renowned percussionist John Santos and the John Santos Quintet. Santos (b. 1955, Fig. 7.7) is well-known as an educator, composer, and promoter of Afro-Latin music. Born in San Francisco, California, to Puerto Rican and Cape Verdean parents, he has conducted research on traditional music in Brazil, Colombia, Cuba, Puerto Rico, and elsewhere and has recorded with an amazing array of renowned figures since the 1970s. He was director of the Orquesta Típica Cienfuegos (1976–1980), the Orquesta Batachanga (1981–1985), and the Machete Ensemble (1985–2006) before forming his quintet and current sextet.

Santos' composition "Alabí Oyó" was released in 2007 on the *Papa Mambo* CD and features piano, bass, flute, *timbales, chéquere, batá* drums

FIGURE 7.7 *John Santos leading the ensemble that performs on CD track 26,* "Alabí Oyó." *Pictured left to right are Marco Díaz (piano), John Santos (chéquere), Saul Sierra (bass), Orestes Vilató (timbales), and John Calloway (flute).* (Photo by Tom Erlich).

(see Fig. 3.2), two *quijadas* (the same instrument as used in the Roldán composition described earlier), bells, and vocals. It represents a fusion of traditional Afro-Cuban religious repertoire with jazz. Specifically, the composition features three distinct *batá* rhythms and two prominent chants dedicated to the Yoruba *oricha* Changó, known as lord of the drums and representing masculinity and vitality. To an even greater extent than other *orichas*, Changó's powerful essence has been transformed into a symbol of African cultural resistance in various parts of the Americas. The phrase "Alabí Oyó" is a reference to Changó's origins in the ancient African city of Oyo, in what is now Nigeria. Harmonically, the composition incorporates chord changes from jazz saxophonist John Coltrane's famous piece "Equinox." Santos states in his liner notes that he dedicates "Alabí Oyó" to those like Coltrane "who advance humanity and spirituality through the positive application of the arts."

ACTIVITY 7.4 *As you listen to CD Track 26, "Alabí Oyó," follow the partial listening guide in the box and the full guide at www.oup.com/us.moore.*

Partial Listening Guide for CD Track 26

"Alabí Oyó"

0:00–0:13

The song begins with Santos on lead vocal singing the first chant, accompanied by piano and a *chéquere* marking beats 1–2 and 4–5 of the 6/8 measure. Flute fills in with improvisations following the end of the first vocal phrase at 0:07; cowbell and ride cymbal play accents in the background.

Alabí Oyó e, Alabí Oyó e	White cloth born of Oyo
Baba Okete Erinle Ka woo	Father of the mountaintop, let us see you

0:14–0:27

The chant repeats, with flute responding again and somewhat louder fills on the cymbal of the *timbales.*

0:28–0:35

A third repetition of the chant; all instruments enter as before behind the voices, and the bass can be heard improvising briefly at 0:32.

0:36–1:29

Batá drums enter here under an extended flute solo, accompanied by a bell pattern similar to the one discussed in CD track 1 (Fig. 1.5), as well as the piano, bass, and a second *chéquere* pattern. The *batá* rhythm in this section is called *ñongo*, one of perhaps thirty common rhythms performers on this instrument must learn. Santos plays all three drums (and all six drumheads!) himself on a stand rather than in a group with other drummers as would be characteristic in ritual contexts.

CONCLUSION

The entire history of music making in the Hispanic Caribbean has revolved around questions of how to resolve the social and cultural divisions left in the wake of colonialism and the Atlantic slave trade. Leaders of Cuba, the Dominican Republic, and Puerto Rico all faced tremendous obstacles following independence from Spain as they attempted to fashion a nationalist project by forging a common sense of identity. Some of the problems arising from this process persist. The ongoing search for meaningful collective cultural representation is evident in the music of these islands, and in fact music is one of the primary sites where disputes over identity have been manifest, especially those revolving around the role of African-derived heritage within national expression. During the colonial period, strict divisions between the races and classes had their counterpart in the equally distinct musical styles cultivated by colonial elites and laborers or slaves. Slowly, as marginal groups gained greater access to education, as barriers of racism and segregation began to erode, new forms of music emerged that reflected a greater reconciliation of African and European forms. And as increasing segments of the population now travel in and out of the region and interact with hemispheric and global cultures, entirely new cultural influences have appeared to further diversify local expression.

Various phases characterize the development of musical creolization in Latin America and the Caribbean. The first phase, which began in the early colonial period and extended through the early twentieth century, is characterized by a rejection of non-European culture on the part of elites. For some time, European immigrants retained close ties with the countries they and their families had emigrated from and continued to view themselves as Europeans rather than part of a new culture in the Americas. To the extent that dominant society recognized or engaged with African-derived expression, it tended to be in the form of parody or ridicule, of which blackface musical comedy is representative. A second phase of the process took place in the early to mid-twentieth century, characterized by a gradual recognition on the part of elites that African-influenced traditions represented a vital element of Caribbean heritage and needed to be reflected in national culture. Of course, European- and African-influenced musics had been blending for centuries in genres performed by the working classes, but only in the mid-twentieth century did conservatory-trained composers begin to embrace Afro-Caribbean culture as their own.

In the later twentieth and twenty-first centuries, questions of how the islands of the Hispanic Caribbean should represent themselves through music continue to be a concern. But the decades since the 1970s have given rise to much more serious interest in the study of Afro-Caribbean heritage and to a breakdown of earlier rigid and confining distinctions between notions of classical, popular, and folk musics. The increasing fluidity of such categories and a greater appreciation for once marginal forms of music make recent trends in the region especially exciting. Of course, the entire world has become more interconnected of late with advances in technology, communication, and travel; but the Caribbean, with its centuries-old history of cultural exchange and creolization, may still have important lessons to share with others. In the years to come, Hispanic Caribbean composers will draw from diverse traditions and experiment with them more freely than ever before. Contemporary music making has the potential to be a liberating force, a means of disseminating new racial projects and subjectivities. It can engage significant sectors of populations and regions, bind them together, and help to challenge social division. Armed with a knowledge of the past in all its diversity and complexity, musicians and composers are more capable than ever of redressing cultural misperceptions and speaking to ongoing concerns of the present.

Glossary

Abakuá. The term for music, dance, and ritual of Efik origin in Cuba, influenced by cultures of the cross-delta region between present-day Nigeria and Cameroon. *Abakuá* societies consist exclusively of men. The musical traditions involve public masked dancing and street processions, as well as more secretive events held in private homes.

Abwe. See *chéquere.*

Afro. A popular song genre from the early twentieth century in which lyrics and music tried to evoke aspects of the black Caribbean experience.

Aggregate melodies. A prominent characteristic of much Afro-Caribbean and West African music is that the melodies of a given piece often derive from the interaction of various individual melodies played together. The simultaneous performance of individual, minimalist melodies forms an aggregate melody that is perceived by the listener as a single unit.

Aguinaldo. A common type of Puerto Rican *música jíbara*, generally sung at Christmastime with religious themes. *Aguinaldos* are also common in the Dominican Republic. One might think of them as Christmas carols, following traditions adopted from Spain.

Apambichao **style.** A style of *merengue* that incorporates a syncopated bass style similar to that of the Cuban *son.*

Areíto [also *Areyto*]. A communal, religious song-and-dance form of the native populations living in the Caribbean at the time of the Spanish conquest.

Aria. A featured song within an opera composition.

Arpeggiation. The outlining of the individual notes in a chord one at a time, usually in a sequence from low to high or high to low.

Asaltos navideños. Literally "Christmas assaults." A practice common in Puerto Rico similar to Christmas caroling. Singers travel from house to house singing *aguinaldos* and then demanding food and drink from those for whom they have performed.

Bachata (plural: *bachatas*). A prominent form of Dominican popular dance music derived from the Latin American *bolero*. The music is relatively slow and is danced by couples in a tight embrace.

Bachatero. A performer or consumer of *bachata* music.

Balada. A recent variant of the *bolero* genre that emerged in the 1960s. It is characterized by a fusion of elements of the "classic" *bolero* of the 1950s with others derived from international pop music.

Bandurria. A Spanish-derived string instrument common in Puerto Rican *música jíbara* and Cuban *música guajira*.

Batá drumming. One of four major Yoruba-derived musical traditions in Cuba. It involves performance on three double-headed, hourglass-shaped drums that lay across the legs of seated performers. *Batá* drumming is a complex and virtuosic tradition, very difficult to play.

Bhangra. A style of music originally from the Punjab, on the border between India and Pakistan. Since the 1980s, rhythms associated with this traditional musical genre have been fused with electronica to create a modern dance beat.

Blackface minstrelsy. One of the most popular forms of stage entertainment in the United States in the nineteenth and early twentieth centuries. It most typically involved white Americans painting their faces black and parodying the music, speech, and behavior of black Americans.

Bolero. A romantic vocal genre of the Hispanic Caribbean. The style is characterized by extended harmonies and accompaniment by particular rhythms played on the *claves*, *maracas*, and other percussion instruments. The Latin American *bolero* developed in late nineteenth-century Cuba but quickly spread throughout Latin America.

Bomba. This term can refer to the jokey verbal interludes in *seis bombeao*. Alternately, it denotes a kind of Afro-Puerto Rican music and dance style involving hand drumming or can refer specifically to the lead drum used to perform that music.

Bomba sicá. One of the more common subgenres of Afro-Puerto Rican *bomba* music heard in Puerto Rico today and the one that has been most influential on commercial dance music.

Bombazos. Modern urban events that blend traditional *bomba* drumming and dance with influences from rap, hip-hop, break dance, and other commercial expressions.

Bombo. A large bass drum, often double-headed, that is used in Afro-Cuban carnival bands.

Boogaloo (also spelled ***Bugalú***). A form of 1960s dance music fusing elements of the Cuban *son* and cha-cha-cha with R&B music. Its primary advocates were Puerto Ricans living in the New York area.

Buleador (plural: ***Buleadores***). The lower-pitched drum used in Afro-Puerto Rican *bomba* music, one of at least two in the ensemble. It plays a relatively static, supporting pattern against which the lead drum (known as the *primo* or *bomba*) improvises.

Cabildo. Literally, "council." With the permission of colonial authorities, slaves and free blacks from virtually every West African ethnic group represented in the Americas formed these organizations as a means of helping each other accustom themselves to their new environment. *Cabildos* served as an important means of perpetuating African cultural practices, especially languages, religions, and music.

Caja. Literally, "box." A term often used to refer to the lowest drum or percussion instrument in an Afro-Cuban performance ensemble.

Cajón. Another term for "box," this one referring to an actual box used as a percussion instrument in parts of Latin America.

Cajón para los muertos. Literally, *cajón* performance for the dead. The term for a Kongo-derived ceremony in Cuba celebrating the spirits of particular dead individuals or ancestors.

Canción. Literally, "song." The *canción* is a pan-Latin American romantic song genre that emerged in the early nineteenth century, a Spanish-language counterpart to European art song. It was cultivated largely by the middle classes and influenced the development of the *bolero*.

Canciones de amargue. Literally, "songs of bitterness." A phrase used to describe early *bachata* repertoire in the 1970s and 1980s.

Canto. Literally, "chant." One of various terms used to describe the strophic song section that begins the Cuban *son*.

Cantos de palo. Palo songs. Religious songs of Kongo origin performed in Cuba and associated with the Palo Monte religious sect.

Cáscara. Literally, "shell." A rhythmic pattern played by two sticks. It can be performed on the side of a drum, on a wood block or piece of bamboo, or on the sides of the *timbales*.

Chachachá. A form of Cuban dance music dating from in the early 1950s.

Champeta. A style of popular dance music from the Caribbean coast of Colombia. Many pieces are quite similar in overall sound to *reggaeton*, with a constant *habanera* beat used to accompany rapped vocals or short choral refrains.

Charanga. A term for a dance band group consisting of piano, bass, *güiro*, *timbales*, flute, and violins, in addition to other wind instruments on occasion. *Charanga* bands tend to play *son*-influenced repertoire but use wind instruments and strings associated with nineteenth-century dance bands.

Chéquere (also *abwe* or *güiro*). A Yoruba-derived musical instrument. It consists of a roundish dried gourd that has been varnished; the end is also cut off, and all the seeds are removed. Finally, a net of beads or seeds is tied around the instrument so that it can be shaken to produce rhythmic sounds.

Cinquillo. Literally, "little group of five." A common rhythmic figure found in the Caribbean and circum-Caribbean consisting of five pulses.

Clave. An instrument, a pair of rounded, resonant sticks made of hard wood.

Clave rhythm. A constantly repeating figure, usually two measures in length, that serves as the structural basis for the rest of a piece's rhythms and melodies. Various *clave* rhythms exist in the Hispanic Caribbean.

Cofradía. See *cabildo*.

Comparsa. Cuban carnival music, featuring Afro-Cuban percussion of many sorts in addition to trumpet and other instruments. Various distinct *comparsa* traditions exist across the island.

Conga drums. Large hand drums made of strips of wood nailed together and topped with a skin head. They are derived from Afro-Cuban traditions of Bantu-Kongo origin.

Conguero. A conga player.

Contradanza. The Spanish term for *contradance*. A form of secular dance music derived from Europe that became popular throughout the Caribbean in the eighteenth and nineteenth centuries.

Controversia candente. Literally, "burning controversy." A moment in improvisational sung dueling in which one singer "snatches away" an improvised poem from another, rhyming his or her initial line with another before the first singer can finish.

Convite. The name of a Dominican *nueva canción* collective of the 1970s. The term *"convite"* refers to a work effort in which participants help other members of their community without payment.

Creolization. Creolization refers to the fusion or blending of different racial and cultural groups over time and the creation of something new and different out of those components.

Creolized music. Music that fuses elements from two or more distinct sources, such as traditional West African drumming and European folk song.

Cuá (also *fuá*). An instrument used in Puerto Rican *bomba* music. It consists of a pair of sticks that play a constantly repeated *cinquillo* pattern on a wood block or similar object.

Cuatro. A small folk guitar from Puerto Rico with ten metal strings, the majority strung in double courses. It is a prominent feature of *música jíbara* and a national cultural symbol.

Cuerpo. Literally, "body." A term used to describe the initial strophic song-like section of the Dominican *merengue*.

Dancehall. A form of Jamaican dance music performed largely in clubs. It is characterized by driving and rapid rhythms, electronically generated sounds, and in many cases lyrics with overtly sexual content.

Danza. A form of music that accompanied figure dancing and that that gained popularity throughout the Hispanic Caribbean in the nineteenth century. It contributed to the development of various styles of music such as the *danzón*.

Danzón. A form of Cuban ballroom dance music for couples. It developed in black middle-class dance salons in the 1870s, heavily influenced by genres such as the *contradanza* and *danza*.

Danzón clave. A two-measure alternating rhythmic pattern associated with the Cuban *danzón*. It consists of a *cinquillo* followed by four quarter notes.

Décima. A ten-line. Spanish-derived poetic form prominent in *música guajira* and *música jíbara*.

Dem Bow. A Jamaican dance rhythm developed in the studio that strongly influenced the development of *reggaeton*.

Diaspora. A term used to reference various cultural formations including African-influenced cultures of the Americas. It implies three core elements: the movement or displacement of populations, notions of a shared homeland that displaced groups have left behind, and a degree of boundary maintenance that displaced groups retain in social and cultural terms from others.

Eleggguá. A Yoruba deity in the Santería religion. Eleggguá is a childlike trickster figure. He is also the messenger of the *orichas*, guardian of the crossroads, and the opener and closer of doorways, spiritual and otherwise.

El Perreo. See *Perreo, el.*

Enramada. The name for a thatch-covered lean-to in the Dominican Republic associated with *velación* celebrations. *Enramadas* are constructed outdoors. They serve as a focal point for secular music and dance activity after more formal devotional songs have been sung.

Espinela **form**. A poetic rhyme scheme developed in medieval Spain. It is the most common rhyme scheme found in present-day *décimas*.

Ethnicity. This term is used to characterize to the cultural heritage of minority groups in modern, urban, multicultural societies. Those asserting their ethnicity attempt to reassert cultural difference rather than conform to mainstream behavior.

Fiestas patronales. Patron saint festivals. Annual events held in honor of various Catholic saints, often involving music and dance.

Filin (also *feeling*). A variant of the *bolero* that developed in Cuba in the late 1950s. It is characterized by complex and extended harmonies, the extensive use of vocal improvisation, and a *rubato*-style vocal.

Folk Catholicism. Catholic practices that do not conform to orthodox Catholicism. Many forms of music in the Hispanic Caribbean are influenced by folk Catholicism that often blends Spanish traditions with those from Africa or elsewhere.

Fuá. See *cuá.*

Gallego. A Spaniard from the northwestern province of Galicia. The *gallego* was one of three stock characters in the Cuban comic theater at the turn of the twentieth century.

Grito de Lares. Cry of Lares. The name of a Puerto Rican rebellion against Spanish colonial rule that took place in 1868.

Guayo. See *güira.*

Güira. A ridged metal scraper used in the Dominican Republic.

Güiro. A term for a hand-held scraper made of gourd or metal or the large round gourds fitted with nets of beads that are used in Afro-Cuban religious events.

Habanera **rhythm**. A rhythm related to the *tresillo* and found in variation throughout Latin America, as well as in *reggaeton*. It may derive from West African sources, from the Arab world, or both.

Hermandad. Literally, "brotherhood." See *cabildo.*

Hispaniola. The name given initially by Columbus to the second largest island in the Caribbean, currently divided into the nations of Dominican Republic and Haiti.

Independentista. An advocate of political independence for the island of Puerto Rico.

Inle. A minor deity in the Santería pantheon who is a hunter, fisherman, and doctor. He symbolizes health and abundance and is represented by the image of a fish.

Jaleo. Literally, "tug" or "pull." A term used to describe later sections of the Dominican *merengue* that are faster and more improvisatory and usually incorporate interlocking melodies from the trumpets and saxophones as well as call–response singing.

Kongo. A term for Bantu-Kongo groups in central sub-Saharan Africa.

Luás. See *misterios.*

Mangulina. A form of folkloric dance music from the Dominican Republic in 6/8 time, which appears to have been influenced by the Spanish *zapateo.*

Marímbula. An instrument of Shona origin in sub-Saharan Africa. It consists of a resonator box, to which strips of metal are attached; the strips are plucked to produce various tones.

Martillo. Literally "hammer." The name for the basic pattern performed on the bongo drums in Cuban *son.*

Mayohuacán. A "slit drum" percussion instrument used by native peoples of the Caribbean.

Melismatic. An adjective to describe melodies that stretch a single syllable of text over many different notes.

Merengue. The national music and dance of the Dominican Republic since the 1930s.

Merengue típico. A folkloric form of *merengue* that originated in the Cibao (central northern) region of the Dominican Republic.

Misterios (also *luás*). A term similar to *orichas.* It refers to ancestor spirits and other supernatural forces worshiped in Dominican Vodú ceremonies.

Modernism. A pan-artistic movement that first emerged in Europe at the turn of the twentieth century. It is associated with aggressive experimentation in an attempt to expand the horizons of classical music practice.

Moña. Literally, "ribbon." A repeated melodic phrase played by the horn section in salsa songs and used to generate additional excitement during the hotter sections of the *montuno.*

Mongó. A small drum used by *salve* percussionists in the Dominican Republic. It is held between the knees and played vertically with two hands.

Montuno. Literally, "from the mountains." The term is used to describe the latter sections of Cuban *son* pieces that are faster and more improvisatory and incorporate call–response singing.

Mulata. A female *mulato. Mulatas* appear often in Caribbean prose and culture; Spanish men often viewed them as beautiful, hypersexual beings. In many ways they represent a symbol of Caribbean identity.

Mulato. One of dozens of racial categories common in the Hispanic Caribbean. It refers to a racial mixture of African and European.

Música guajira. The term for rural Spanish-derived music in Cuba, associated with string instruments and poetic forms such as the *décima.*

Música jíbara. Country music of Puerto Rico, featuring a number of distinct string instruments and in general demonstrating significant influence from Spanish folk traditions.

Negrito. Literally, "little black man." The generic term for a blackface actor in the Cuban comic theater.

Negro. One of many words for a black person in the Spanish-speaking Americas.

Negro bozal. The colonial term for a recently arrived African slave who did not yet speak Spanish well. The *negro bozal* became a prominent character type in Cuban literature and on the stage of the comic theater.

Negro catedrático. The "schooled" black. Similar to the Zip Coon of the U.S. minstrelsy stage, this figure from the Cuban comic theater was portrayed as an urban dandy who liked to display his sophistication by using big words he couldn't pronounce.

Nonliturgical *salve.* See also *salve.* An Afro-Dominican musical genre that blends Spanish-derived *salves de la Virgen* with percussive accompaniment such as *palo* or *pandero* frame drumming.

Novenas. Nine-day festivals associated with folk Catholicism in the Hispanic Caribbean. They typically involve the performance of both sacred and secular repertoire, prayers to particular saints, and music for dancing.

Nueva canción. Literally, "new song." A form of socially conscious music that emerged in Latin America and the Hispanic Caribbean in the 1960s.

Nueva trova. The Cuban term for *nueva canción*.

Nuyorican. A person of Puerto Rican descent born in the New York area.

Ochosi. A Yoruba deity of the hunt who is worshipped in Santería ceremony.

Ochún. A Yoruba goddess of beauty and love recognized in Santería ceremony.

Oggún. A Yoruba deity of iron and the forge who is worshipped in Santería ceremony. Oggún is a fierce warrior known for his dogged determination.

Orichas. Ancestor deities/spirits/forces of nature who are worshipped in the Santería religion.

Ostinato. A short, repeated harmonic, melodic, or rhythmic figure used as the structural basis for creating a piece of music.

Palo. Literally, "stick." A term used in the Dominican Republic to refer to drumming ensembles that accompany many forms of sacred and secular music making. The typical *palo* ensemble consists of two long, single-headed *palo* drums as well as a metal *güiro* scraper and other percussion.

Panderetas (also *panderos*). The name for the hand-held frame drums used in Puerto Rican *plena* music.

Panderos. See *panderetas*.

Parranda. One of many Latin American terms for "party." In Puerto Rico it can refer to musical street processionals during the Christmas season.

Paseo. Literally, "promenade." An introductory instrumental section in nineteenth-century dance music such as the *danza* and *danzón* and in the Dominican *merengue*.

Peña. A small, informal artistic gathering, usually in a private home or a café.

Perreo, el. "Doggy-style" dancing. A form of dancing associated with *reggaeton* music. It involves a couple locking hips and gyrating together in an erotic manner.

Plena. A creolized form of music in Puerto Rico typically employing frame drums, various melodic instruments, and vocals.

Program music. An instrumental composition inspired loosely by an image, event, or idea and attempting to evoke it through sound.

Punto. The general term used in Cuba for sung *décimas* in the *música guajira* tradition.

Punto libre. A form of *punto* in which the pulse of the song is not constant throughout but instead stops and starts to accommodate verbal improvisation.

Quijada. A musical instrument made from the jawbone of a donkey. The instrument is either struck with a fist so that the teeth rattle or the teeth themselves are scraped with a stick.

Quinto. The highest-pitched lead drum in the *rumba* ensemble. This is the drum that improvises against more static parts played by others.

Racial formation. This concept refers to the overarching ways in which societies are organized and experienced racially, the historical frames within which racial categories are created, experienced, and ultimately transformed over time.

Racial project. This refers to an interpretation or representation of race that aims to alter existing racial dynamics. It implies social activism within an existing racial formation.

Rap consciente. Socially conscious rap. The term developed among Cuban rappers to distinguish their artistic goals from those of more commercially oriented performers.

Reggae-español. A Spanish-language version of reggae and dancehall music from Jamaica that first became popular in Panama in the 1970s and 1980s.

Reggaeton. A popular form of dance music in the Hispanic Caribbean that has developed since about 1998. It is based on the *habanera* rhythm.

Regla de Ocha. "The rule of the *orichas*." Another term for Santería.

Romance. Epic narrative ballads derived from Spanish traditions that date back to the Middle Ages.

Rondo. A term for a "rounded" musical form that begins and ends with the same A segment of music, as well as playing it between the introduction of other segments. Its most typical form is ABACA.

Rubato. Literally "robbed," referring to tempo. Rubato passages do not follow a strict meter but slow down and speed up as appropriate to the interpretation of the piece.

Rumba. A secular form of Afro-Cuban music and dance. Its instrumentation includes only percussion of various sorts and vocals. It developed in the urban slums of Havana and Matanzas in the late nineteenth century.

Rumba guaguancó. The most commonly performed subgenre of *rumba*. It has been very influential in the development of *son* and salsa, especially in terms of *cáscara* rhythms performed on the *timbales*.

Salsa. A commercial label that emerged in New York in the 1960s to describe dance music derived from the Cuban *son* but containing many influences from Puerto Rican folklore, jazz, and other sources.

Salsa dura. "Hard salsa." A name for early, raw-sounding salsa repertoire of the 1970s.

Salsa monga. "Limp salsa." See ***salsa romántica***.

Salsa romántica. "Romantic salsa." A type of salsa associated with the 1980s and early 1990s. It has a more slick and highly produced sound than earlier *salsa dura* and may have introductions or interludes written in the style of romantic ballads.

Salsero. A performer or a fan of salsa.

Salve. A devotional music genre from the Dominican Republic. *Salves* exist in many forms, some sounding very Spanish and consisting only of vocals, others incorporating numerous African-derived percussion instruments.

Salve con versos. A form of creolized *salve*. It includes new text in various sections added to the original Catholic prayer and is often performed in a more rhythmic fashion than *salves* to the Virgin.

Salve de la Virgen. Another name for the *Salve Regina* in the Dominican Republic.

Salve Regina. Literally, "Save Our Queen." A Catholic chant in praise of the Virgin Mary that dates from the Middle Ages.

Santería. A religion practiced in Cuba and more recently in Puerto Rico, the United States, and elsewhere. It consists of Yoruba traditions fused with elements of Catholicism.

Scherzo. Literally, "joke." The term is used by classical composers to describe compositions that are playful, rhythmic, and lively.

Seguidilla. A strophic song form derived from Spanish traditions.

Seis. The term used in Puerto Rico for sung *décimas* in the *música jíbara* tradition.

Seis bombeao. A *seis* subgenre that involves jokey *bombas* or poetic recitations between segments of instrumental music.

Seis chorreao. The most common subgenre of *seis*. It often accompanies couple dancing. The dancers' feet are said to slide low against the floor so that they look like they're *chorreando* or "flowing."

Septeto. "Septet." A group consisting of seven members that plays "classic" Cuban *son* in the style of the 1930s, with the addition of a trumpet.

Sexteto. "Sextet." A group consisting of six members that plays "classic" Cuban *son* in the style of the 1920s.

Soca. The Trinidadian equivalent of dancehall, *soca* is an electronic dance music that developed in the 1970s and 1980s. Its fundamental repeated pulse is very similar to the *habanera* rhythm.

Son. A creolized form of dance music from Cuba. Although derived from the eastern side of the island, it developed into its commercial form in the 1920s in Havana. *Son* contributed significantly to the development of present-day salsa music.

Soneos. One of various terms for the improvised lead vocals sung by salsa singers.

Subido. Literally, a raising or heightening. A term used to describe moments of intense, ecstatic performance during Afro-Dominican *salves*.

Syncretism. A term similar to "creolization." Syncretism implies fusion of two distinct sets of cultural practices into a single system. The distinct beliefs persist but are perceived as a single unit.

Tambor. A generic term for "drum." An Afro-Cuban religious event may also be described as a *tambor*, a "drumming."

Tambora. A double-headed drum used in the Dominican Republic to accompany folkloric and popular music, including the *merengue*.

Tamborita. See *mongó*.

Timbales. A percussion instrument created in nineteenth-century Cuba and used today in salsa bands. It consists of two drums with metal frames set on a stand, usually played in tandem with a woodblock, various bells, and a cymbal.

Típico moderno. A format for playing *merengue* music. It is based on the rural *merengue típico* style but adds saxophone and conga drums, and often features more elaborate arrangements.

Tira tira. Literally, "shootout" or "gunfight." The term is used in Cuban *punto* to describe aggressive verbal dueling between two singers. See also *controversia candente*.

Toque. Literally, a "touching" or "playing." A generic term for an Afro-Cuban religious event. A *toque* can also refer to a specific rhythm.

Tratado. Literally, "treatment." A series of short songs in call–response format dedicated to a particular *oricha* or *orichas* and used as part of worship in Santería ceremonies.

Tres. Literally, "three." A folkloric string instrument from Cuba that has three courses of doubled strings.

Tresero. A *tres* player.

Tresillo. A rhythmic figure consisting of three eighth notes that is characteristic of much Caribbean and circum-Caribbean music.

Triethnic heritage. The notion that African, European, and indigenous peoples have all blended over time to create modern Latin American populations and that all have contributed culturally to the region.

Tumbadora. The Spanish term for conga drum.

Verso. "Verse." One of the terms for the strophic song section of the Cuban *son*.

Vodú. An Afro-Dominican religious tradition with roots in present-day Benin and Dahomey. It developed as the result of the influences of Haitian traditions, along with significant elements derived from Catholicism and other European practices.

Yoruba. A term used to describe various ethnic groups in present-day Nigeria and Cameroon, especially those associated with the Oyó Empire in the eighteenth and nineteenth centuries.

Zapateado (also *zapateo*). A style of Spanish-derived dance involving a stiff torso and movement primarily from the waist down, similar to flamenco or Mexican folk dancing.

Resource Guide

∞

Note: Written resource materials in English and Spanish, and additional lists of audio-visual resources, can be found at the Global Music Series Web site (www.oup.com/us.moore).

CDs and Recorded Music
General

Blades, Ruben
1992   *The Best*. Globo Records CDZ 80718. Miami, FL: Sony.

Cruz, Celia
1993   *Azúcar negra*. New York: Sony International.

Cruz, Celia and Ray Baretto
1995   *Ritmo en el corazón*. Charly CD 172. New York: Sonido, Inc.

Cruz, Celia and Johnny Pacheco
2006   *Celia y Johnny*. (Re-issue of the 1974 Vaya LP) Miami, Florida: EMusica.

Dane, Barbara
1970   *Canción protesta: Protest Songs of Latin America*. Paredon Records CD PAR01001. Distributed by Smithsonian Folkways.

Pacheco, Johnny
2005   *Johnny Pacheco. Entre amigos*. Bronco Records CD BR175. Puerto Rico: Bronco Records.

Roberts, John Storm
1978   *Black Music of Two Worlds*. Smithsonian-Folkways CD FW04602.

Santos, John
2007   *The John Santos Quintet. Papa Mambo*. Machete Records CD M206. Berkeley, CA: Machete Records.
2008   *Perspectiva Fragmentada. The John Santos Quintet and Friends*. Machete Records CD M208. Berkeley, CA: Machete Records.

Various artists
1993   *Africa in America. Music from Nineteen Countries*. Corason 3-CD set MTCD 1157. Cambridge, MA: Rounder Records.

1993   *The Original Mambo Kings*. Verve CD 314 513 876-2. New York: Polygram Records.

2002   *Latin Jazz: La combinación perfecta*. Smithsonian Folkways CD SFW40802.

2003   *Reggaeton Hits*, Vol. 1. New York: Cutting Records CD CMD5021.

Cuba

Azúcar Negra
2000   *Andar andando*. Bis Music CD 215. Havana: Artex.

Cabrera, Lydia
2001   *Havana, Cuba, ca. 1957: Rhythms and Songs for the Orishas.* Smithsonian Folkways CD SFW 40489.

2003   *Havana & Matanzas, Cuba, ca. 1957: Batá, Bembé, and Palo Songs from the Historic Recordings of Lydia Cabrera and Josefina Tarafa*. Smithsonian Folkways CD SFW 40434.

Chappottín, Félix
2003   *Conjunto Chappottín y Sus Estrellas: Una Nueva Generación*. Camajuan compact disc. Havana: Camajuan.

Conjunto Folklórico Nacional de Cuba
1996   *Música yoruba*. Bembé CD 2010-2. Redway, CA: Bembé Records.

Milanés, Pablo
1996   *Años III*. Spartacus CD SLD22137. Havana: PM Records.

Mompié, Haila
2003   Haila. *Tributo a Celia Cruz.* Pimienta Records CD 245 360 567-2. Havana: Bis Music.

Moré, Benny
1987   *Romántico*. BMG Music CD 6647-2-RL. New York: RCA.

NG La Banda
1994   *Simplemente lo mejor de NG La Banda*. Caribe Productions CD 9435. Havana: EGREM.

Piloto, Giraldo
1997   *Juego de manos*. Euro Tropical EUCD-3. Canary Islands, Spain: Manzana Productions.

Rodríguez, Silvio
1995   *Al final de este viaje*. Spartacus CD 22103. Mexico City: Spartacus.

Santos, John
1982   *The Cuban Danzón, Its Ancestors and Descendants*. Smithsonian Folkways CD FW 04066.

Schloss, Andrew
1981   *Carnival in Cuba*. Smithsonian-Folkways CD FW04065.

Septeto Habanero
1995   *Septeto Habanero: 75 Years Later.* Corason CD. Cambridge, MA: Rounder Records.

Various Artists
1990   *Routes of Rhythm. A Carnival of Cuban Music,* Vol. 1. Rounder CD 5049.
1990   *Septetos Cubanos: Sones de Cuba.* Corason 2-CD set MTCD113/4. Distributed in the U.S. by Rounder Records.
1994   *Afro-Cuba. A Musical Anthology.* Rounder Records CD 1088. Cambridge, MA: Rounder Records.
1994   *Casa de la Trova de Santiago de Cuba.* Corason CD COCD120. Cambridge, MA: Rounder Records.
1995   *Sacred Rhythms of Cuban Santería.* Smithsonian-Folkways CD SFW40419.
1996   *Cuba: Contradanzas & Danzones.* Nimbus Records NI 5502. Charlottesville, VA: Nimbus Communications International.
1997   *Cuba in Washington.* Smithsonian-Folkways CD SFW40461.
2001   *Cuba guajira y son. Caña, tabaco y ron,* vol. II. Orfeon CD 25CDTR-833. Re-released by Orchard.com.
2008   *A Tribute to Gonzalo Asencio, "Tío Tom."* Smithsonian-Folkways CD SFW40543.

Dominican Republic

Austerlitz, Paul
1997   *Merengue: Dominican Music and Dominican Identity.* Rounder CD 1130.

Bolívar, Gómez and Eric Ramos
1997   *Música raiz 1.* Santo Domingo: Fundación Cultural Bayahonda CD.

Días, Luis
2003.   *Luis Días y las maravillas.* Diasong.

Domínguez, Leonardo
2004   *Quisqueya en el Hudson.* Smithsonian-Folkways CD 40495.

Durán, Blas
1997   *Estelares de Blas Durán.* J&N Records CDL82461. Miami, FL: Sony.

Expresión Joven
2006   *Dominican Republic: ¡La hora está llegando! The Time Is Coming.* Paredon LP PA1025. Re-released by Smithsonian Folkways 1974. Washington, D.C.: Smithsonian Institute.

Fortuna, Xiomara
2001   *Kumbajei.* New York, NY: Circular Moves.

Gills, Verna
2001a   *Music from the Dominican Republic. The Island of Quisqueya, Vol. 1.* Smithsonian-Folkways CD FE 4281 (1976).
2001b.   *Music from the Dominican Republic. The Island of Española, Vol. 2.* Smithsonian-Folkways CD FE 4282 (1976).
2001c.   *Cradle of the New World.* Smithsonian-Folkways CD FE 4283 (1976).
2001d.   *Music from the Dominican Republic. Songs from the North, Vol. 4.* Smithsonian-Folkways CD FE 4284 (1978).

Gills, Verna and Daniel Pérez Martínez
2000   *Rara in Haiti/Gagá in the Dominican Republic.* Smithsonian-Folkways CD FE 4531 (1978).

Guerra, Juan Luis
1990   *Bachata Rosa.* Miami, FL: Karen Records.
1992   *Areíto.* Miami, FL: Karen Records.
1996   *Grandes éxitos de Juan Luis Guerra.* Karen CD KRD 30177. Miami, FL: Karen Publishing.

Lora, Huchi and Rafael Chaljub Mejía
2005   *Ripiando el perico: Antología del merengue típico.* Santiago, Dominican Republic: Grupo León Jimenes.

Marks, Morton
2006   *Afro-Dominican Music from San Cristóbal, Dominican Republic.* Smithsonian-Folkways CD FE 4285 (1983).

Méndez, Kinito
2001   *A palo limpio.* New York: Sony International.

Núñez, Enerolisa
2001   *Enerolisa Núñez y el grupo de salve de Mata los Indios. Música Raiz,* Vol. 2. Roldán Mármol, prod. Santo Domingo: Fundación Cultural Cofradía.

Roberts, John Storm
1998   *Caribbean Island Music: Songs and Dances of Haiti, the Dominican Republic and Jamaica.* Nonesuch CD H-72047 (1978).

Saldaña, Francisco and Víctor Cabrera
2003   *MasFlow.* San Juan, Puerto Rico: V.I. Music.

Sánchez, Edis
2000   *El gran poder de Dios.* Santo Domingo: Drumayor.

Ulloa, Francisco.
1993   *Francisco Ulloa y su Conjunto Típico Moderno. ¡Ultramerengue!* Green Linnet CDGLCD 4004. Danbury, CT: Green Linnet Records Inc.
1995   *Pegaito.* Miami, FL: Karen Records.

Vargas, Wilfrido
1995   *Los años dorados.* Karen CD KRD 148. Miami, FL: Karen.

Various artists
2001   *Bachata Hits 2001.* J&N Records CD JNK 83754. New York: Sony.
2005   *Fiesta en Banica.* Earth Partners CD. Makanda, IL: Magnetic Art Productions

Puerto Rico

Brown, Roy
1970   *Basta ya, revolución.* Puerto Rico: Disco Libre.
2005   *Yo protesto.* San Juan, Puerto Rico: Tierrazo (1981).

Feliciano, José
1995   *20 éxitos.* BMG CD 74321-33382-2. New York: BMG Music.

Gran Combo de Puerto Rico
2002   *40 aniversario.* Sony International CD. New York: Sony.

Jiménez, Andrés
1992   *En la última trinchera.* Producciones Cuarto Menguante DCM-85. San Juan, Puerto Rico: Producciones Cuarto Menguante.

Palmieri, Eddie
1996   *La perfecta.* Fania Records CD LPA 8170.

Paracumbé
1996   *Paracumbé.* San Juan, Puerto Rico: Paracumbé, Inc.

Pleneros de la 21, Los
1990   *Puerto Rico, mi tierra natal.* Shanachie CD 65001. Newton, NJ: Shanachie Records.

2005   *Para todos ustedes.* Smithsonian-Folkways CD SFW40519.

Rivera, Ismael and Rafael Cortijo
2008   *Ismael y Cortijo, grandes éxitos,* Vols. 1 and 2. Armanda y Fernández CD AF 8006. Miami, FL: Big World Distributors.

Rodríguez, Pete "El Conde"
2007   *Este negro sí está sabroso.* Fania Records CD 00489 (1976).

Roldán, Sandra
1978   *Boricua Roots/Raices Boricuas.* Smithsonian-Folkways CD FW05446.

Toro, Puli
1985   *Puli Toro Sings Favorite Hispanic Songs.* Smithsonian-Folkways CD FW08730.

Various artists
1971   *Folk Songs of Puerto Rico.* Smithsonian-Folkways CD FW04412.
1978   *¡Viva Puerto Rico libre!* Paredon Records PAR01035. Distributed by Smithsonian-Folkways.

1992   *Bomba: Music of the Caribbean.* Monitor CD MON61355. Distributed by Smithsonian-Folkways.

1996   *Puerto Rican Music in Washington.* Smithsonian-Folkways CD SFW 40460.

1997   *Puerto Rico Tropical.* Latitudes CD LAT 50608. Chapel Hill, NC: Music of the World.

2001   *Lamento borincano. Early Puerto Rican Music: 1916–1939.* Arhoolie Records 2-CD set 7037–38.

2003   *Jíbaro hasta el hueso: Mountain Music of Puerto Rico by Ecos de Borinquen.* Smithsonian-Folkways CD SFW40506.

2004   *Viento de agua unplugged: Materia prima.* Smithsonian-Folkways CD SFW 40513.

Yurchenko, Henrietta
1971   *Folk Songs of Puerto Rico.* Smithsonian-Folkways CD FW 04412.

References

Ꝏ

Books and Articles

Abreu, Christina D.
2007   "Celebrity, 'Crossover,' and *Cubanidad*: Celia Cruz as 'La Reina de la Salsa,' 1971–2003." *Latin American Music Review* 28(1):94–124.

Aparicio, Frances
1998   *Listening To Salsa: Gender, Latin Popular Music, and Puerto Rican Cultures.* Hannover, CT: Wesleyan University Press.

Austerlitz, Paul
1997   *Merengue: Dominican Music and Dominican Identity.* Philadelphia: Temple University Press.
2005   *Jazz Consciousness. Music, Race, and Humanity.* Middletown, CT: Wesleyan University Press.

Béhague, Gerard, ed.
1994   *Music and Black Ethnicity. The Caribbean and South America.* New Brunswick, NJ: Transaction Publishers.

Benítez-Rojo, Antonio
1996   *The Repeating Island: The Caribbean and the Postmodern Perspective,* 2nd ed. Durham, NC: Duke University Press.

Bettelheim, Judith, ed.
2001   *Cuban Festivals: A Century of Afro-Cuban Culture.* Princeton, NJ: Marcus Wiener Publishers.

Bilby, Kenneth
1985   "The Caribbean as a Musical Region." In *Caribbean Contours,* ed. Sidney Mintz and Sally Price. Baltimore, MD: Johns Hopkins University Press, pp. 181–218.

Brubaker, Rogers
2005   "The 'diaspora' diaspora." *Ethnic and Racial Studies* 28(1):1–19.

Buisseret, David et al.
2000   *Creolization in the Americas.* College Station: Texas A&M University Press.

Chaudenson, Robert, ed.
2001   *Creolization of Language and Culture.* New York: Routledge.

Chávez Alvarez, Ernesto
1991   *El crimen de la niña Cecilia. La brujería en Cuba como fenómeno social (1902–25).* Havana: Editorial de Ciencias Sociales.

Davis, Martha Ellen
1981   *Voces del purgatorio: estudio de la salve dominicana.* Santo Domingo: Museo del Hombre Dominicano.

Dufrasne González, Emanuel J.
1994   *Puerto Rico también tiene...¡tambó!* Río Grande, Puerto Rico: Paracumbé.

García Canclini, Néstor
1995   *Hybrid Cultures: Strategies for Entering and Leaving Modernity,* trans. Christopher L. Chiappari and Silvia L. López. Minneapolis: University of Minnesota Press.

Gilroy, Paul
1993   *The Black Atlantic. Modernity and Double Consciousness.* New York: Verso.

Glasser, Ruth
1995   *Music Is My Flag. Puerto Rican Musicians and Their New York Communities, 1917–1940.* Berkeley: University of California Press.

Helg, Aline
1990   "Race in Argentina and Cuba, 1880–1930: Theory, Policies, and Popular Reaction." In *The Idea of Race in Latin America.* ed. Richard Graham. Austin: University of Texas Press, pp. 37–70.
1995   *Our Rightful Share: The Afro-Cuban Struggle for Equality, 1886–1912.* Chapel Hill: University of North Carolina Press.

Jorge, Bernarda
1982   *La música dominicana: siglos XIX–XX.* Santo Domingo: Publicaciones de la Universidad Autónoma de Santo Domingo.

Kubik, Gerhard
1994   "Ethnicity, Cultural Identity, and the Psychology of Culture Contact." In *Music and Black Ethnicity. The Caribbean and South America.* ed. Gerard Béhague. New Brunswick, NJ: Transaction Publishers, pp. 17–46.

Lane, Jill
2001   *Blackface Cuba, 1840–1895.* Philadelphia, PA: University of Pennsylvania Press.

León, Argeliers
1991   "Of the Axle and the Hinge: Nationalism, Afro-Cubanism, and Music in Pre-Revolutionary Cuba." In *Essays on Cuban Music: North*

American and Cuban Perspectives. ed. P. Manuel. Lanham, MD: University Press of America, pp. 267–282.

Lord, Lewis
1997   "How many people were here before Columbus?" *U.S. News & World Report*, 08/18/97, Vol. 123 Issue 7, p. 68.

López Cruz, Francisco
1967   *La música folklórica de Puerto Rico.* Sharon, CT: Troutman.

Malavet Vega, Pedro
1993   *Historia de la canción popular en Puerto Rico (1493–1898).* Ponce, Puerto Rico: Editorial Corripio.

Manuel, Peter, ed.
2009   *Creolizing Contradance in the Caribbean.* Philadelphia: Temple University Press.

Martínez Furé, Rogelio
1991   "Tambor." In *Essays on Cuban Music: North American and Cuban Perspectives*, ed. Peter Manuel. Lanham, MD: University Press of America, pp. 27–47.

Miller, Ivor
2000   "A Secret Society Goes Public: The Relationship Between Abakuá and Cuban Popular Culture." *African Studies Review* 43(1):161–188.

Omi, Michael and Howard Winant
1986   *Racial Formation in the United States: From the 1960s to the 1980s.* New York: Routledge & Kegan Paul.

Ortiz, Fernando
1947   *Cuban Counterpoint; tobacco and sugar.* New York: A. A. Knopf.

Pacini Hernández, Deborah
1989   "Social Identity and Class in 'Bachata,' an Emerging Dominican Popular Music." *Latin American Music Review* 10(1):69–91.
1991   "*La lucha sonora*: Dominican Popular Music in the Post-Trujillo Era." *Latin American Music Review* 12(2):105–123.
1995   *Bachata. A Social History of a Dominican Popular Music.* Philadelphia: Temple University Press.

Patterson, Enrique
1996   "Cuba: Discursos sobre la identidad." *Revista Encuentro de la cultura cubana* 2 (otoño de 1996), pp. 49–67.

Perna, Vincenzo
2005   *Timba: The Sound of Cuban Crisis.* London: Ashgate.

Piper, Daniel C.
        forthcoming "Musical mobility, religious networks, and creative process in Afro-Dominican salves and palos performance." Ph.D. dissertation, Brown University.

in press "Palos", "Salves." *Encyclopedia of Popular Music of the World*, Vol. IX, New York: Continuum Books.

Quintero Rivera, Angel "Chuco"
1999   *Salsa, Sabor y control: sociología de la música tropical*. San Juan, Puerto Rico: Siglo Veintiuno Editores.

Rivero, Yeidy
2005   *Tuning Out Blackness. Race and Nation in the History of Puerto Rican Television*. Durham, NC: Duke University Press.

Rondón, César Miguel
2008   *The Book of Salsa. A Chronicle of Urban Music from the Caribbean to New York City*. Chapel Hill: University of North Carolina Press.

Scott, James C.
1985   *Weapons of the Weak: Everyday Forms of Peasant Resistance*. New Haven, CT: Yale University Press.

Stewart, Charles, ed.
2007   *Creolization: History, Ethnography, Theory*. Walnut Creek, CA: Left Coast Press.

Tallaj, Angelina
In press "Afro-Dominican fusion Music." In *Encyclopedia of Latin American Popular Music*, ed. Jorge Torres. Westport, CT: Greenwood Publishing.

Thompson, Donald, ed.
2002   *Music in Puerto Rico. A Reader's Anthology*. Lanham, MD: Scarecrow Press.

Turino, Thomas
2003   "Nationalism and Latin American Music: Selected Case Studies and Theoretical Considerations." *Latin American Music Review* 24(2):169–209.

Wade, Bonnie
2004   *Thinking Musically*. New York: Oxford University Press.

Audio-Visual Materials Cited

Acebal, Sergio. "La negra monguita." Victor 78 record #46073-1, 1928. "Monologue." Sergio Acebal (composer and singer) with pianist Sergio Pita.

Gillespie, Dizzy. *Live at Royal Festival Hall*. Dizzy Gillespie and the United Nations Orchestra. Red Ink CD B00005QKGG, 1989.

Marre, Jeremy. *Salsa: Latin Music of New York and Puerto Rico*. BBC "Beats of the Heart" series DVD. Newton, N.J.: Shanachie Records, 1979.

Masucci, Jerry and León Gast. *Our Latin Thing (Nuestra Cosa)*. London: Vampisoul, 2004 (1971).

Pérez-Rey, Lisandro. *La Fabri-K: The Cuban Hip-Hop Factory*. Miami, FL: Gato Films, 2005.

Ranks, Shabba. *Just Reality*. New York: VP Records, 1991.

Singer, Roberta and Ashley James. *Bomba, Dancing the Drum*. New York, NY: Searchlight Films, 2000.

Zeig, Susan, prod. *Plena Is Work, Plena Is Song*. Susan Zeig, prod. New York: Cinema Guild, 1989.

Index

∞

231